THE
BEST BOOKS OF THE DECADE
1936-1945

THE BEST
BOOKS OF THE DECADE

1936-1945

ANOTHER CLUE TO THE LITERARY
LABYRINTH

By

ASA DON DICKINSON

Author of "One Thousand Best Books,"
"Best Books of Our Time, 1901-1925,"
"Best Books of the Decade, 1926-1935," etc.

NEW YORK
THE H. W. WILSON COMPANY
1948

To

H. H. T.,

For Whom Books Have Come Alive

There was a time when Sydney Smith could say: "Who reads an American book?" Today we could say: "Who does *not* read an American book?"

—André Maurois

PREFACE

This volume is my fourth "clue to the literary laby-rinth" [1]—a fourth attempt to designate the best books produced for readers of English in a given period. In its preparation I have been again diverted by the verbal contortions of most list-makers in their determined avoidance of that terrible word *best*. They all *mean* best of course, but most of them seek to avoid the slurs of cavillers by recourse to less irrevocable adjectives such as "outstanding," "noteworthy," "memorable," "important," etc. For months I have been humbly following the somewhat timorous footsteps of these my betters. Now my time has come. The reckonings have been cast up. I take my courage in both hands and, as on previous occasions, declare with a loud voice that the books described in the following pages are the best produced in the decade, 1936-45. Is this brazen effrontery? Well, not really. Always, you see, one can dodge behind the concluding paragraph of this preface. 'Tis an ever present help in time of trouble.

A book of this sort cannot afford to ignore Professor Henri Peyre's *Writers and Their Critics* (1944), wherein he calls attention to the sins, negligences and ignorances of critics and reviewers, and cites chapter and verse to show that in every age and country they have failed to recognize budding genius. This direful truth would seem to cut the ground from under a book of this kind. Yet the author can still find comfort and reassurance in the idea that lies at the core of this volume and its three predecessors: "in the *multitude* of counsellors there is safety." Any critic now and then can and does go wrong, but this need not trouble us too much for we put not our trust in any one individual opinion, but seek and follow a *consensus* of the best opinion obtainable.

[1] The figure on the backstrap of this book was copied from a very ancient Cretan coin. It would seem to indicate that there is basis of fact for the legends of King Minos of Crete and *his* labyrinth.—A. D. D.

In comparing this book with its three predecessors two trends are noteworthy: the steadily increasing proportion of American titles among the best books, and the decreasing proportion of fiction titles since 1925. This is made evident by the accompanying tables.

	Books before 1900	1901-25	1926-35	1936-45
American ..	22.5%	52%	73%	76%
British	49.5%	38%	18.5%	13%
Foreign	28%	10%	8.5%	11%
Non-Fiction .	63%	42%	65%	71.5%
Fiction	37%	58%	35%	28.5%

This volume has one new feature that I hope may prove consoling to readers who fail to find one or more of their favorites listed among our select Four Hundred titles. As the compiler's records contain the "scores" of thousands of books which failed to make the grade, we now list in an appendix the runners-up, giving author, title, score and date of the six hundred books which most nearly attained the one hundred points necessary for admission to our Four Hundred's ranks.

Except as noted above, this book follows exactly the plan of its immediate predecessor in the series, *The Best Books of the Decade 1926-1935*. For new readers we reprint below the preface of the preceding book, changing only such facts, dates and figures as need alteration to fit them to this latest volume.

Many years ago, at an impressionable age, I came across a book which interested and I think permanently influenced me. It was *Self-Measurement*, by William DeWitt Hyde, President of Bowdoin College. With its help a serious, conscientious young person—I will not say prig—can evaluate himself as a member of society. Has he a snub nose, red hair, and freckles? Then he is a liability not an asset in the aesthetic *ensemble*. Better mark him down *minus forty.* Has he a pleasing tenor voice and the ability to read music? He scores *plus fifty* for potential value in the village choir. . . . It now sounds rather silly perhaps, but in rosy-cheeked youth I found the computation of my individual score a thrilling experience and I think a usefully stimulating one.

Since that day I have confessed a weakness for all schemes to weigh imponderables and hold a tape-line to infinity. This book is one of them.

One Thousand Best Books, a descriptive list and comparative rating of the choicest books of all time as selected by a consensus of expert opinion, was published in 1924. This was followed four years later by *Best Books of Our Time, 1901-1925*—a work on the same plan, also listing a thousand titles. Then came *Best Books of the Decade, 1926-1935.* It listed four hundred titles and was published in 1937. This present book lists and describes the four hundred "best" books, published 1936-1945. It accomplishes its aim more nearly, I believe, than any of its predecessors. In the multitude of counsellors there is wisdom, and more "best-book lists" by competent authorities were discovered and have contributed to the making of this volume than were available for any of its predecessors. (This would seem to indicate a continuing, nay, even an increasing public interest in essays at best book selection.) Moreover, an admitted defect in the two earlier lists has been corrected in the two later ones. In the earlier works old books had an indubitable advantage over new ones, for the former had had more time than the latter to accumulate a stock of endorsements; and it was by the size of this stock that the books were rated.

In the present work and its predecessor a title is at first rated ten points for each list upon which it appears. If the list is a lengthy one which not only sets down the most important titles but indicates also which are considered the stars among the most important, a book thus doubly honored is accorded a double credit—twenty points.

To overcome the handicap of lack of time in which to gather endorsements the ratings of books published in 1945 are marked up twenty per cent; those of 1944, fifteen per cent; 1943, ten per cent; and 1942, five per cent. The records of 1941 and 1940 books stand without adjustment; while those of 1939 books are cut five per cent; those of 1938, ten per cent; 1937, fifteen per cent; and 1936, twenty per cent. With these modifications the newest books probably have a slight advantage over the oldest ones. But it is a very slight one for the average adjusted score of the 1945 books exceeds that of the 1936 books by only a few points. Without adjustment the average score of the 1936 books would exceed that of the 1945 books by a considerable amount.

The equity of the adjustment is further evidenced by the fact that roughly the same number of books each year attains the required minimum adjusted rating—one hundred points.

The main body of the work consists of a single arrangement, alphabetical by authors, of all the four hundred titles included in the list. There will be found the essential, identifying facts about each author, as well as a thumb-nail description and evaluation of each book. One may always check the latter against the book's numerical score, to discount the personal, idiosyncratic prejudice or enthusiasm of the compiler.

The table of contents is a key to other groupings according to comparative excellence, form, subject matter, or nationality.

The number in bold-face type which accompanies each title is its adjusted rating according to a consensus of the best obtainable critical opinion. These "scores" range between a minimum of 100 and the maximum of 680. For economy of space this number takes the place of the list of endorsers given in two of the three earlier books, as part of each title's description. If any reader wishes to know which sponsors have endorsed a given title, this information will be furnished provided the enquirer encloses a stamped, addressed envelope.

The initials B.R.D. (for *Book Review Digest*), followed by numerals and plus and minus signs, appear after the publication date of each title. B.R.D. 6+, 3–, for example, would mean that in the *Book Review Digest* six favorable reviews are cited and three unfavorable ones.

A descriptive list of the authorities, on whose endorsements our ratings are based, immediately precedes the main text.

The reader is particularly asked to remember that throughout this book the word *best* means *selected by a consensus of expert opinion as most worthy the attention of today's intelligent American readers, with at least a high school education or its equivalent.*

A. D. D.

CONTENTS

"In the multitude of counsellors there is safety."

Proverbs xi:14

THE
BEST BOOKS OF THE DECADE

1936-1945

A CITATION OF THE HUNDREDS OF BEST-BOOK LISTS ON WHICH THIS BOOK IS BASED

A. L. A. *catalog*, in two volumes covering respectively 1932-36 and 1937-41, lists and annotates some thousands of excellent books published in the decade, 1936-45, all of which are recommended by the American Library Association.

AMERICAN Library Association issued in January 1939, a list of one hundred "books which every American should read." (Six of the titles were published during the decade, 1936-45.) This list was supplemented by Thomas M. Iiams in the *Library Journal.* April 1, 1944.

AMERICAN *Library Association Bulletin*, in 1945 and 1946, published lists of fifty outstanding books of 1944 and 1945, as selected by the A.L.A. membership.

AMERICAN Writers Congress, at their meeting in June 1939, chose by ballot the "best published writing" of the preceding year. *Publishers' Weekly*, for June 10, 1939, lists the eight titles in each classification which received the highest number of votes.

AMERICAN *yearbook* contains in each year's issue a review of the year's important books. This report consists usually of about fifty pages.

AMERICANA *annual* for 1937 and its yearly successors contain an article, "Literature," which lists and briefly characterizes the most important books published during the preceding year.

ANNUAL *register*, of London, contains each year a chapter entitled "Retrospect of literature, art, and science." After an inclusive summary of the year's important publications in the literary field, follow a dozen pages wherein about a score of titles are deemed worthy of special notice. Many even of these, however, are not of prime interest to American readers.

BEACH, J. W. *American fiction, 1920-40*. 1941. This book deals chiefly with eight authors: Dos Passos, Hemingway, Faulkner, Wolfe, Caldwell, Farrell, Marquand and Steinbeck.

BEARD, Charles A. In the *Yale Review* for December 1939, he lists twelve books of history published 1930-39 that had "intensely interested" him.

BENNET, Whitman. *Practical guide to American book-collecting*. 1941. The authors included are in a sense classics.

BOOK of the Month Club asked "a hundred and fifty-nine leading critics" to name the outstanding books of 1940. Their choice is listed in *New Republic*, February 24, 1941.

"BOOKLIST BOOKS" was an annual selection from the American Library Association's periodical, *The Booklist*. This yearly winnowing of the best from the very good ceased with the issue covering the year 1940.

BOOKS. See *New York Herald Tribune Weekly Book Review*.

BRAND, Millen. In "What to read," he named in *The Writer* (August 1940) the ten books which he advises writers to read.

BRENNER, Rica. *Poets in our time*. 1941. The author considers the following worthy of special consideration: S. V. Benét, McLeish, Lindsay, Eliot, Teasdale, Auden, Spender, Wylie and Yeats.

BRICKELL, Herschel. His choice of books published in 1937 is set forth in *Publishers' Weekly* for January 1, 1938.

BRITANNICA *Book of the year,* in the ten volumes for 1937-46, lists and comments upon the choice books of 1936-45. They are set forth in separate articles headed "American literature," "English literature," etc.

CANBY, H. S. He selected for *Life*, in 1944, the outstanding books of 1922-44. They appear in the issue for August 14.

CARDOZO, Benjamin Nathan. "Justice Cardozo's reading" is described by George S. Holloway in the *Saturday Review of Literature* of February 24, 1940. Besides a list of fifty titles published in 1936 and 1937, the article quotes the judge's salty comments on many other recent books.

CLEVELAND Public Library chose sixty books of 1940 as "well written, authentic and eminently readable." The annotated list appears in the *National Education Association Journal* for March 1941.

COMMONWEAL, annually in December, comments upon the year's harvest of important books.

COMMONWEAL published on April 9, 1943, a list of "twenty-four basic war books."

CORDELL, William H. and Cordell, K. C. *American points of view.* 1937. An anthology of important essays and articles published in 1936.

CUFF, R. P. *Guide to the literary reading of college freshmen.* 1938. Contains a useful "Freshman Reading List."

CURRENT *History's* Literary Advisory Council listed annually from 1936 to 1940 the year's "ten most outstanding non-fiction works."

DICKINSON, Asa Don. "Best books of 1937-39," is made up of three annotated lists of about forty titles each which appeared in the *National Education Association Journal* during the springs of 1938-40.

ENOCH Pratt Free Library of Baltimore selected its choice of the "Readable Books" of 1941 and 1943. The lists are printed in the National Education Association *Journal's* February issues for 1942 and 1944.

ESSAY *Annual*, 1936-41, 6 vols., edited by Erich A. Walter, is a "yearly collection of significant essays."

FADIMAN, Clifton, in the *Yale Review* for December 1939, named eleven novels published 1930-39 that had specially pleased him.

FREEMAN, Margaret B., in *Library Journal* for February 1939, published an excellent article on "1939 books for young adults." About 100 titles are recommended.

FREEMAN, Marilla, Librarian of the Cleveland Public Library, contributed to the *Wilson Library Bulletin* for June 1938, an annotated list of nine specially valuable recent books.

GANNETT, Lewis, critic of the *New York Herald Tribune*, named twenty-five American and English books of 1936 "interesting and outstanding."

He found twenty-seven of the 1937 books "specially significant" as each of them appeared on all three of the select lists chosen by *The Nation, New Republic* and *Time*.

His own "Christmas lists" for 1940 and 1943 included respectively sixteen and twenty-two items.

GEISMAR, Maxwell. *Writers in crisis: the American novel between two wars.* 1942. This study deals chiefly with Lardner, Hemingway, Dos Passos, Faulkner, Wolfe and Steinbeck.

GOOD *reading*, edited by the Committee on College Reading of the National Council of Teachers of English. 1946. An excellent list, well annotated.

GRAHAM, BESSIE. *Bookman's manual*, 5th ed., 1941. Though originally designed for the guidance of booksellers, librarians and bookmen generally have found this carefully compiled and revised volume extremely useful.

GRAY, G. W., in the *Yale Review* for December 1939, listed thirty-two books of science, published 1930-39, as being those which appealed most strongly to him.

HACKETT, A. P. *Fifty years of best sellers, 1895-1945.* 1945. An interesting book, though not exactly in our field. For each year are listed the ten best sellers—fiction, and the ten best-sellers—non-fiction.

HANSEN, Harry, of the *New York World-Telegram*, in January each year, surveys and comments upon the literary high-spots of the year preceding.

"INVITATION to learning," the programs on world books of the Columbia Broadcasting System included one book published in 1940: Leonardo da Vinci's *Notebooks*.

JOHNSON, Alvin, in *Yale Review* for December 1939, listed seven notable books on economics published, 1930-39. Three of these appeared in 1936-39.

JOHNSON, Merle. *American first editions.* 4th ed. 1942. The authors included are all in a sense American classics.

LAMONT, Thomas W., in the *Saturday Review of Literature*, in December 1943, gave well-considered commendation to ten or twelve recent books.

LAMONT, W. H. F., of Rutgers University, released in January 1947, four select lists, all of which contain titles published 1936-45. These are "Sixty great novels of all time," "Fifty outstanding biographical writings," "Fifty modern Continental and South American novels" and "Fifty contemporary American and British novels."

McCORD, David, in *Yale Review* for December 1939, listed twenty-four books of poetry published 1930-39 as those which he considers most important.

LOVEMAN, Amy, in *Saturday Review of Literature*, December 2, 1944, commented on those she considered the outstanding titles of 1944.

LOVEMAN, Amy, in the *Saturday Review of Literature* for December 1, 1945, selected and commented upon nearly a hundred titles of 1945 which she considered most notable.

LOVEMAN, Amy, in the *Saturday Review of Literature* for September 1, 1945, published her choice of about four-hundred "basic books" for the home library. About forty of these appeared during the decade 1936-45.

McCOMBS, Charles F., Chief bibliographer, New York Public Library. *Books published in the United States, 1939-1943.* 1945. A general list of about 1400 titles "recommended to reference libraries in the war areas."

MANTLE, Burns, and his successors. *Best plays of 1936-45.* 10 vols. 1937-46. Each year's volume contains about ten plays by Americans.

MICHIGAN, University of. *Alumni reading lists*: 3rd series: What to read. 1939. Annotated.

MILLET, F. B. *Contemporary American Authors.* 1940. "Contemporary" is equivalent to Twentieth Century. The book includes a list of about 250 titles in the field of *belles lettres*.

NATION publishes annually, usually in the first December issue, a list of the year's most "notable" books. These lists comprised from fifty-six to two hundred and twenty-nine titles in the years 1936-45. Only the list for 1936 is annotated.

NATION's *citation.* "A roster of Americans who deserve the applause of their countrymen." The group for 1936 included six authors of new books. That for 1937 included four.

NEW *International yearbook* for 1936 and its successors each contains an article "Literature: English and American" which names the year's important publications in the English language. These lists usually include five hundred or more titles with little comment.

New *Republic* publishes annually in December a list of "One hundred notable books" of the year. The editors explain guardedly that they are not necessarily the "best" books, but those "that have the most interest for our own times." They are not annotated.

New *York Herald Tribune Weekly Book Review* (formerly *Books*), in the first issue in December, each year, cites three favorite recent books of each of about fifty leading authors and other distinguished readers. Such persons as Ellen Glasgow, Edmund Wilson, Stephen Vincent Benét, Frank Sullivan, Wendell Willkie, Thomas Craven, Donald Culross Peattie, Stuart Chase, Douglas Freeman, Kenneth Roberts, George Fielding Eliot, Walter Millis, Hendrick Willem Van Loon, William Lyon Phelps, Edna Ferber, Carl Sandburg, Branch Cabell, Franklin P. Adams, Lin Yu-tang, Carl Von Vechten, Van Wyck Brooks, Louis Bromfield, Vincent Sheean, H. L. Mencken, Sinclair Lewis, Clifton Fadiman, William Allen White, John Erskine, Alexander Woollcott, André Maurois, Walter Prichard Eaton, and many others contributed to this symposium in 1940, a typical year.

New *York Herald Tribune Weekly Book Review* in December 1939, named the year's ten titles which were most often recommended by seventy selected writers and other public figures.

New York Public Library's list of "Ten books for Christmas" appeared in *Publishers' Weekly*, November 28, 1936.

New York Public Library in March, 1945, published the useful "Have you read these?—a selection of books, 1935-1945." It comprises about a hundred titles, and is annotated.

New York (State) University publishes each year in its *Bulletin to the Schools* (usually in the November issue) a reading list of new books, comprising 100 to 150 titles. These lists are prepared by the Book Information Section of the New York State Library.

NEW *York Times Book Review* sometimes lists in an early December issue the ten best books of the year as chosen by a group of competent critics.

NEW *Yorker*, in its issue for December 14, 1940, listed, with annotations, its choice of the year's best books.

NEWSWEEK, in its issue for December 14, 1942, selected twelve of the year's books as particularly worth recommending. In its issue for December 19, 1936, twenty-six such titles are named; and in that of December 16, 1940, twenty outstanding titles.

O. HENRY memorial award: prize stories of 1936-45 selected and edited by Harry Hansen and others. Three prize stories of each year are selected.

O'BRIEN E. J. ed. *Best short stories.* 10 vols. 1936-45.

O'BRIEN, E. J. ed. *Fifty best American short stories, 1915-39.* 1939.

ONE *hundred significant books* is the title of a list compiled by the Committee on College Reading for the National Council of Teachers of English and published in the *National Education Association Journal* in December 1941. All but a very few were published before 1936-45.

OXFORD *companion to American literature*, by J. D. Hart. 1941. Includes a "Chronological index" listing the prominent literary landmarks of each year.

PHELPS, William Lyon. A list of his favorites among recently published books appeared in *Newsweek*, September 13, 1937.

PHELPS, William Lyon, in July 1936, published in *Scribner's Magazine* an annotated list of a hundred books issued "since June 1, 1935."

PORT Washington Public Library, in 1942, asked a group of distinguished authors, critics and publicists to name the books which had "most profoundly affected the thoughts and actions of mankind" during the preceding half-century. Only a small minority of the titles that appear on the resultant list were published 1936-45.

"PRESIDENTS should read books." Columbia University's *Pleasures of Publishing* polled its readers in 1940 to ascertain what titles should be recommended to our Presidents. The ten most often suggested are listed in *Publishers' Weekly*, June 29, 1940.

PUBLISHERS' *Weekly*, published in vol. 131, page 117, its selection of the "Distinguished books of 1936."

PUBLISHERS' *Weekly* collated the best-book-of-the-year lists published at the end of 1939 by *Nation, New Republic, Commonweal, Saturday Review of Literature* and *Time* and in its issue for December 16, 1939, named sixty-seven titles as mentioned most frequently in these lists.

PULITZER Prize winners may generally but not quite always be safely numbered among the best books. Leading critics were polled each year, 1937-41, to ascertain their nominations for the Pulitzer prize winners.

RASCOE, Burton, in *Newsweek*, December 26, 1938, published a list of twenty titles—his favorites among the books of 1938.

RICHARDSON, Louise, in *Recreation* (August 1938) writes of "Books and the more abundant life." Of those she lists only about ten were published during 1936-45.

ROTARIAN, in one or other of its January issues, 1937-46, has published annotated lists of the previous year's ten best or twenty best books. From 1937 to 1943 those lists were compiled by William Lyon Phelps; thereafter by John T. Frederick.

"S. R. O: the most successful plays in the history of the American stage," compiled by Bennett Cerf. 1944. Includes three plays published 1936-45.

SATURDAY *Review of Literature*, December 2, 1939, selected fifty-two of the year's publications to recommend for Christmas. Similarly in December of the years 1941 to 1945 some twenty to sixty titles were endorsed by their reviewers as the year's best for Christmas giving.

SCOGGIN, Margaret S., of the New York Public Library, recommends some of the 1944 and 1945 "Books for young adults" in the *Library Journal* for October 15, 1944, and October 15, 1945.

SHAW, Charles B. *List of books for college libraries, 1931-1938*, published in 1940, is a supplement to his basic list which appeared in 1931. About 3600 titles are included. "The simple fact of inclusion implies a high degree of merit and of usefulness in the specified sphere of this publication." Like the original work the list was published by the American Library Association, with the aid of the Carnegie Corporation.

STANDARD *catalog for public libraries*, 1940 edition, is an annotated, classified list of 12,000 titles. Very important books—about one fifth of the titles—are starred. Of these the *most* important — about one fifth — are double-starred. In checking this list we have disregarded all but the starred and double-starred titles.

Supplement, 1941-1945, lists 3,900 important books of these years, again starring the more important and double-starring the most important. As in the original work we have disregarded all but the starred and double-starred titles.

TIME, 1937-45, lists each year in a December issue the year's "outstanding titles." The books listed have varied in number from sixty-two to eighty-six. The last five lists have been annotated.

TORONTO Public Library, at the end of 1945, published an annotated list of "150 books, 1943-1945," which met with wide approval. The 14th edition of this list was current in September 1946.

WHITE, William Allen, in the *Yale Review*. December 1939, listed twenty-two notable biographies of the decade, 1930-39. Seven of these were published 1936-39.

THE
BEST BOOKS OF THE DECADE
1936-1945

Adamic, Louis   1899-

American author. Born in what is now Yugoslavia; educated at the Gymnasium, Ljubljana; came to the United States, 1913; served in the U.S. Army, 1917-20; naturalized, 1918; married Stella Sanders, of New York, 1931; Guggenheim Fellow, 1932-33.

FROM MANY LANDS. 1940. B.R.D. 4+, 0– Harper. $3.50.   **100**

Tells the stories, sketches the characters, reveals the personal philosophies and individual problems of a number of Americans who were born in foreign lands.

Adams, Franklin Pierce ("F. P. A.")   1881-

The famous columnist of the "Conning Tower" was born in Chicago and educated at the Armour Scientific Academy and the University of Michigan. Since 1938 he has become even better known as a member of the cast of "Information Please."

INNOCENT MERRIMENT; AN ANTHOLOGY OF LIGHT VERSE. 1942. B.R.D. 7+, 0– McGraw. $3.   **105**

Burlesque, parody, nonsense rhyme and satire; translation, paraphrase, song and story. These selections are about as good as they come, and a surprising number first appeared in the "Conning Tower." "A highly salubrious volume," says W. R. Benét, "I want this book to be widely distributed."

Adams, Henry   1838-1918

Descendant of two Presidents of the United States; brother of Charles Francis Adams. Member, American

Academy of Arts and Letters. Author of the famous "Education" (1918) and of "Mont St. Michel and Chartres" (1913).

LETTERS (1892-1918); edited by Worthington C. Ford. 1938. B.R.D. 7+, 3- Houghton. $4.50.   144

He was one of the great letter writers, thoughtful and dowered with ample leisure. The type is now practically extinct. Says *The Springfield Republican*, "Adams' pessimism was part of the fun. His friends expected him to grumble and he grumbled magnificently for their pleasure and his own."

LETTERS (1858-91) was published in 1930.

Adams, J. Donald   1891-

Author, editor, anthologist. He was born in New York City and educated at Harvard. His career as a journalist was interrupted by two years' service in World War I. Editor of the *New York Times Book Review* from 1925 to 1943, he still writes an editorial in each issue.

SHAPE OF BOOKS TO COME. 1944. B.R.D. 5+, 2- Viking. $2.50.   103

In these essays Mr. Adams surveys American literature since 1900. With no apologies, but without smugness, he takes his stand on the side of the angels.

Adams, Samuel Hopkins   1871-

Journalist, and author of many books about the American scene. He was born in New York City and educated at Hamilton College.

A. WOOLLCOTT, HIS LIFE AND HIS WORLD. 1945. B.R.D. 7+, 2- Reynal. $3.50.   156

"Alexander Woollcott, despite everything, supplied an enlivening moment in a racy and enlivening chapter of American culture, and the Adams biography serves him well."—*New Republic*.

"Neither prettified nor knife-in-the-back, . . . gives a detailed picture of the man, friend and enemy, showman and salesman."—*Kirkus Bulletin.*

Adler, Mortimer Jerome   1902-

Born in New York City; educated at Columbia University, 1920-1928; professor of the philosophy of law, University of Chicago.

How to Read a Book: the Art of Getting a Liberal Education. 1940. B.R.D. 6+, 2– Simon. $2.50
                                                            130

About learning and thinking, how and what to read, and the why of it; about the obligations of citizens in a democracy.

"These four hundred pages are packed full of high matters which no one solicitous for the future of America can afford to overlook."—Jacques Barzun, in the *Saturday Review of Literature.*

Agar, Herbert (Sebastian)   1897-

Journalist and author. Born in New Rochelle, N.Y.; educated at Columbia and Princeton Universities; served in Naval Reserve, 1917-18, and was later lieutenant commander; was Special Assistant to American Ambassador, London, and Director, British Division, Office of War Information.

Time for Greatness. 1942. B.R.D. 8+, 3– Little. $2.50.
                                                            137

A classification of America's problems of war and peace.

"How the weaknesses which we as individuals permitted to develop in our society at last invited attack upon us." One critic remarks that a better title for the book would be *Pater peccavi.*

"An outstanding document of our time. It reflects brilliantly the feeling of liberal Americans who do not like war, yet like slavery and barbarism even less."—*Saturday Review of Literature.*

Aldington, Richard, editor   1892-

English poet and man of letters; served in World War I, 1916-1918.

Viking Book of Poetry of the English-Speaking World, 1941. B.R.D. 11+, 8– Viking. $3.50.
120

In round numbers here are 1,300 poems by 300 authors who have written during the last thousand years. The critics have found many flaws, as is usual in the case of anthologies, yet W. R. Benét hails the collection as being "in general, a superior achievement," while *New Republic's* critic, Malcolm Cowley, prefers it to the "Oxford Book of English Verse."

Andrews, Mrs. H. M. *See* West, Rebecca, pseud.

Andrews, Roy Chapman   1884-

American zoologist and explorer. Born, Beloit, Wisconsin; educated at Beloit College; formerly Director, American Museum of Natural History; leader of many scientific expeditions; most important work was that done in the Gobi Desert where dinosaur eggs and fossils were found.

Under a Lucky Star; a Lifetime of Adventure. 1943. B.R.D. 4+, 2– Viking. $3.
110

Not a scientist's memoirs. Such a book is often stodgy. There are here, rather, good-humored recollections of adventurous travel, written for the general reader, "closer to Frank Buck than to William Beebe."

Armstrong, Margaret (Neilson)   1867-1944

Born in New York City. Artist and illustrator till 1930; thereafter, biographer and specialist in murder mysteries.

FANNY KEMBLE: A PASSIONATE VICTORIAN. 1938. B.R.D. *792.069*
    12+, 1– Macmillan. $3.   **162** *K31A*

"It's Fanny Kemble's final triumph that she has found a biographer worthy of her."—*Books.*

"A beautiful and judicious biography. Reading it is like reading a piece of great fiction set against a background of social and intellectual history on both sides of the Atlantic, through most of the nineteenth century."—W. E. Garrison, in *Christian Century.*

TRELAWNEY; A MAN'S LIFE. 1940. B.R.D. 12+, 7–
    Macmillan. $3.   **170**

This extraordinary Cornish adventurer, intimate of Byron and Shelley, has a secure place in the history of English literature.

"Eminently readable, this book will appeal especially to men."—*Library Journal.*

"His life is the very stuff of romance, and Miss Armstrong has written a biography that reads like a novel."—*Commonweal.*

"Those who are not yet acquainted with his fabulous life, have something in store for them in the reading of this book."—John Erskine, in *Books.*

Arvin, Newton   1900–

American author and teacher. Born, Valparaiso, Indiana; educated at Harvard; Guggenheim Fellow, 1935-36; has taught English at Smith College since 1922.

WHITMAN. 1938. B.R.D. 9+, 4– Macmillan. $2.75.
                                                100

Less a biography than an able, critical, social and political interpretation, with some Left Wing coloration.

Asch, Sholem   1880–

This Polish-American novelist, who is said to write always in Yiddish, came to America in 1910 and was naturalized in 1920. He lives in Stamford, Connecticut.

THE APOSTLE; translated by Maurice Samuel.   1943.
    B.R.D. 12+, 7– Putnam. $3.   **198**

Yale Review calls this novel about St. Paul "the culminating, finest step in Jewish religious development."

"It is reverent and deeply felt . . . but remember that it is fiction, not doctrine."—*Commonweal.*

"A sequel to *The Nazarene* and, like many sequels, inferior to its predecessor. It is a lesser book, just as Paul, its subject, is a lesser figure than his Master."—Clifton Fadiman, in the *New Yorker.*

THE NAZARENE; translated by Maurice Samuel.   1939.
    B.R.D. 11+, 2– Putnam. $2.75.   **152**

Scholarly story of the life and times of Christ, retold from three different points of view.

"Judged purely as a novel, *The Nazarene* is a superb achievement. . . Papini's *Life* is thin beside it."—John Cournos, in *Atlantic.*

"It is a book which every Christian will wish to read. . . . There are no biographies of Christ which bring so vividly to life the figure of Jesus."—*Churchman.*

Auden, Wystan Hugh   1907-

English poet, educated at Oxford; lives in England and United States; Professor of English at University of Michigan; writes often in collaboration with Christopher Isherwood.

COLLECTED POETRY. 1945. B.R.D. 5+, 2– Random.
    $3.75.   **199**

"This volume firmly establishes Mr. Auden as the most exciting poet of his generation."—*Atlantic.*

"This collection certainly confirms Auden's great reputation."—*Nation.*

"Auden, it has for some time been apparent, has succeeded Eliot as the strongest influence in American and British poetry."—Louise Bogan, in *New Yorker.*

Audubon, John James   1785-1851

Franco-American artist and ornithologist. Born in Santo Domingo; reared in France; came to United States in 1803.

BIRDS OF AMERICA; introduction and descriptive text by William Vogt. 1937. B.R.D. 6+, 1– Macmillan. $12.50. (Reprint, 1947, $6.95).   **119**

First popular edition of a century-old classic with five hundred color plates.

"Looking at the book in sum, with five hundred reproductions of the most famous paintings of birds ever made, one can only call it superb."—*Saturday Review of Literature.*

AUDUBON'S AMERICA: NARRATIVES AND EXPERIENCES; edited by Donald Culross Peattie. 1940. B.R.D. 9+, 1– Houghton. $6.   **240**

"Should have a wide appeal as biography and travel, as natural history, and as a broad picture of the America of his day as only Audubon could have written it."—*Library Journal.*

"Mr. Peattie culls from Audubon's memoirs and hard-to-get-at journals the freshest and liveliest of his impressions, whether of grackles or Daniel Boone. This he edits with lively insight."—Clifton Fadiman, in *New Yorker.*

Baker, Mrs. Dorothy (Dodds)   1907-

Born, Missoula, Montana; educated in California; lived in France; has been a teacher of Latin.

YOUNG MAN WITH A HORN. 1938. B.R.D. 7+, 3– Houghton. $2,50.   **100**

"The strangely touching story of a swing musician."

Not forgetting the inevitable limitations of the subject, Clifton Fadiman is willing to "step up and announce clear and loud that *Young Man with a Horn* is practically perfect."

"[The story] has the firm lines of a sculptured figure; the quality and pathos that Charlie Chaplin gave, playing the little fellow in a large industrial plant. . . . Rick's last words, though they were never spoken, are as haunting as the song of the heart-broken clown in 'Pagliacci.' "—*Boston Transcript*.

Barnard, Harry   1906-

Journalist and biographer of American statesmen. Born in Pueblo, Colorado, "the son of Dr. David Kletzky," an eye specialist. Educated at the University of Denver and the University of Chicago. He has written a life of Senator Couzens of Michigan and is now (1948) studying the career of Rutherford B. Hayes.

THE EAGLE FORGOTTEN; the Life of John Peter Altgeld. 1938. B.R.D. 6+, 1- Bobbs. $4.   **100**

It was the hero-worshipping poet, Vachel Lindsay, who called Altgeld the eagle forgotten. Here is the truth about the poor German boy who became Governor of Illinois and pardoned the Haymarket rioters. The truth needed telling. Altgeld was neither a snake of anarchism nor a saint of labor. The evidence is fairly considered and both sides are given praise and blame as deserved.

Barzun, Jacques Martin   1907-

Professor of history at Columbia University since 1929. Born in Paris, he came to the United States in 1919 and was naturalized in 1933.

TEACHER IN AMERICA. 1945. B.R.D. 11+, 0- Little. $3.   **204**

This book is really about teaching, rather than teachers —what is taught and why and how, and what can be done to improve teaching. Education may be the dullest of subjects but there are no dull pages in this book. It should interest laymen too for it is not burdened with the jargon and mechanics of pedagogy. Educators who will consult Mr. Barzun, says Dean Gauss, may perhaps "learn something to their advantage."

Beard, Charles Austin   1874-

American author and college professor. Born at Knightstown, Indiana, and educated at DePauw University, Oxford, Cornell and Columbia. He taught political science at Columbia from 1904 to 1917, when he resigned in support of academic freedom; advised the Japanese on municipal affairs for some years before and after the great earthquake; helped to found the New School for Social Research, New York City. He lives now at New Milford, Connecticut, where he operates a large dairy farm. He is a member of the National Institute of Arts and Letters.

342.733
B36r

THE REPUBLIC: CONVERSATIONS ON FUNDAMENTALS. 1943. B.R.D. 7+, 2– Viking. $3. **209**

"An inspiring course on the fundamental issues of government and democracy. . . . It should revolutionize the teaching of American government both on the college and adult education levels."—*Nation*.

"He who reads the first of these conversations will read all of the twenty-one that are recorded in this book." —*New York Times*.

(But watch out for the one on foreign affairs. It turns into a somewhat noisy and bitter cat-fight.)

**Beard, C. A.   (1874-   ) and Beard, Mary Ritter
1876-**

973
B36a

AMERICA IN MIDPASSAGE. 1939. B.R.D. 14+, 7– Macmillan. $3.50. **237**

This is vol.3 of *The Rise of American Civilization* and covers our history from Coolidge (1924) to 1938.

"Better books of contemporary history than this may yet be written, but not many of them."—*American Political Science Review*.

"It is a brilliant, comprehensive and masterly analysis of the America it considers."—*Christian Science Monitor.*

John Dewey says nobody but the Beards could have done this job.

Beard, C. A. and Beard, M. R., editors

973
B366

BASIC HISTORY OF THE UNITED STATES. 1944. B.R.D. 6+, 2– Garden City. 69c. **126**

"Perhaps, all in all, the best one-volume history that has even been written about the United States."—*New Yorker.*

"An impressive short work which rounds off a lifetime of brilliant studies of American civilization."—*New York Times.*

"It is surely a wonderful thing that millions of Americans can now read their own history at so small a cost."—*Commonweal.*

Beard, Mary Ritter. *See* Beard, C. A. jt. auth.

Beard, Miriam (Mrs. Alfred Vagts)   1901-

Daughter of C. A. and M. R. Beard; husband was officer in German army in World War I.

650.9
B36

HISTORY OF THE BUSINESS MAN. 1938. B.R.D. 9+, 3– Macmillan. $5. **100**

"An extremely important book."—*Saturday Review of Literature.*

"Well written, in an easy and readable style, lightened by numerous amusing anecdotes."—*Annals American Academy.*

"The task is well done. No historian need pass this way again."—Stuart Chase, in *Books.*

Benét, Stephen Vincent   1898-1943

Member, National Institute of Arts and Letters. Born, Bethlehem, Pennsylvania; the son and grandson of American army officers; educated at Yale and the Sorbonne; died in New York City. Author of the narrative poem, "John Brown's Body," which won Pulitzer prize, 1928, and of the folk tale, "Devil and Daniel Webster," (1937).

WESTERN STAR. 1943. B.R.D. 6+, 1– Farrar. $2.
165

This is the beginning of the great epic that was to have shown the westward migration of those who founded this nation. "One feels," says Leonard Bacon, "that even 'John Brown's Body' was but a prologue to the great story he hoped to tell." The author goes only so far as to describe the settling at Plymouth and at Jamestown. Won Pulitzer prize, 1944.

Benét, William Rose   1886-

American poet. This elder brother of Stephen Vincent Benét was born at Fort Hamilton, now in New York City, and educated at the Sheffield Scientific School (Yale). Since its beginning in 1924 he has been a member of the editorial staff of the *Saturday Review of Literature*. He has been four times married; his second wife was the poet Elinor Wylie. He is a member of the National Institute of Arts and Letters.

DUST WHICH IS GOD. 1941. B.R.D. 7+, 3– Dodd.
$3.50.   **160**

This autobiographical novel in verse won a Pulitzer prize, 1942. It presents a detailed picture of a period, 1900-1940.

"One of the great documents of our time."—J. G. Fletcher, in *Poetry*.

"If the American audience would suspend their distaste for poetry for just one book, and began to read this one, it would go through the country life a prairie fire."— *New York Times*.

Blodget, Mrs. A. S. *See* Skinner, Cornelia Otis

Booth, Clare (Mrs. Henry R. Luce)   1903-

Born in New York City; educated at the Cathedral School of St. Mary, Garden City. She has been both actress and play-wright. Lives at Greenwich, Connecticut, and was a member of Congress, 1943-47.

EUROPE IN THE SPRING. 1940. B.R.D. 7+, 1- Knopf. $2.50.   **100**

This traveler's observation of Europe and Europeans from February to June, 1940, is called a "sane, sad, disturbing recital" by the *New York Times*.

Miss Booth conveys a sense of the apathy, false confidence and despairing criticism which characterized London, Paris, Amsterdam and Brussels on the eve of catastrophe."—*Atlantic*.

"It has all the impressionistic charm of a Colette or a Katherine Mansfield, but also at times the deep significance of a Siegfried or a Madariaga."— A. Maurois, in *Saturday Review of Literature*.

Borgese, Giuseppe Antonio   1882-

Author and university professor in Italy and the United States. Born in Sicily, he came to the United States in 1931 to escape Fascism, became an American citizen in 1938, and married Elizabeth, daughter of Thomas Mann, in 1939.

GOLIATH; THE MARCH OF FASCISM. 1937. B.R.D. 5+, 1- Viking. $3.   **128**

"History of Italian culture and politics from Dante to Mussolini, portraying the background and rise of modern fascism."—*Book Review Digest*.

"Borgese was eminently qualified for this task. He has written a book to which future historians will turn for inspiration as well as instruction."—Alvin Johnson, in *Yale Review*.

Botkin, Benjamin Albert, editor   1901-

Born in Boston; editor of *Folk-Say* (1929-32) and of *Space* (1934-35). He is folk-song adviser to the Library of Congress and president of the American Folklore Society.

TREASURY OF AMERICAN FOLKLORE; STORIES, BALLADS AND TRADITIONS OF THE PEOPLE, with a foreword by Carl Sandburg. 1944. B.R.D. 7+, 1– Crown. $3.   138

398
B74t

"A literary storehouse of the stories, legends, tall tales, ballads and songs of the American people."—J. A. Lomax, in *Saturday Review of Literature.*

"The general impression one gets is of the sheer lustiness of Americana. Cowboys, bad men, lumberjacks and big Negro laborers rollick through its pages."—*Christian Science Monitor.*

"Most imposing volume of American folklore. . . . If you have funds for only one book a year, buy this."—*Library Journal.*

Bowen, Catherine Drinker   1897-

Born in Haverford, Pennsylvania; lives in Bryn Mawr.

YANKEE FROM OLYMPUS; JUSTICE HOLMES AND HIS FAMILY. 1944. B.R.D. 12+, 2– Little. $3.   380

340
H25B

The Holmeses of Massachusetts from 1763 to 1935. And it was only three generations: Abiel, the man of God, Oliver the man of medicine, and Oliver, Junior, the man of law.

"A book to understand America by."—S. D. Hayakawa, in *Book Week.*

"First and last a work of art. It has the structure and movement of a well-built novel rather than the undirected flow of a biography."—*Columbia Law Review.*

Bowen, Elizabeth (Mrs. Alan Cameron)   1899-

Lives at Bowen's Court, Cork, Ireland, and in London.

DEATH OF THE HEART. 1939. B.R.D. 15+, 3- Knopf.
$2.50.   133

A distinguished novel in the tradition of Henry James
and Proust. The critics say: "It makes no concession to
the popular taste"; "it is cold and brittle like a diamond,
and it cuts as mercilessly"; and "there are certain things
too painful to be the subject of fiction."

"By far her best· book and as satisfying a novel
as has come out of England for some time."—Clifton
Fadiman, in *New Yorker*.

Bowers, Claude G.   1879-

Journalist, author, diplomat. A former ambassador
to Spain and to Chile. He has written much on American
history, especially on Jackson and Jefferson.

973.46
B78j

JEFFERSON IN POWER: THE DEATH STRUGGLE WITH THE
        FEDERALISTS. 1936. B.R.D. 9+, 4- Houghton.
        $3.75.   152

Sequel to *Jefferson and Hamilton*, 1925 (see *Best
Books of Our Time*); covers the eight years of Jefferson's
presidency. J. T. Adams published his *Living Jefferson*
the same year as *Jefferson in Power*, so his opinion of the
latter is interesting. He says "Mr Bowers' present book
shows a marked advance over his previous ones not only in
style but also in fairness and balance. . . . Though not his
most exciting, it is, I think, his best."

973.46
B78y

YOUNG JEFFERSON; 1743-1789. 1945. B.R.D. 13+, 3-
        Houghton. $3.75.   156

From his birth to his return from Europe to become
Washington's Secretary of State.

"The third and completing Jefferson volume of Bowers,
who wrote his biography backward. One can see why. The
farther back into the colonial record, the harder to add flesh
and blood to the narrative."—*Boston Globe*.

"An eye for the significant detail, the revealing anecdote,
the apt quotation, makes his pages glow with life and movement."—*New York Times*.

Bowman, Peter

Author and mechanical engineer. With Anaconda Copper Mining Company, 1939-41. Associate editor of *Popular Science Monthly* since 1942; with Combat Engineers, 1943.

BEACH RED. 1945. B.R.D. 8+, 2– Random. $2.50.
120

This war book is something of a curiosity, a fictional narrative poem describing a modern ordeal by battle. There is literally one line to the second, one chapter to the minute.

"Mr. Bowman has found something of his own which is not professional belles-lettres and yet not, in a bad sense, journalistic."—Edmund Wilson, in *New Yorker*.

"This is the story not only of a landing on a tiny, unnamed Pacific island but, indeed, of all war everywhere." —*Saturday Review of Literature*.

Brogan, Denis W.   1900-

Professor of political science. Born in Glasgow, he lives in Cambridge, England, and has written much on American history and government.

AMERICAN CHARACTER. 1944. B.R.D. 11+, 2– Knopf. $2.50.
150

A book designed to make more intelligible to the British public certain American principles and attitudes.

"He is one of a very few men—whether foreigners or citizens of the country—who knows the United States." —H. Agar, in *Spectator*.

"Anyone hoping for a better understanding of what, who and why the United States is, will value this book highly, especially if the seeker for understanding be an American."—*Christian Science Monitor*.

Bromfield, Louis   1896-

American novelist. Born in Ohio, his education was disrupted by World War I in which he served with the

French Army. Since then he has lived much of the time in France and India but is now back on his Ohio farm. He is a member of the National Institute of Arts and Letters.

630.1
B86p

PLEASANT VALLEY. 1945. B.R.D. 8+, 2– Harper. $3.
130

In part autobiographical reminiscences of sophisticated life in the cities of the United States, France and India, and in part exposition of his theories of farming and the blessed American farm life. The critics use mostly pleasant adjectives in their comment: delightful, wise, beautiful, charming, entertaining, romantic. 'Tis a far cry indeed from the feverish *Night in Bombay* to a summer morning in *Pleasant Valley*. The *Saturday Review of Literature* says that this book is "straight from the heart with no eye on the box office."

Brooks, Van Wyck   1886-

American man of letters. Member American Academy of Arts and Letters. Born in Plainfield, New Jersey, and educated at Harvard; he taught English at Stanford University and has done much editorial work for publishers. He edited *The Freeman*, 1920-24. His *Ordeal of Mark Twain* (1919) provoked controversy. With four books among the "Four Hundred Best," his is by far the largest score, 1711 points, made by the decade's authors.

810.9
B87f

FLOWERING OF NEW ENGLAND, 1815-1865. 1936. B.R.D.
15+, 3– Dutton. $4.   510

About the men whose portraits still decorate schoolroom walls throughout the nation: Longfellow, Emerson, Hawthorne, Thoreau, Lowell, etc. He describes in beautiful prose, distinguished by scholarship and penetration, the life which produced these figures of the Golden Age of American letters. The book won him a Pulitzer prize in 1937, and was designated "the most distinguished non-fiction book of 1936" by American Book Sellers Association.

"Van Wyck Brooks has produced a masterpiece."—*Catholic World.*

"If he continues and finishes his task on the same scale as this, and with the same knowledge, range, insight, precision and grace, he will have written not only the best history of American literature, but one of the best literary histories in any language."—Carl Van Doren.

NEW ENGLAND: INDIAN SUMMER, 1865-1915. 1940. *810.9*
    B.R.D. 11+, 1– Dutton. $3.75.   560 *B87n*

The second part of his literary history. The foremost figures among the hundreds described are four almost great men, all in some degree frustrated: Henry Adams, Henry James, Francis Parkman and William Dean Howells.

"A must book for libraries large and small."—*Library Journal.*

"It confirms once more the indubitable position of Van Wyck Brooks as the premier literary historian now at work in the United States."—*New Yorker.*

"This is not merely another book; it is an event in literature."—*Springfield Republican.*

OPINIONS OF OLIVER ALLSTON. 1941. B.R.D. 4+, 2– *818.5*
    Dutton. $3.   170 *B87o*

The "opinions" are mostly literary opinions of course. Oliver Allston appears to be just a harmless necessary stooge for the author.

"One of the most thoughtful and dynamic books in recent American writing. These are qualities, to be sure, that we long since came to expect in the work of Van Wyck Brooks, but they are present here in a more concentrated and, at the same time, a more widely applied way than in any other book we have had from him."—J. Donald Adams, in *New York Times.*

"Because this book plumbs the depths and shallows of vital problems, it should be widely, slowly and thoughtfully read."—*Saturday Review of Literature.*

WORLD OF WASHINGTON IRVING. 1944. B.R.D. 9+, 0–
    Dutton. $3.75.   **471**

This third title in the author's series of works on
American literary history covers the years 1800 to 1840
and all of the United States except New England.

"The average reader in all likelihood will consider this
the most exciting of the author's books."—*Catholic World.*

"'Tis a wonderful period to go back to and Mr. Brooks
has written about it what seems to me so far the most
attractive volume of the series. . . . For the reader who is
curious about cultural phenomena there is not a dull page
or a dull foot-note."—Edmund Wilson, in *New Yorker.*

"Mr. Brooks makes clear the enduring importance of
authors who have long been honored but unread—for who
now reads Brockden Brown or Cooper or Simms or Bryant
or even Irving, aside from his legends?"—H. S. Commager,
in *Weekly Book Review.*

Brown, Cecil   1907-

American radio commentator, lecturer, war correspondent. Born, New Brighton, Pennsylvania; educated at
Western Reserve and Ohio State Universities. He sailed
as a seaman on freighters, 1938-39, and was sunk by Japanese in the South China Sea in 1941.

SUEZ TO SINGAPORE. 1942. B.R.D. 8+, 4– Random.
    $3.50.   **126**

Adventures—and they were adventures—of a radio
commentator from April, 1940, in Rome, to March, 1942,
when he was homeward bound for America.

"Timely, important and, above all, exciting reading."—
Saturday Review of Literature.

"Contains the fullest, the most vivid, the angriest account that anyone has written of the fall of Singapore."—
New Republic.

Brown, Harry Peter M'Nab   1917-

Born in Portland, Maine, this American author of fiction, criticism and verse served in World War II, part of the time on the staff of *Yank*.

WALK IN THE SUN. 1944. B.R.D. 12+, 2– Knopf.
      $2.   253

"This short novel describes a few hours with a few men on a beachhead in Italy. The book is by a soldier, who is also a poet, and it is very good indeed."—John Hersey, in *Weekly Book Review*.

"The whole book is beautifully compact; it is witty; it has none of the sentimental toughness of much American writing; its style is nearer to Thurber than to Hemingway."—*New Statesman*.

"Nothing so far in war literature has equalled this little story in showing the heights to which American boys can rise in meeting a situation. It is a gripping little tale."—*Christian Science Monitor*.

Brown, John Mason   1900-

Dramatic critic, lecturer and war correspondent. Born in Louisville, Kentucky, and educated at Harvard and Williams. Served in U.S. Navy, 1942-44, during invasions of Sicily and Normandy, and was awarded a Bronze Star for his conduct in the latter. He has written many books on the theatre.

MANY A WATCHFUL NIGHT. 1944. B.R.D. 3+, 1– McGraw. $2.75.   126

Personal account of pre-invasion England and the events leading up to D-day, of the landing in Normandy and the subsequent battles.

"A book that should last far beyond the ephemera of most reports on the war in Europe."—*Saturday Review of Literature*.

Buchan, John (Lord Tweedsmuir)   1875-1940

British explorer, novelist, publisher; Governor-General of Canada.

PILGRIM'S WAY; AN ESSAY IN RECOLLECTION.   1940.
        B.R.D.   12+, 0– Houghton. $3.   260

The English title is "Memory Hold-the-Door."

"A distinguished addition to the few first-rate autobiographies in the English language."—*New York Times*.

"Contains, besides an account of his life, a fine gallery of portraits of those with whom he was intimately or well acquainted."—*Commonweal*.

"A study of living. What has life done to me? Is the adventure worth while? These questions are asked and answered courageously."—*Boston Transcript*.

Buck, Paul H.   1899-

Historian. Born in Columbus, Ohio. In 1926 he joined the educational staff at Harvard, where he is now Dean of the Faculty and professor of history.

ROAD TO REUNION.   1937. B.R.D. 7+, 2– Little. $3.25.
                                                        102

This survey of American history from 1865 to 1900 was awarded the Pulitzer prize for history in 1938.

"A distinctive contribution to American literature."— N. B. Cousins, in *Current History*.

"A brilliant performance . . . a real contribution to our understanding of how an America, almost riven, has become almost one again."—G. F. Milton, in *New Republic*.

Buck, Pearl S. (Mrs. Richard John Walsh)   1892-

American novelist. Born at Hillsboro, West Virginia; spent her youth with missionary parents in Chinkiang on the Yangtse; educated by her mother at home, at boarding-school at Shanghai, and at Randolph Macon College. She married in China a young American teacher of rural economics and shared his life of teaching in various parts of

China. She is now the wife of Richard J. Walsh, her publisher. Member, National Institute of Arts and Letters. Won Pulitzer prize in 1932, Nobel prize in 1938.

DRAGON SEED. 1942. B.R.D. 13+, 4– Day. $2.50. *F*
B9226
147

A story of China under the Japanese invader.

"The strongest and most instructive story yet written of China at war."—*Time*.

"I doubt if Pearl Buck was ever better than in her new novel, *Dragon Seed*."—Edward Weeks, in *Atlantic*.

"A vivid portrayal of family solidarity and devotion amid the horrors and terrors of modern warfare."—*Library Journal*.

"A propaganda novel concerned with a little group of farmers who decided not to flee westward before the advancing Japanese, but to hold on to the land as long as they could."—*Catholic World*.

FIGHTING ANGEL: PORTRAIT OF A SOUL. 1936. B.R.D. *266*
8+, 2– Reynal. $2.50. *5982B*
104

"A thoroughly admirable and sympathetic account of her father's stalwart faith and indefatigable labors both in scholarship and evangelism."—*Commonweal*.

"Both as a study of a man who had absolute belief in the rightness of his principles and of a missionary of the period in which the subject carried on his work in China, Mrs. Buck's book is in all respects an admirable piece of work."—*Review of Reviews*.

THE PATRIOT. 1939. B.R.D. 8+, 2– Day. $2.50. **123**

Story of Chinese nationalism in the making.

"Twelve years in the life of a young Chinese—his experiences with the Communists, his sojourn in Japan and his marriage with a Japanese girl, his eventual return to his own country to fight under Chiang Kai-shek."—*Book Review Digest*.

Burman, Ben Lucien   1895-

American author and journalist. Born at Covington, Kentucky, educated at Harvard. Wounded at Belleau Wood in World War I, he served as a correspondent in World War II. As a journalist and writer of short stories he was only moderately successful till one of his Mississippi River stories was published. Since then he has become "the man who made America river-conscious."

BIG RIVER TO CROSS: MISSISSIPPI LIFE TODAY.   1940.
   B.R.D.   10+, 3-   Day. $3.   100

Anecdotal account of the Mississippi River, the boats of various kinds which navigate it, and the people who float on its waters or live on its banks.

"A fine, lazy, slightly overwritten book that brings Mark Twain up to date. . . . Local stuff at its most ingratiating."—*New Yorker*.

"An unusually good book for reading aloud."—*Library Journal*.

Burnham, James   1905-

Born in Chicago, he was educated at Princeton and Oxford, and is now professor of philosophy at New York University. He was formerly a Marxist or Trotskyite.

MANAGERIAL REVOLUTION; WHAT IS HAPPENING IN THE
   WORLD. 1941. B.R.D. 6+, 3- Day. $2.50.   130

What is happening? The author says we are in the midst of a social revolution, during which power is passing from the hands of the capitalists to those of the *administrators* in business and government. The new order, he thinks, will be neither socialism nor the rule of labor.

"His demonstration of the certain emergence of the managerial state is interesting and compelling."—*Commonweal*.

"Here is a volume which is worth reading . . . not for the conclusions it imparts, but for the disturbance to habitual thought patterns which it will engender."—Ordway Tead, in *Survey Graphic*.

Butler, Nicholas Murray   1862-1947

Born at Elizabeth, New Jersey. He lived, learned, taught, administered, at Columbia University from 1882 to his death in 1947; President from 1901 to 1945; President Emeritus, 1945-1947.

ACROSS THE BUSY YEARS; RECOLLECTIONS AND REFLEC-
    TIONS. 2 vols. 1939-40. B.R.D. 8+, 2– Scrib-
    ner. $7.50.   **100**

The first volume covers his childhood, youth and education, and deals with his experience at Columbia and in national affairs; the second volume deals chiefly with his interests in international affairs from 1893 to 1939.

"Invaluable to the future social historian, these memoirs of the great and the prominent are designedly and frankly full-dress." —*New Yorker*.

"For all his characteristic reticence and his great discretion, he has given us a book entitled to a place in political Americana."—*Commonweal*.

Byrd, Richard Evelyn   1888-

American naval aviator and explorer. Born in Winchester, Virginia, of a distinguished and historic Virginia family. Travelled alone around the world at the age of twelve; was educated at the United States Naval Academy; in charge of Navy Department's training camps in 1917 and of American naval forces in Canadian waters the following year. After World War I, he devoted himself to scientific aviation as a means of Arctic and Antarctic exploration. He has flown over both Poles, but his explorations in the Antarctic form his greatest achievement. Served in Pacific naval aviation in World War II; commanded great Antarctic expedition in 1946.

ALONE. 1938. B.R.D. 4+, 0– Putnam. $2.50.   **135**

The account of his self-imposed isolation at Advance Base in the Antarctic in 1934.

"There never was a book like it, because there never was an adventure quite like it. If it took courage to survive the ordeal, it has likewise taken courage to tell about it."—*Christian Science Monitor*.

"This pitiful, glorious tale . . . a book worthy to go on the shelf with Captain Scott's dairy."—*Times* (London).

Caldwell, Erskine   (1903-   ) and White, Margaret Bourke   (1906-   )

Mr. Caldwell was born at White Oak, Georgia. He has been undergraduate, cotton-picker, professional footballer, stage hand; and author of the novel, *Tobacco Road*, etc., and has lectured on "Southern Tenant Farmers" at the New School for Social Research. He is a member of the National Institute of Arts and Letters. Miss Bourke White was born in New York City. She has taken striking photographs in twenty-one countries. The authors were married in 1939 and divorced in 1942.

YOU HAVE SEEN THEIR FACES. 1937. B.R.D. 3+, 0- Viking. $5.   **119**

Here is stirring commentary, and striking photographs of Southern sharecroppers, black and white.

"What Miss Bourke White's camera says in this book is beyond argument."—N. B. Cousins, in *Current History*.

"I don't know that I've ever seen better photography, but Mr. Caldwell's comment . . . pretty much makes the book his own by main force and conviction."—Robert Van Gelder, in *New York Times*.

Canby, Henry Seidel   1878-

American critic. Born in Wilmington, Delaware, of an old Quaker family; educated at Friends' School, Wilmington, and at Yale, where he was given charge of Freshman English as soon as he received his doctor's degree. He continued to be a member of the Yale faculty for many years and has lectured at many other universities at home and abroad. Formerly editor successively of the *Literary Re-*

view, *Saturday Review of Literature* and the *Yale Review*, he has been since 1926 Chairman of the Board of Judges, Book-of-the-Month Club, and is now Secretary of the National Institute of Arts and Letters.

THOREAU. 1939. B.R.D. 13+, 5– Houghton. $3.75. *818.31*
                                            399 *T488c*

"Mr. Canby's long-awaited biography of Thoreau is the first life of the Man of Walden which has ever made that man plain to me. . . . Mr. Canby has shown why he has been at his task these many years. He has thought so long and so well that line after line is an epigram."—D. C. Peattie, in *Atlantic*.

"One of the very best of recent literary biographies, . . . a book that without any question will remain the standard life for a long time to come."—*Books*.

"Out of the shadows of print and the wraiths of inveterate misinterpretation he has drawn forth a substantial man, three-dimensioned, believable, and has placed him in the front rank of American prose masters."—*Nation*.

WALT WHITMAN, AN AMERICAN; A STUDY IN BIOGRAPHY. *811.3*
    1943. B.R.D. 7+, 2– Houghton. $3.75.   **176** *W615c*

"A sensitive, highly useful, and of course thoroughly scholarly biographical study of Whitman as artist and personality, and particularly of his grandeur and limitations as a pioneer spokesman of the central theme of American democracy."—*New Yorker*.

"Mr. Canby has written worthily of a great and demanding subject. 'When you read Whitman,' he says, 'think of the Bible first and of Longfellow not at all.' "— *Weekly Book Review*.

Canfield, Dorothy. *See* Fisher, Dorothy Canfield.

Carlson, John Roy (pseudonym of Arthur Derounian) 1909-

Writer, lecturer and first-hand observer of Fascist activities in the United States. Born in Greece, brought to America in 1921, naturalized in 1926, educated at New York and Columbia Universities.

351.74
D43u

UNDER COVER. 1943. B.R.D. 5+, 2– Dutton. $3.50.
187

"These intimate glimpses of traitors, sincere fanatics and secret agents at work, show something which even their trials have lacked—the psychology and motives of such men and women. It is a gallery of trolls."—Will Irwin, in *Saturday Review of Literature*.

"Better editing would have improved the book; but it should be read."—*Library Journal*.

Carmer, Carl Lamson   1893-

917.47
C28

American author. Born, Cortland, New York; educated at Hamilton College and Harvard. Taught English at Hamilton and at Syracuse, Rochester and Alabama Universities, 1915-1927. Served in World War I as lieutenant of artillery. Has devoted himself to writing since 1927.

THE HUDSON. 1939. B.R.D. 4+, 0– Farrar. $2.50.
171

Collection of Hudson facts and legends of Hudson folk and their folklore and folkways.

"Marrying history, travel and biography to geography he has given us a splendid impressionistic picture of one of the great valleys of America, from the days of Father Jogues to those of Father Divine." —*New York Times*.

Caruso, Mrs. Dorothy Park (Benjamin)

Daughter of Park Benjamin, the author, lawyer and scientist. She married Caruso, the great operatic tenor, in 1918, three years before his death.

780.92
C329C

ENRICO CARUSO, HIS LIFE AND DEATH. 1945. B.R.D. 3+, 0– Simon. $2.75.
156

"Not only an intensely human document but one which, undoubtedly because of its rarely wonderful subject, seems to approach unconsciously the stature of art."—*New York Times*.

"Mrs. Caruso's lovingly drawn portrait of her husband is that of a great singer, who was also an extraordinarily picturesque and amiable character."—*Saturday Review of Literature*.

Cather, Willa Sibert   1876-1947

American novelist. Member, American Academy of Arts and Letters. Born near Winchester, Virginia, she was reared on a ranch in Nebraska and educated in a country high school and the University of Nebraska. After graduation came newspaper work in Pittsburgh, teaching in the Alleghany High School, and editing *McClure's Magazine* (1906-1912). Her first book, *April Twilights* (verse), was published in 1903. She was awarded the Pulitzer prize for fiction in 1923, the Prix Femina ten years later and a gold medal in 1944 from the National Institute of Arts and Letters. *My Antonia* is perhaps her best and most characteristic book.

SAPPHIRA AND THE SLAVE GIRL. 1940. B.R.D. 11+, 4–
    Knopf. $2.50.   210

A story of Virginia before the Civil War.

"One finds in this novel that delicate yet powerful art of brief and significant narrative, where all that is needed is included and all that is needless is left out. . . . It is the French art of the *nouvelle*, in which Voltaire triumphed, and the Russian Turgeniev excelled. Miss Cather has triumphed in it also."—H. S. Canby, in *Saturday Review of Literature*.

Cecil, Lord David   1902-

Son of Marquis of Salisbury; educated at New College, Oxford; has written several books about leading figures in the Victorian age of English letters.

942.08
M51C

THE YOUNG MELBOURNE, AND THE STORY OF HIS MAR-
RIAGE WITH CAROLINE LAMB. 1939. B.R.D. 15+,
1– Bobbs. $3.   133

"The story of this marriage of incompatibles is told by
Lord David Cecil with great charm in the Lytton Strachey
style, purified from the worst vices of the master. It is
as good as a novel; in fact it is a novel."—*Manchester
Guardian.*

"Perhaps the best, certainly the raciest and most absorbing biography since Lytton Strachey's *Queen Victoria.*"—
Time.

"As much a diagnosis of the symptoms of decadence in
an aristocracy as a personal character study; and for that
purpose the subject is ideal."—*Books.*

Chamberlain, John   1903-

Reporter, columnist, literary editor, author, lecturer,
professor. Born in New Haven, Connecticut; graduate of
Yale. His books have been chiefly concerned with public
affairs in America.

AMERICAN STAKES. 1940. B.R.D. 5+, 1– Carrick.
$2.75.   100

Eight essays on contemporary American problems in
politics and economics, such as isolationism, the third term,
consumers' cooperatives, unemployed youth.

Mr. Chamberlain has shown that he is still young enough
to change his mind, but he remains a leftist sort of liberal.
Conservative reviewers compliment him on his sanity and
fairness and good humor. As Clifton Fadiman puts it, "He
doesn't hate half enough those who disagree with him.
Mark you, he hath *not* a lean and hungry look. Such men
are dangerous."

Chapman, John Jay   1862-1933

American man of letters, crusader and "aristophile."
His friend Owen Wister called him a belated abolitionist.
To guide his pen he framed the homely motto: "What
don't bite ain't right."

JOHN JAY CHAPMAN AND HIS LETTERS, edited by M. A. DeWolfe Howe. 1937. B.R.D. 8+, 1– Houghton. $4.   **161**

"Mr. Howe has chosen from a wealth of letters and a volume of reminiscences material which reveals the man . . . and has supplemented this material with a commentary of his own which fills out biographical detail and weaves disjointed correspondence into a chronological whole."—Amy Loveman, in *Saturday Review of Literature*.

"Whoever misses this biography loses hours of enjoyment. . . . Don't do it, even if you think biography does not interest you. This one will."—*Boston Transcript*.

Chase, Mary Ellen   1887-

American novelist, teacher, lecturer. Born, Blue Hill, Maine; educated at the Universities of Maine and Minnesota. Taught English at Minnesota, 1918-1926, and since then at Smith College. She has spent most of her vacations in travel and study in England. The novel, *Mary Peters*, is perhaps her best known book.

GOODLY FELLOWSHIP. 1939. B.R.D. 5+, 1– Macmillan. $2.50.   **173**

These autobiographical chapters are chiefly concerned with her experiences, from Maine to Montana, as a teacher of English. She seems to enjoy teaching—almost to glory in it.

"Believing as I do, that there is no profession more adventurous, more exciting, more thrilling than that of teaching, it is a pleasure to read this autobiographical testimony. I have never read a book more refreshingly honest."—William Lyon Phelps, in *Saturday Review of Literature*.

WINDSWEPT. 1941. B.R.D. 11+, 2– Macmillan. $2.75.   **130**

The family chronicle of the Marstons for three generations (1880-1939) in their big stone house on the Maine coast. A story full of courage and vitality.

"This is Mary Ellen Chase's finest novel."—R. S. Hillyer, in *Atlantic*.

"*Windswept* becomes a symbol of the kind of life America at its wisest and best can produce—a tolerant, kind, broad, humorous, human, stirring, humble—in short—a civilized life."—*Saturday Review of Literature*.

Chase, Stuart   1888-

A public official who has written a score of books—mostly on American public affairs—in as many years. He was born at Somersworth, New Hampshire; educated at Massachusetts Institute of Technology and Harvard; and became a Certified Public Accountant in 1916. He says, "Fun for me is economic research and writing about it."

RICH LAND, POOR LAND; A STUDY OF WASTE IN THE NATURAL RESOURCES OF AMERICA. 1936. B.R.D. 11+, 3− McGraw. $2.50.   **128**

A profoundly disturbing book on the disastrous effects of wind and water erosion.

"A dramatic narrative that is as readable as the average novel and infinitely more important."—M. W. Childs, in *Books*.

"A grand book by a man who knows what he is talking about."—*Forum*.

"I wish it could be required reading in all colleges, in all women's clubs and men's clubs too."—*Yale Review*.

TYRANNY OF WORDS. 1938. B.R.D. 10+, 8− Harcourt. $2.50.   **117**

A popularization of the branch of philosophy known as semantics which deals with the meaning of meaning. The book's gospel is to the effect that when one uses an abstraction in speaking, one should be on one's guard to know exactly what one is talking about. Have Marshall and Molotov (and their interpreters) meant always the same thing in uttering the word democracy?

Cheney, Sheldon   1886-

American exponent of modern art and the modern theatre. Born in Berkeley, California; educated at the University of California. He has been a professed critic of art and the drama since 1910. In 1916 he founded the *Theatre Arts Magazine*, continuing as its editor till 1921. His first book was published in 1914 and has been followed by a dozen others.

WORLD HISTORY OF ART. 1947. B.R.D. 4+, 1− Viking. $5.   **161**

709
C51w

All inclusive; copiously illustrated.

"The difference between Mr. Cheney's work and Mr. Van Loon's is the difference between a photograph and a painting. Mr. Cheney is the historian; Mr. Van Loon the interpreter. Appropriately Mr. Cheney uses photographs to illustrate his book, Mr. Van Loon his own drawings."— N. B. Cousins, in *Current History*.

"The author's style and his use of English are delightful and there is a freshness and vividness about the whole book that are characteristic of a task done for the first time."—*New York Times*.

Chesterton, Gilbert K.   1874-1936

Prolific journalist, dramatist, poet, novelist and critic; Priest of Paradox; professional Catholic and mediævalist.

AUTOBIOGRAPHY. 1936. B.R.D. 9+, 1− Sheed. $3.   **152**

824.91
C525

"The mind behind this book must be praised. It is one of the most attractive minds let loose in our time, and this book is one of its completest expressions."— Mark Van Doren, in *The Nation*.

Childs, Marquis W.   1903-

Author of political and economic best sellers; born in Clinton, Iowa. This Washington and foreign correspondent and lecturer traveled fifteen thousand miles with Franklin Roosevelt in his 1936 campaign.

SWEDEN: THE MIDDLE WAY. 1936. B.R.D. 12+, 3– Yale. $2.50.   154

"An able and up-to-date discussion of cooperation, co-operative housing, the state power system, state railways, state ownership of industries, government monopolies, liquor control, central agricultural cooperatives."—*American Political Science Review*.

"Probably the season's most useful publication."—*Forum*.

"Striking observation, faithful reporting, vigorous journalism of a high order."—H. G. Leach, in *Books*.

Churchill, Winston Spencer   1874-

After "Munich" (1940) England in her extremity called him at sixty-six to head the Government. The rest is history. He saved England, and England and America saved the world, at least for a time.

BLOOD, SWEAT AND TEARS. 1941. B.R.D. 13+, 0– Putnam. $3.   150

The historic speeches of the Prime Minister from May, 1938 to February, 1941.

"This is the voice of a great leader and a great fighter for democracy, standing alone in one of the greatest crises in the history of the world."—Walter Millis, in *Books*.

"In general the speeches give an accurate survey of the course of the war, and their cumulative effect is tonic and bracing."—*Atlantic*.

"Churchill was right nine times out of ten in his judgment of the various phases of the world crisis. . . . Much of this book is history."—Clifton Fadiman, in *New Yorker*.

"Churchill has earned the right to be called the best public speaker in the world today."—M. Cowley, in *New Republic*.

Clark, Walter Van Tilburg   1909-

Born in Maine, but reared in Nevada, he is a graduate of the State University at Reno, where his father was president.

Ox-Bow Incident. 1940. B.R.D. 8+, 1– Random. $2.
                                                                    120

This first novel is a rousing tale of the cattle country in the eighties. There are rustlers in it and a lynching. Mr. Weeks of the *Atlantic* likes it for its beauty, its naturalness and its excitement. The characters are real people—not just appendages to shooting irons.

"Not to put too fine a point upon it, I think it's what you might call a masterpiece."—Clifton Fadiman, in *New Yorker*.

Commager, Henry S.   (1902-) and Nevins, Allan (1890-), editors

Mr. Commager is an American historian, and until recently associate editor of the *American Scholar*. Born in Pittsburgh, Pennsylvania, he was educated at the University of Chicago and has taught history at New York University and Columbia since 1926. Mr. Nevins, journalist, teacher and author, was born at Camp Point, Illinois, and educated at the University of Illinois. He has been professor of American history at Columbia since 1931. Author of twenty books and editor of many others, he is a member of the National Institute of Arts and Letters.

Heritage of America. 1939. B.R.D. 5+, 1– Little.
          Student's edition, $2.40.   133

Collection of two hundred and fifty-two original documents, in whole or in part, making plain what America is and has been about. The range is from Leif Ericson to Franklin Roosevelt. The extracts abound in human interest and are very readable.

Costain, Thomas Bertram   1885-

Born at Brantford, Ontario, he came to the United States in 1920 and has long been an American citizen. He was associate editor of the *Saturday Evening Post*, 1920-34, and became advisory editor at Doubleday's in 1939.

BLACK ROSE. 1945. B.R.D. 5+, 2– Doubleday. $3.
108

"Romantic tale of thirteenth century England and the Orient."—*Book Review Digest*.

"Mr. Costain has painted a picture book all his own. As such you are free to enjoy it, and by no means unlikely to have a whale of a time; but high-brows better keep out."—*Saturday Review of Literature*.

Covarrubias, Miguel   1902-

Caricaturist, painter, author. Born in Mexico City and entirely self-taught, he spent two years in China, Java and Bali; was a Guggenheim Fellow in 1940. He now divides his time between New York City and Mexico.

ISLAND OF BALI; with an Album of Photographs. 1937. B.R.D. 5+, 1– Knopf. $5.   127

"One of the most beautiful books of the year."

"The art and culture, the background and the everyday life of the Balinese as seen through the sympathetic and understanding eyes of an artist."—*Book Review Digest*.

"As superb a piece of reporting, of anthropological and artistic understanding, as you will find in a dozen campus-fulls of pompously scientific work."—*Books*.

Cozzens, James Gould   1903-

Born in Chicago of New England antecedents. Mr. Cozzens was raised on Staten Island, spent two years at Harvard and was a major in the Army Air Forces in World War II. He lives now on a New Jersey farm.

THE JUST AND THE UNJUST. 1942. B.R.D. 7+, 2– Harcourt. $2.50.   **105**

This not-at-all-lurid novel tells the story of a three-day murder trial in a New England country town. There is no hero, no heroine—just good objective characterization of not very remarkable people seen against a convincing legal background. Yet it was a best seller and won the praise of critics. Joseph Hergesheimer said in the *Saturday Review of Literature* that he had read it "at a sitting, or rather in bed, through a night of intolerable heat. It was the source and form of unbroken pleasure."

Craven, Thomas, editor   1889-

Born in Salina, Kansas; educated at Kansas Wesleyan University, 1908, and studied art in Paris and London. He has written and lectured a great deal on art since 1925, traveling much and observing the artistic development of America.

TREASURY OF ART MASTERPIECES, FROM THE RENAISSANCE TO THE PRESENT DAY. 1939. B.R.D. 7+, 5– Simon. $10.   **161**

One hundred and forty-four new color plates, each accompanied by a page of commentary. "Some of these are little masterpieces of compression."

"The one American publication of its type that we would place at the top of its class. The editor's contributions add mightily to its popular value."—*Boston Transcript*.

Cronin, Archibald Joseph   1896-

British novelist and physician. Born at Cardross, Dumbartonshire, Scotland; educated at Glasgow University. His medical training was interrupted by naval service during World War I. In 1931 he gave up a lucrative London practice to follow his natural bent for literature. Visited America during World War II on a government mission to study the hospitalization of soldiers.

F
C947c

THE CITADEL. 1937. B.R.D. 9+, 3– Little. $2.50. **127**

Study of the character development of a young Scottish doctor.

"All who enjoy a good novel for its own sake will find it an engrossing, finely written story that needs no justification whatever."—*Saturday Review of Literature.*

GREEN YEARS. 1944. B.R.D. 9+, 4– Little. $2.50. **127**

Story of an orphan childhood in a Scottish town. The elderly and unsophisticated, at any rate, will find its Dickensian flavor very much to their taste.

"He writes the way all people hope their doctor sees and feels. No wonder he is successful!"—Dorothy Hillyer, in *Boston Globe.*

KEYS OF THE KINGDOM. 1941. B.R.D. 11+, 6– Little.
$2.50. **130**

Appealing story about a tolerant. Scottish priest in China. "Best of the year's best sellers."

"Even if this novel goes the way of most best sellers— and I do not think this will happen—it deals with that which has eternal and redemptive values for our tragic world."—Frank Fitt, in *Christian Century.*

Cross, Wilbur L.   1862-

Grand Old Man of Yale—and Connecticut. Born at Mansfield, Connecticut, of old New England stock and educated at Yale, where he served successively as instructor, professor, dean of the Graduate School and provost, from 1894 till his retirement in 1930. (Incidentally he was also editor of the *Yale Review.*) The first year of his retirement he signalized by beginning at sixty-eight the first of four terms as the Democratic governor of a Republican state. He is also the ex-Chancellor of the American Academy of Arts and Letters.

974.6
C 951

A CONNECTICUT YANKEE. 1943. B.R.D. 8+, 1– Yale.
$5.   187

About half of this autobiography is devoted to his
long academic career at Yale, the remainder to his eight
years of stalwart wrestling with Connecticut politics.

"The straightforward story of a good American."—
Library Journal.

"One of the best of all portrayals of New England life
and character."—*Springfield Republican.*

Cummings, Edward Estlin   1894-

Born in Cambridge, Massachusetts, son of a professor
of English at Harvard, educated at Harvard. He served
in World War I and since then has lived mostly in Paris
and New York's Greenwich Village, studying and practic-
ing art and painting and writing.

COLLECTED POEMS. 1938. B.R.D. 2+, 0– Harcourt.
$3.   117

"Cummings is really easy to read; his typographical
humor is not at all an obstruction, and the matter is far
more important, one sees, than the manner. Cummings is
fresh in both senses, and the recognition too long obscured
by impatience, now that it must come, will be because of
that freshness."—John Holmes, in *Atlantic.*

"Here are collected some of the finest lyric poems of
our day. . . . This is the poetry of a man of complete
artistic integrity."—Dudley Fitts, in *Saturday Review of
Literature.*

Curie, Eve   1904-

Musician, author, lecturer, war correspondent. Born
in Paris, the daughter of Pierre and Marie Curie, the dis-
coverers of radium, she served in World War II as an
officer of the Fighting French in the Women's Division of
their forces. She speaks fluent English, French and Polish.

940.538
C97j

JOURNEY AMONG WARRIORS. 1943. B.R.D. 9+, 1–
    Doubleday. $3.50.   187

Miss Curie visited the war fronts around half the world:
Africa, the Near East, Russia, Iran, China and India.

"To call Miss Curie's book the best one any woman has
written on this war is inadequate praise, because never
before has the whole panorama of the world at war been
so honestly, so skillfully and so beautifully presented."—
W. L. White, in *New York Times*.

546.432
C96c

MADAME CURIE, A BIOGRAPHY; translated by Vincent
        Sheean, 1937. B.R.D. 6+, 0– Doubleday. $3.50.
                                                    212

The life of the patient, laborious discoverer of radium,
written by her younger daughter.

"The actual record of Marie Curie's life is epic. Eve
Curie writes that epic movingly."—*Chicago Daily Tribune*.

"A book so moving, so finished, so profoundly affecting
that one comes to think of Mme. Curie's life as material
for a symphony—by Beethoven, perhaps, or by Sibelius."—
New York Times.

Curti, Merle (Eugène)   1897-

Born at Papillon, Nebraska, and educated at Harvard
and the Sorbonne, he has been professor of history at
many American colleges since 1921, and was a Guggenheim Fellow, 1929-30. High in the councils of many
learned societies he has written several books on American history and public affairs.

917.3
C97g

THE GROWTH OF AMERICAN THOUGHT. 1943. B.R.D. 8+,
        3– Harper. $5.   121

A social history of American thought from Jamestown
to Pearl Harbor.

"This is an important event in the history of American
scholarship. It is also an important event in the development of American democracy. Not since the appearance
of Parrington's *Main Currents in American Thought*, in

1927, has there come from our press a work of comparable significance in this field."—J. S. Counts, in *New Republic*.

"In the midst of glittering generalities and naïve hosannas concerning 'the American way of life,' this book comes like a refreshing breeze, with its cool dispassionate analysis of the sole basis for the characteristics that make our nation unique."—*Scientific Book Club Review*.

Daniels, Jonathan   1902-

This son of Josephus Daniels (Southern editor, ambassador to Mexico, and Woodrow Wilson's Secretary of the Navy) was born at Raleigh, North Carolina, and educated at the University of North Carolina and Columbia Law School. He has been a Guggenheim Fellow, a trustee of Vassar College, assistant director of the Office of Civilian Defense, and administrative assistant to President Truman.

SOUTHERNER DISCOVERS THE SOUTH. 1938. B.R.D. 9+, 0- Macmillan. $3.   207

917.5
D18

"Mr. Daniels throws light on many questions, presenting perhaps the best available summary of Southern problems as they stand to-day."—*Annals, American Academy*.

"A tolerant, highly readable, amusing and urbane book." —*Atlantic*.

"The best book on the modern South that has yet been written."—*Books*.

SOUTHERNER DISCOVERS NEW ENGLAND. 1940. B.R.D. 12+, 2- Macmillan. $3.   100

912.4
D18s

"I am a teacher, and I know a good teacher when I see one. . . . Mr. Daniels is the best of teachers. . . . I know far more about New England than I did two days ago, even after fifty years' acquaintance; and I am grateful for the information and more for the illumination of Mr. Daniels' lesson sheet."—Mary Ellen Chase, in *Boston Transcript*.

"A sympathetic and thoughtful book. . . . If it is somewhat gloomy, that is not Mr. Daniels' fault, for New England when he saw it, was facing disillusion."—J. P. Marquand, in *Saturday Review of Literature*.

Dark, Eleanor (O'Reilly) (Mrs. Eric Dark)   1901-

Australian novelist, winner of two gold medals from the Australian Literature Society for the best Australian novel of the year—*Prelude to Christopher* in 1934, and *Return to Coolami* in 1936.

TIMELESS LAND. 1941. B.R.D. 11+, 2- Macmillan. $2.75.   **100**

This is Australia in fiction—a novel about the early days (1787-92) of the colony at Sydney, with special attention to picturing the reactions of the aborigines.

"Mrs. Dark has something of the power of Isak Dinesen, a sheer respect for language and the rhythmic progress of sentences. . . . A rare, beautiful book rich with authentic history and the best of fiction."—*Nation*.

"A novel of stern beauty and profound reality which unquestionably ranks among the best books of the year."—*Saturday Review of Literature*.

Davenport, Marcia (Gluck) (Mrs. Russell W. Davenport)   1903-

Musical critic and novelist. Born in New York City; the daughter of Alma Gluck; on the editorial staff of the *New Yorker*, 1928-31.

VALLEY OF DECISION. 1942. B.R.D. 6+, 3- Scribner. $3.   **126**

Story of five generations of a mine-owning family in Pittsburgh.

"A novel in the spacious tradition whereby your circle of friends and range of experience are widened; it is, moreover, as enjoyable as it is distinguished."—*Books*.

"A truly monumental work which never for one instant loses its quality of stirring human interest."—*New York Times*.

Davenport, Russell W.   1899-

Publicist and poet. Born in South Bethlehem, Pennsylvania. The husband of Marcia Davenport. Served as private first class in World War I, 1917-19. A member of the editorial staff of *Fortune*, 1930-41, and of *Life*, beginning 1943. He helped greatly to nominate Wendell Willkie.

MY COUNTRY. 1944. B.R.D. 3+, 2- Simon. $1.50.
                                                           127

811.5
D24m

This long patriotic poem "is the song of the internationalist who knows that if he is not bold, not generous, not committed to the brotherhood of man, then the flowers will not grow in his own plot of ground, . . . his own roof will give way, . . . and there will be no more kindly dreaming beside the heap of rubble that was once his fireplace."

"It's time that what is said here should be said in this way. We need songs of faith as well as tanks and heavy guns. An emotion that makes the pulses beat like drums and the eyes grow misty may not be unmanly—it may be the strongest, the most practical thing in the world."—R. L. Duffus, in *New York Times*.

Davies, Joseph Edward   1876-

Publicist and diplomat. Born in Watertown, Wisconsin; educated at University of Wisconsin. Entrusted with many governmental missions, 1913-41; economic adviser to Woodrow Wilson at Versailles.

MISSION TO MOSCOW. 1942. B.R.D. 13+, 2- Simon. $3.   105

327.73
D25m

This is the record of the mission (1936-38) pieced together from the contemporary evidence and confidential dispatches and personal diary and correspondence.

"One of the best informed books to appear in recent years on Soviet Russia."—*Foreign Affairs*.

"A book of exceptional importance for the understanding of the main international developments of our time. . . . It marks the first time that the State Department has opened its contemporary files to the public."—*Pacific Affairs*.

Day, Clarence   1874-1935

American author. Born in New York City; educated at St. Paul's School, Concord, New Hampshire, and at Yale. Served in Navy in Spanish-American War, and there fell a victim to arthritis. He was an undaunted invalid for many years before his death.

LIFE WITH MOTHER. 1937. B.R.D. 4+, 1- Knopf. $2.
                                                                119

"I know of no book of the last few years so full of gayety and sympathy, so certain to draw a chuckle, so pungent, so incisive, and yet so kindly as *Life with Mother*, unless it be its predecessor, *Life with Father*."—A. Loveman, in *Saturday Review of Literature*.

Delacroix, Eugène   1798-1863

French artist of great versatility, passion, virility. A great colorist, but an indifferent draughtsman.

JOURNALS. Translated from the French by Walter Pach; illustrated with reproductions of the paintings and drawings of the artist. 1937. B.R.D. 4+, 2- Covici. $7.50.   119

"From the first jotting of 1822 to the last considered note of 1863, the year of his death, Delacroix told the truth as man and artist."—*Book Review Digest*.

"Through the luminous translation of Mr. Pach, himself an artist in his own right, the *Journals* make delightful and instructive reading. The indiscretions of the youthful confessions retain their Gallic lightness while the technical passages have a clarity that will make them valuable to artist and layman alike."—Frances Winwar, in *New York Times*.

Derounian, A. *See* Carlson, J. R.

De Voto, Bernard 1897-

American author. Born, Ogden, Utah; educated at the University of Utah and Harvard. Served as second lieutenant, Infantry, 1917-1918; taught English at Northwestern University, 1922-1927, and at Harvard, 1929-1936. He has edited *Harvard Graduates' Magazine, Saturday Review of Literature*, etc., and is the author of a dozen books. He is a special student of the work of Mark Twain.

YEAR OF DECISION, 1846. 1943. B.R.D. 8+, 2– Little. $3.50.   176

The true story of "some people who went west in 1846" —the year that saw the culmination of the whole westward migration from the Atlantic to the Pacific.

"1846 was a year of crass territorial annexation, yet it was also a year of purified national emotion, in which we decided as a people to change our way of life."—Clifton Fadiman, in *New Yorker*.

"De Voto's best book to date. And that makes it good enough to become a part of the permanent literature of the nation."—*Saturday Review of Literature*.

Dewey, John 1859-

Born in Burlington, Vermont. Educated at the University of Vermont and Johns Hopkins, he has taught over the years at the University of Michigan, University of Minnesota, University of Chicago, and Columbia. Mr. Dewey is the father of the Progressive School movement and "dean of American philosophers." He was the first president of the American Association of University Professors and is a past president of the American Psychological Association and of the American Philosophical Society, a member of the National Academy of Sciences and a corresponding member of *L'Institut de France*.

321.8
D51f

FREEDOM AND CULTURE. 1939. B.R.D. 3+, 0– Putnam. $2.   100

"Study of the conditions on which true democratic culture is based." —*Book Review Digest*.

"Few oldsters and no youngsters can afford complacently to say that they will get nothing out of *Freedom and Culture*. It plumbs the fundamentals of the problem of democracy."—*New York Times*.

Dodd, William E.   1869-1940

Born Clayton, North Carolina; professor of history, diplomat, author of books about the South and Southerners. He helped R. S. Baker to edit Woodrow Wilson's "Papers," 1924-26, and became our Ambassador to Berlin.

AMBASSADOR DODD'S DIARY, 1933-1938. 1941. B.R.D. 12+, 3– Harcourt. $3.50.   120

"Daily notes of the gathering storm."

"No future study of World War II will be complete without full cognizance of Dodd's diary."—*Nation*.

"His diary is prophecy as well as history."—*New Republic*.

"A valuable contribution to our knowledge of how the Diplomatic Corps in Berlin was thinking in those days, especially as it is written by a man who had access to so much and dared to write it."—*Spectator*.

Dos Passos, John   1896-

American novelist. Born in Chicago; educated at Harvard. During World War I he served in various ambulance corps, 1917-19. He has lived in New York, Washington, London, Brussels, Madrid and Paris. A Guggenheim Fellow in 1939. He has a lively, sympathetic interest in Soviet Russia, the common soldier and the masses. He is a member of the National Institute of Arts and Letters.

BIG MONEY. 1936. B.R.D. 9+, 6– Harcourt. $2.50.
144

This story about the postwar boom of the 1920's, much applauded by radicals, is among the most important and distinguished novels of the year.

"There are few novelists in this country whose craftsmanship is as secure and whose sense of American life is as understanding. . . ."—*Atlantic.*

"Establishes his position as the most incisive and direct of American satirists."—Horace Gregory, in *Books.*

STATE OF THE NATION. 1944. B.R.D. 8+, 3– Houghton. $3. 138

An objective first-hand report on America in wartime with special attention to labor-management relations. He traveled from Maine to Seattle, from San Francisco to Mobile. Some readers will regret, and be annoyed by, some of his characteristic mannerisms.

Douglas, Henry K. 1840-1903

Born in Shepherdstown, West Virginia, Mr. Douglas rose from private to brigade-commander in the army of the Confederate States and was an aide-de-camp to Stonewall Jackson. After the war he lived in Maryland and became a judge.

I RODE WITH STONEWALL. Ed. by Fletcher Melvin Green. 1940. B.R.D. 6+, 0– University of North Carolina. $3. 100

A valuable addition to the shelf of personal narratives of the Civil War.

"A book of rare quality. Its primary distinction lies in the intimacy, frankness and discernment with which it treats Stonewall Jackson, substituting a series of graphic undress photographs for the conventional portrait in oils. . . . The author, who knew Jackson from Bull Run to the tragic end at Appomattox, makes him human, likable and understanding."—*Saturday Review of Literature.*

Duhamel, Georges   1884-

Physician, poet, playwright, novelist. Born in Paris, in 1907, he lived, loved, printed and wrote at "The Abbaye," a sort of French Brook Farm on the Marne. He served as surgeon through World War I. At the beginning of World War II he was given charge of French radio broadcasting.

F
D869p

PASQUIER CHRONICLES. 5 pts. 1938. B.R.D. 6+, 2–
    Holt. $3.50.   **116**

To him who would know France and the French "a careful reading of the *Pasquier Chronicles* will be more enlightening than a Cook's tour through La Belle France."

"An excellent picture of French life and character, but it is not full of obvious glamor nor in any way strange to us."—*Saturday Review of Literature*.

"These are men and women—hear them quarrel, watch them eat, see how touchingly ridiculous a good man can be."—*Books*.

**Du Maurier, Daphne (Mrs. F. A. M. Browning)
    1907-**

Born in London; the grauddaughter of George Du Maurier, author of *Trilby*, and daughter of Gerald Du Maurier, the actor. She married in 1932 Lieutenant-Colonel (now General) F. A. M. Browning, who served in World War I, 1914-18. They live in Cornwall.

REBECCA. 1938. B.R.D. 6+, 4– Doubleday. $2.75. **117**

An absorbing story. Its drama now and then lapses into melodrama as happened in another tale of a second marriage, called *Jane Eyre*. The critics often bring up the Brontës in estimating this book.

"An ingenious, exciting, and engagingly romantic tale."
—*Times* (London).

"Miss Du Maurier's plot is undoubtedly the kind of thing which the three girls of Haworth Parsonage would have liked to thrash out as they paced the dining-room arm-in-arm after Papa had gone to bed."—Kate O'Brien, in *Spectator*.

Durant, Will   1885-

American author. Born in North Adams, Massachusetts; educated by French Catholic nuns and by the Jesuit fathers of St. Peter's College, Jersey City. He earned his doctor's degree at Columbia. He studied for the priesthood, but later gave himself to the socialist movement and to adult education. Director of the Labor Temple School, New York City, from 1914 to 1927, he is now first of all a historian.

LIFE OF GREECE; with an introduction on the prehistoric culture of Crete. 1939. B.R.D. 3+, 0– Simon. $3.95.   133

This book is volume 2 of his 8-volume *Story of Civilization*.

"A large handsome book, written in the grand manner." —*Boston Transcript*.

"Eminently suited to the needs and tastes of one who comes almost virgin-minded to the great feast of Greek life and literature." —*New York Times*.

CAESAR AND CHRIST, A HISTORY OF ROMAN CIVILIZATION AND OF CHRISTIANITY FROM THE BEGINNINGS TO A.D. 325. 1944. B.R.D. 6+, 1– Simon. $5.   161

This is volume 3 of his *Story of Civilization*.

"It combines a high regard for scholarship with a sense of drama and it ought to be widely read. Handsomely illustrated."—*New Yorker*.

"Merits a place of honor in a world that has enjoyed Gibbon, Mommsen and Ferrero. . . . Scholarly research has rarely been translated into such a lively, yet stimulating and accurate history."—*Saturday Review of Literature*.

Edmonds, Walter D.   1903-

Novelist. Born at Boonville, New York, where he still lives. Educated at private schools and Harvard. The scene of his novels is up-state New York, often with the Erie Canal in the background.

Drums Along the Mohawk. 1936. B.R.D. 11+, 3-
    Little. $2.50.   136

"The full flavor of the pioneer days is here."—*Boston Transcript*.

"A very American book. . . . If it had been published before the world was deluged with print it might have had its chance of being an American classic."—*Forum*.

"A novel without dull moments, of drama, poetry and understanding. It deserves to survive."—R. L. Duffus, in *New York Times*.

Einstein, Albert   (1879-) and Infeld, Leopold (1898-)

Einstein is a theoretical physicist of German-Swiss antecedents. Originator of the theory of relativity. He came to the United States in 1933 and became a citizen in 1940. He is a life member of the Institute for Advanced Study at Princeton and was awarded the Nobel Prize in 1922.

Infeld was born at Cracow, Poland. He has learned and taught at Polish, English, American and Canadian universities.

530.9   Evolution of Physics: the Growth of Ideas from
    Early Concepts to Relativity and Quanta.
    1938. B.R.D. 8+, 0- Simon. $2.50.   108

A book that, eschewing mathematics, is written for the general reader; but it will be well for that personage if he gird his loins before tackling it.

"Deals almost exclusively with the fundamental concepts of physics, and it considers these concepts only as *leading ideas* serving to coordinate experience."—*Nation*.

"An admirable and important book on some of the knottiest problems ever attacked by the human mind."—*New Republic*.

Eliot, George Fielding   1894-

Born in Brooklyn, this author and commentator on military subjects is a graduate of Melbourne (Australia) University; served with the Australian forces in World War I, 1914-18; with the Canadian "Mounties," 1919-21, and in the U.S. Army's Military Intelligence Reserve, 1922-30.

RAMPARTS WE WATCH. 1938. B.R.D. 6+, 0– Reynal. $3.   100

This book is a study of the problems of our national defense. It is an interesting exercise to read, after the fact, an exposition written *before* the fact. That is the kind of book this is.

"His description is sane, unsensational and of sober interest to all citizens. Also the Major writes with great clarity and precision."—*New Yorker*.

"A well-documented study, the recommendations of which, if adopted, might make war against this country an impossible or certainly a risky undertaking."—*Saturday Review of Literature*.

Eliot, Thomas Stearns   1888-

Anglo-American poet. Born in St. Louis of New England ancestry; educated at Harvard, the Sorbonne and Merton College, Oxford. He married an Englishwoman, became a British subject in 1927, and joined the Anglo-Catholic church. He returned to America in 1932 after eighteen years, to teach poetry at Harvard. His *Waste Land* (1922), wail of the "lost generation," stands as an important landmark in American literature.

811.5
E42c

COLLECTED POEMS. 1909-1935. 1936. B.R.D. 1+, 0-
    Harcourt. $2.50   **120**

"A valuable and fascinating book because it gives
a birdseye view of Mr. Eliot's poetic progress, from his
early but derivative excursions right up to the present day."
—*New Statesman.*

"A body of verse that is eloquent of the lost generation.
It has a technical excellence equaled by the fewest of his
contemporaries. His accomplishment may be measured
by the very violence of the reaction against him."—Babette
Deutsch, in *Books.*

811.5
E42f

FOUR QUARTETS. 1943. B.R.D. 8+, 1- Harcourt. $2.
                                                   121

Some critics have considered these religious poems his
best work and they have been declared the best creative
writing of the year

"You do not read great poetry unprepared, ignorant or
carelessly. Mr. Eliot's poetry is exacting: it has the right
to be." —*Commonweal.*

"Elizabeth," (pseudonym of Mary Annette Beauchamp Russell, Countess Russell)   1866-1941

Born in Sydney, Australia. Considered one of the first
wits of her time, she was a cousin of Katherine Mansfield.
Her first husband was Count von Arnim, junker of East
Prussia. After his death she lived and wrote for some
years in Switzerland. In 1916 she married Earl Russell,
elder brother of the present Earl whom we know as Bertrand Russell. They separated after three years. At the
start of World War II she came to America where she
remained until her death in 1941 near Charleston, South
Carolina.

MR. SKEFFINGTON. 1940. B.R.D. 9+, 2- Doubleday.
    $2.50.   **100**

"This is Elizabeth at her best, and those who have for so
many years waited impatiently for each new book know
how good that can be."—*Times* (London).

"It is moist with sentimentality, it is basically snobbish, it is—but there's no use: charm's charm and Elizabeth has it."—Clifton Fadiman, in *New Yorker*.

Emerson, Ralph Waldo   1803-1882

"There is no man living to whom, as a writer, so many of us feel and thankfully acknowledge so great an indebtedness for ennobling impulses. . . . We look upon his as one of the few men of genius whom our age has produced, and there needs no better proof of it than his masculine faculty for fecundating other minds."—James Russell Lowell, 1868.

LETTERS, 1813-1881, edited by Ralph L. Rusk. 6 vols. 1939. B.R.D. 7+, 2– Columbia. $30.   142

814.3
E53L

"These letters are from a nineteenth century mind who presumably rivals Lincoln as one of the two or three seminal minds of the age. . . . More abundantly than the formal 'Essays' or the 'Journals' this encyclopedic edition of Emerson's letters fills interstices in his outer and, to a lesser extent, his inner life."—*Yale Review*.

"The letters complement the journals by revealing the range of a social life that touched most of the elements of his time and country. . . . They make much more real and concrete a character whose outlines have been somewhat shadowy and vague."—Van Wyck Brooks, in *New Republic*.

"F. P. A."   *See* Adams, F. P.

Fairfield, Cecily.   *See* West, Rebecca, pseud.

Fast, Howard   1914-

Born in New York City, he was educated in the New York public schools and the National Academy of Design, while working part time in the New York Public Library. He gave up art when he sold his first story at eighteen. He served overseas in governmental assignments, 1942-44, and as a newspaper correspondent in 1945. His published works have been chiefly fiction or biography. They are never too conservative.

CITIZEN TOM PAINE. 1943. B.R.D. 8+, 3– Duell. $2.75.   **154**

A novelized biography.

"Paine appears as a fool on occasion, a bad politician always, but also as one of the few men of his time (Franklin was another) who understood the Revolution, who understood the inevitability of America."—*New Yorker*.

Faulkner, William   1897-

Novelist. Born in New Albany, Mississippi, of a distinguished Southern family. For two years he attended the state university, leaving to join the Canadian Flying Corps in World War I, wherein he served till the Armistice. Months of tramping in Europe followed, and then came a sojourn with Sherwood Anderson and journalism in New Orleans, before a return to his permanent home in Oxford, Mississippi.

THE HAMLET. 1940. B.R.D. 1+, 4– Random. $2.50.   **110**

"Chronicles of decay, of viciousness, of perversion, of cruelty."

"For extremely limited library purchase because of its abnormalities and its tortured style."—*Library Journal*.

"In *The Hamlet* his peculiar power is at its best. . . . Here is all the earthy force that Mr. Faulkner can summon, like a spirit out of the ground, when he chooses to do so."— S. V. Benét, in *Saturday Review of Literature*.

THE UNVANQUISHED. 1938. B.R.D. 7+, 2– Random. $2.50.   **126**

The Sartoris family during Civil War and Reconstruction.

"Choice of normal subject matter and simplification of style enable Mr. Faulkner to attain a new vigor in his writing."—*Springfield Republican*.

"Few stories of the War and the Reconstruction period have pierced further below the surface or have been more self-authenticating in mood and interpretation."—*Christian Century*.

WILD PALMS. 1939. B.R.D. 3+, 3− Random. $2.50.
114

The book contains two stories without obvious connection.

"It is a disturbing sort of performance, with something of nightmare quality about it."—*Times* (London).

"It is very good Faulkner, not the best, but a fair example of this sensational talent—genius if you like, I should not gainsay the word—in story telling"—P. M. Jack, in *New York Times*.

"After a while this bestiality becomes merely ludicrous; one begins to feel not that Mr. Falkner is trying his darndest to see how much misery he can make his characters stand but also that he is trying to see how much misery he can make his readers stand."—Clifton Fadiman, in *New Yorker*.

Federova, Nina (pseudonym of Antonina Riasanovsky) 1895-

Born in Poltava, Russia, she was educated at the University of Petrograd and the Y. M. C. A. College, Harbin, Manchuria. Married in 1923, she now lives in Eugene, Oregon, a citizen of the United States.

THE FAMILY. 1940. B.R.D. 9+, 0− Little. $2.50. **110**

This story of White Russians in China in 1937, before and during the Japanese invasion, won the *Atlantic's* $10,000 prize.

"This novel is one of the most engaging stories that this reviewer has read in years."—*New York Times*.

"A distinguishied novel . . . written in the tradition of the great Russian novelists. . . . Neither Tolstoi nor Dostoievski would be loath to give a smile of brotherhood to Nina Federova."—*Books*.

Ferber, Edna   1887-

American fictionist and playwright. Member National Institute of Arts and Letters. Born of Jewish parents in Kalamazoo, Michigan. Her formal education ended with graduation from high school, when she began work on a country newspaper. Most at home in her native Middle West, she now lives in and near New York.

PECULIAR TREASURE. 1939. B.R.D. 8+, 0– Doubleday. $3.   **161**

A frank, good-humored and entertaining autobiography. She loves America and its institutions.

"She just shows what happened to as amusing and wholehearted and impressive a person as any she has created, Edna herself."—Mary Ross, in *Boston Transcript*.

"It is only in the life of individuals that we can grasp the significance of the great American experiment, and Miss Ferber's lively and generous career seems to be one of the more successful results of that experiment."—*Boston Transcript*.

Field, Rachel Lyman (Mrs. Arthur Pederson)   1894-1942

Novelist and poet. Born in New York City; educated in public schools of Stockbridge and Springfield, Massachusetts, and as special student at Radcliffe College. Awarded, 1929, John Newbery Medal for most distinguished contribution to literature for children, for *Hitty, Her First Hundred years*.

ALL THIS AND HEAVEN TOO. 1938. B.R.D. 8+, 2– Macmillan. $2.50.   **180**

A novel based on events in her own family history. She is the great-niece of her heroine who was the

defendant in a murder trial which was a *cause célèbre* at
Paris in 1847. After her acquittal the defendant came to
America to live happily ever after as the wife of a New
England clergyman.

"I have read over many years few more intriguing
novels than this one, few so well done, few so worth doing."
—Mary Ellen Chase, in *Commonweal*.

Fisher, Dorothy Canfield   1879-

American novelist. Member, National Institute of
Arts and Letters. Born at Lawrence, Kansas, of old
Vermont stock. Her father had been president of two
state universities before he became Librarian at Columbia.
The daughter graduated at Ohio State and earned a doctor's
degree at the Sorbonne and Columbia. Before and during
World War I she lived much in France, but for many years
now she has dwelt among her ancestral hills.

SEASONED TIMBER. 1939. B.R.D. 12+, 3– Harcourt.
    $2.50.   114

This novel about a Vermont academy and its principal
has been called an anti-Fascist allegory. "This is no flat
parable Dorothy Canfield has written. It is a fine, strong,
rounded novel, enriched with her learning and her keen
sense of what stirs men's hearts and minds."—*Forum*.

"Miss Canfield has finely brought her New England
skillfully and inevitably into the current of a changing
time."—*Saturday Review of Literature*.

Fisher, Vardis   1895-

Born at Annis, Idaho, of old Mormon stock, Mr. Fisher
was educated at the Universities of Utah and Chicago. He
served as a corporal in World War I and later taught English at the University of Utah and New York University.

CHILDREN OF GOD; AN AMERICAN EPIC. 1939. B.R.D.
    6+, 4– Harper. $3.   133

A novel which tells the story of the first fifty years of
Mormonism.

"One of the most extraordinarily interesting stories I have ever read. . . . I have rarely encountered a book whose faults one is more eager and easily able to condone."— Clifton Fadiman, in *New Yorker*.

Fitzgerald, F. Scott Key   1896-1940

Born at St. Paul, Minnesota, he left Princeton to join the army in 1917 and served as second lieutenant, first lieutenant, and aide-de-camp to a general till 1919. He has often been called the voice of his generation—the "lost generation."

CRACK-UP, WITH OTHER UNCOLLECTED PIECES, NOTEBOOKS AND UNPUBLISHED LETTERS, edited by Edmund Wilson. 1945. B.R.D. 6+, 1– New Directions. $3.50.   **144**

"This book is . . . the perfect tribute to his life and work, for it is incomplete, romantic, full of verve and promise, full of love, yet somehow tragically unsatisfying." —*Book Week*.

"The critic will find the material useful and readers interested in Fitzgerald will find in the autobiographical essays some of his best writings."—*U. S. Quarterly Booklist*.

THE LAST TYCOON, AN UNFINISHED NOVEL, TOGETHER WITH THE GREAT GATSBY AND SELECTED STORIES. 1941. B.R.D. 5+, 0– Scribner. $2.75.   **120**

The unfinished novel is a striking story about Hollywood and the movies. "The Great Gatsby," here reprinted, is a novelette about life, fast and furious, on Long Island in the days of Prohibition.

"This volume presents the best of Fitzgerald. The notes which reveal the ending ôf the unfinished story are extremely interesting for the glimpse they give into the process of a writer at work."—*Nation*.

Flavin, Martin   1883-

American playwright and novelist. Born in San Francisco, he was a student at the University of Chicago, 1903-05. After twenty years in business he turned definitely to writing—plays from 1923 to 1937; since then chiefly novels. His second wife died by falling into the sea from their home on a rocky point near Carmel, California.

JOURNEY IN THE DARK. 1943. B.R.D. 5+, 3– Harper. $2.75.   **121**

This story won the Harper Prize and also the Pulitzer Prize for fiction.

"He has taken a superficially uninteresting man and made him interesting. That alone is no mean achievement. He has also made a plain Middle Western business man a symbol of all these United States."—*New York Times.*

Flexner, Simon   (1863-1946)   and   Flexner, James Thomas   1907-

Simon Flexner was born in Louisville, Kentucky, and has spent his life studying and teaching in medical schools and laboratories in the United States and Europe. He has been a trustee of the Carnegie Institution, the Rockefeller Foundation and Johns Hopkins University. James Thomas Flexner, also a medical scholar, is his son.

WILLIAM HENRY WELCH AND THE HEROIC AGE OF AMERICAN MEDICINE. 1941. B.R.D. 9+, 0– Viking. $3.75.   **110**

"The best history we have read of the birth of medical science in these United States. The Flexners, father and son, have made a worthy contribution to the biography of their time."—*Commonweal.*

"The result of their labors is one of which they may well be proud. . . . This is a book worthy of its great subject."—Hugh Cabot, in *Books.*

Forbes, Esther   1894-

Born in Westborough, Massachusetts, Miss Forbes spent two years at the University of Wisconsin and was for six years a member of the editorial staff of Houghton Mifflin Company. Her ancestry includes both an alleged witch and one bewitched.

PARADISE. 1937. B.R.D. 11+, 2– Harcourt. $2.50.
102

The story of a seventeenth century Massachusetts family who settled in 1639 on an estate twenty miles inland from Boston and called it Paradise. The story ends with an exciting picture of King Philip's War.

"She has taken pains to build her action and setting on a careful study of Puritan life and the events of colonial history."—*Saturday Review of Literature.*

"Miss Forbes has left no blurred edges in the huge and extraordinarily lively scene she has painted; and it is, one feels, a picture that is fair to the fanatical and earnest Puritans who were yet only too subject to human weaknesses."—*Times Literary Supplement.*

PAUL REVERE AND THE WORLD HE LIVED IN. 1942.
B.R.D. 8+, 3– Houghton. $3.75.   273

"The *legendary* Revere . . . succumbs with surprising ease. Miss Forbes does no debunking, she simply tells the truth, and the truth is more real in her telling of it than any legend could be."—*Atlantic.*

"Her biography of Paul Revere takes at once a high and lasting place in American literature."—Carl Van Doren, in *Books.*

"Esther Forbes writes, not so much like a historian who has done creditable research, but as a woman, home-loving but of wide interests, who actually lived in Boston between —say—1757 and 1818."—R. L. Duffus, in *New York Times.*

Fosdick, Harry Emerson   1878-

Baptist clergyman. Born in Buffalo, New York, he has studied and taught and been honored by many universities. He taught homiletics and theology at Union Theological Seminary and was pastor of Riverside Church in New York City for many years, until his retirement in 1946. During the past forty years he has written a score of religious, ethical and inspirational books.

ON BEING A REAL PERSON. 1943. B.R.D. 6+, 0– Harper. $2.50.   **100**

A consideration of human problems, the adequate solution of which makes possible the well-organized life.

"Psychologically and religiously sound and constructive. . . . Characterized by that high degree of artistic skill which marks all the author's work."—*Journal of Religion.*

"One of the most helpful books in this field I have ever read."—E. H. Johnson, in *Survey Graphic.*

Fowler, Gene   1890-

Journalist, novelist, biographer and self-styled American peasant. Born in Denver and educated at the University of Colorado. He "managed" Queen Marie of Rumania on her visit to America and knows his way about Hollywood.

GOOD-NIGHT, SWEET PRINCE. 1944. B.R.D. 6+, 1– Viking. $3.50.   **173**

This life of John Barrymore says the *Atlantic*, is "highly recommended for the general reader as well as the theatrically inclined."

"A tasteful, affectionate and impeccably accurate book. . . . To read it is to know the rare and tragic man that was John Barrymore."—*Saturday Review of Literature.*

Freeman, Douglas Southall   1886-

"Scholar, newspaperman, Virginia aristocrat." Born at Lynchburg, Virginia, and educated at Richmond College and Johns Hopkins University. He taught journalism at Columbia, 1934-41, while he was also an instructor at the Army War College and Coast Artillery School. He has been editor of the *News Leader* of Richmond, Virginia, for many years. In 1935 his life of Robert E. Lee won a Pulitzer prize. Member National Institute of Arts and Letters.

LEE'S LIEUTENANTS. 3 vols. 1942-44. B.R.D. 23+, 4–
        Scribner. $15.   **583**

"Not only a military classic but a book so valuable and timely for the general reader that I hope its general audience may be very wide."—S. V. Benét, in *New York Times*.

"The standard of scholarship and literary craftsmanship . . . will not disappoint the many admirers of Dr. Freeman's *R. E. Lee*. As a writer of military biography Freeman has few equals."—*Yale Review*.

"A magnificent job in which men whose names are legendary come and go in their habit as they lived."—*New York Times*.

"It is amazing that so long a work should sustain the interest as well as this does."—*Saturday Review of Literature*.

Frost, Robert   1875-

American poet. Member, American Academy of Arts and Letters. Born in San Francisco of New England parentage, he has lived in New England since 1885, save for three years (1912-1915) in England and two sojourns at Ann Arbor, Michigan. He was an unhappy student first at Dartmouth, later at Harvard; and never finished his college course. Since his maturity he has divided his time between poetry, farming, and more or less informal college teaching. He was awarded the Pulitzer Prize for poetry in 1924, 1931, 1937 and 1943.

COLLECTED POEMS. 1939. B.R.D. 4+, 1- Holt. $5.

Called the most important book of the year, this volume confirmed Frost's reputation as the leading American poet of today. It contains six earlier publications: *A Boy's Will, North of Boston, Mountain Interval, New Hampshire, West-Running Brook, A Further Range.*

"They are the recognitions of a man desperately determined that this is really all there is, and that this will be enough."—Muriel Rukeyser, in *Poetry.*

"One feels on every page . . . the healthy earth-tang soundness of the man—like a ripe Baldwin apple plucked in its prime—the power of his simplicity, the amplitude of his mellow, all-embracing kindliness, his pantheistic attitude toward nature, his sensitive appreciation of the beauty inherent in emotions and things of everyday life."—E. L. Tinker, in *New York Times.*

A WITNESS TREE. 1942. B.R.D. 7+, 1- Holt. $2.

Won a Pulitzer Prize for poetry in 1943.

"Robert Frost at his best. . . . *A Witness Tree* is a wonderful book, for this age—for any age."—Robert Hillyer, in *Atlantic.*

"He has given us enough first-rate poems here to satisfy the most exacting critic, keep us all in his debt, and leave him secure in his enviable place as the dean of American poets."—*Books.*

Glasgow, Ellen   1874-1945

American novelist. Member, American Academy of Arts and Letters. Born in Richmond, Virginia, she grew up in her father's fine library, and was elected to Phi Beta Kappa at the University of Virginia. When we wish to know what sort of "nice people" lived in England around the year 1800, we read the novels of Jane Austen. When future generations are curious as to the life and people of Virginia, 1900-1940, they will turn to the books of Ellen Glasgow.

CERTAIN MEASURE: AN INTERPRETATION OF PROSE FICTION. 1943. B.R.D. 7+, 1– Harcourt. $3.50.   **121**

Essays which formed the prefaces to the Virginia edition of her novels. They provide a picture of Southern manners from 1850 to 1939 and enable one to perceive and understand the author's growth as a writer over the years.

"Her lucid explanations may not be of great value to the creative writer, but to the student of literature and reader of fiction they cast an illuminating ray."—*Christian Century*.

"Writing of the craft of fiction, she has written a notable essay on the craft of life."—Hamilton Basso, in *New York Times*.

IN THIS OUR LIFE. 1941. B.R.D. 12+, 3– Harcourt. $2.50.   **220**

This "most distinguished novel of the year," which won the Pulitzer Prize for fiction, recognizes the rift between the generations while describing the manifestations of kinship among decayed aristocrats in a Southern city.

"This is distinguished writing . . . not so much a work of fiction as it is a testament, a summary, a philosophy of belief. The wisest woman in the South has written her commentary upon us, and we do not yet know how profound that commentary is."—*Saturday Review of Literature*.

"Looking back over a career steadily continuing since her twenties, Miss Glasgow can say, as a mason of the Middle Ages might have said, standing off to get the effect of his tower: 'That's a good bit of work, that is. It'll stand.'"—M. L. Becker, in *Books*.

Goodrich, Marcus   1897-

Journalist and novelist. Born in San Antonio, Texas, he served in the Army, Navy and Air Force, 1914-20, and in the Navy in World War II.

DELILAH. 1941. B.R.D. 10+, 4- Farrar. $2.75.   100

This first novel is about a U.S. destroyer and her crew in the Pacific in the months which preceded the American entry into World War I. It's a man's book, without a single female character except *Delilah*, the ship herself. It's gory and brutal. The implicit theme is victory or death. And William McFee, who surely knows both books and ships, says the writing is magnificent.

Goudge, Elizabeth   1900-

British novelist. Born in Wells, Somerset, Miss Goudge later moved with her family to Ely where her father was a canon in the cathedral, and later to Oxford where her father taught divinity.

GREEN DOLPHIN STREET. 1944. B.R.D. 5+, 2- Coward. $3.   127

This Victorian novel of New Zealand and the Channel Islands won an M. G. M. prize of $125,000.

"The prize-winning novel lacks the sterner graces of good literature, but is as tasty as a marshmallow, and practically written in technicolor."—*Time*.

"It is the New Zealand scenes, in the early years of British colonization of that country which are the making of the novel."—*Times* (London).

Graham, Gwethalyn   1913-

Canadian novelist. Born in Toronto, Miss Graham's home is now in Montreal. She was educated in Switzerland and at Smith College. Received the Governor-General's Award for fiction in 1938 and 1944; also the Anisfield Wolf Award for fiction in 1945.

EARTH AND HIGH HEAVEN. 1944. B.R.D. 8+, 2– Lippincott. $2.50.   **127**

A story of the love of Jew and Gentile in Montreal.

"The power of the story is in the thorough realism and maturity of probing into delicate human relationships which it achieves."—*Atlantic*.

"Miss Graham gives us vivid glimpses of social and professional life in Montreal. Her characterizations are lively and convincing, the portrait of the sensitive hero being especially well done."—*Spectator*.

Graham, Mrs. J. A. Maxtone. *See* Struther, Jan, pseud.

Greenslet, Ferris   1875-

Publisher and biographer. Born at Glens Falls, New York, and educated at Wesleyan and Columbia Universities, Mr. Greenslet was the editor of the *Atlantic*, 1902-07. He has served the Houghton Mifflin Company since the latter date as adviser and director. Member National Institute of Arts and Letters.

UNDER THE BRIDGE. 1943. B.R.D. 9+, 0– Houghton. $3.   **100**

Life of the author as man of letters, friend and sportsman.

"Mr. Greenslet belongs to the dying race of men of letters who quote Latin without self-consciousness, abhor sloppy scholarship, and have editorial standards derived from a lifetime of serious reading. . . . His world lacked many things ours has, but it seems, as ours does not, to have been largely populated by mature people."—Clifton Fadiman, in *New Yorker*.

"This is a book to be read hungrily at one sitting, then tasted at frequent intervals many, many times for tonic reassurance. Life can be good, and fun, and satisfying. That is the welcome testimony of Ferris Greenslet."—*Springfield Republican*.

Grew, Joseph Clark   1880-

Diplomatist. Born in Boston, Mr. Grew is a Harvard graduate and has received honorary degrees from a dozen universities. He began his foreign service in Cairo in 1904 and was assigned later, successively, to Mexico, Russia, Germany, Austria, Denmark, Switzerland, Turkey, and from 1932 to 1941 to Japan. He served in the State Department at Washington, 1942-45.

TEN YEARS IN JAPAN. 1944. B.R.D. 12+, 0– Simon. *327.73*
    $3.75.   **161** *684+*

"*Ten Years in Japan* . . . answers a great many questions. It answers very definitely the important question— Why did Japan attack us?"—Quentin Reynolds, in *Book Week*.

"The book is not only a contribution to the literature of the war; it is mighty good reading."—*Current History*.

"From the technical diplomatic view, his career ended in defeat. But it was a defeat in which his biographers will find honor."—Nathaniel Peffer, in *New York Times*.

Gunther, John   1901-

Author, foreign correspondent and radio commentator on foreign affairs. Born in Chicago and educated at the University of Chicago, Mr. Gunther has worked in London, Berlin, Vienna, Moscow, Rome and Paris. In preparation for his very successful "Inside" trilogy he observed Europe at close range, 1924-36; Asia, 1937-38; London in 1939; South America in 1940-41; and the fronts of World War II thereafter.

INSIDE ASIA. 1939. (Revised edition 1942). B.R.D. 8+, *950*
    3– Harper. $3.50.   **228** *G97i*

A political survey with vivid commentary on issues and personalities.

"*Inside Asia* is, all things considered, a remarkably good job. It is packed with information. It is eminently fair.

It is highly readable. To the reader who does not know as much as he would like to know about the East—Far, Middle or Near—it will prove as pleasant and easy an introduction as any book available."—*Saturday Review of Literature.*

"This is the sole comprehensive treatment of the political struggles, and of the drive for national emancipation, of well over one half of the population of the world."—*Nation.*

940.5
G97ib

INSIDE EUROPE. 1936. (Revised editions 1937, 1938, 1939, 1940). B.R.D. 13+, 5– Harper. $3.50.   256

A widely read survey of conditions just before the deluge.

"A personality study of the world's dictators: Hitler, Mussolini, Laval, Dollfuss, Baldwin, Stalin, and their associates, underlings and rivals."—*Book Review Digest.*

"It is vivid and extremely readable from beginning to end, full of anecdotes, picturesque touches, epigrammatic definitions and moments of profound insight."—*New Statesman.*

980
G97i

INSIDE LATIN AMERICA. 1941. B.R.D. 10+, 5– Harper. $3.50.   120

"The material for *Inside Latin America* was gathered on a plane trip through twenty countries. . . . History, anecdotes, personalities, political trends and scenic descriptions are juxtaposed in vivid, telling patterns that reveal the underlying trends."—*Nation.*

"Thank all the Inca and the Aztec gods, this is a good book! . . . A wide popular understanding of Latin America is of incalculable importance to us. Nobody needs to be told that Mr. Gunther is a superb reporter."—*Saturday Review of Literature.*

Habe, Hans (pseudonym of Jean Bekassy)   1911–

Hungarian journalist and author. Mr. Habe was born in Budapest and educated in Vienna and Heidelberg. An anti-Nazi since 1932, he served as a volunteer with the French army, was captured, escaped and made his way

finally to America, where he lectured at many of our army
camps on "how to lose a war." Enlisted in our army in
1943.

A THOUSAND SHALL FALL. 1941. B.R.D. 10+, 1– Harcourt. $3.   **120**

 This fictional autobiography tells of the battle and retreat of France, of his capture by the Nazis, imprisonment,
escape and flight across France. The book has been
screened under the title "Cross of Lorraine."

 "The most vivid book which World War II has yet
[1941] produced."—*Time*.

 "It tells how forty million Frenchmen were criminally
deceived, not simply by Fascist aggressors, but by their own
political aimlessness and the obscene egotism of their leaders."—*Books*.

Hacker, Louis Morton 1899-

 Historian, economist. Born in New York City to Austrian parents, Mr. Hacker has studied and taught at Columbia and other institutions. He learned to write as an
assistant on the editorial staff of the *New International
Encyclopedia* and *Yearbook*.

TRIUMPH OF AMERICAN CAPITALISM. 1940. B.R.D. 5+,
  3– Simon. $3.   **100**

 This economic history of the United States to 1900
may be said to fall into two sections. The first deals
with the emergence of mercantile capitalism after the
Revolution; the second, the rise of industrial capitalism
after the Civil War.

 "Mr. Hacker has written a remarkable book. . . .
It is an interpretive study, much of it brilliant, and
all of it suggestive, of the main trends in the economic
growth of the nation."—Allan Nevins, in *Books*.

 "A readable, scholarly, freshly documented book. . . .
Belongs on the same shelf with Andrews and the Beards,
though the author forces his thesis a little."—*New Yorker*.

Hackett, Francis   1883-

Born and educated in Ireland, Mr. Hackett came to America in 1901 and engaged in legal and then in newspaper work. He married Signe Toksvig in 1918 and moved to Denmark, his wife's country, in 1937; but was in the United States during the invasion.

914.89
H12i

I Chose Denmark. 1940. B.R.D. 5+, 1- Doubleday. $2.50.   **110**

This book tells why he chose Denmark. He likes the country, its wholesome people, and the nice, clean, conservative socialism that was working so well before the Nazis came.

Hagedorn, Hermann   1882-

Novelist, poet, biographer. Born in New York City, he was educated at Harvard University which has continued a strong element in his life. He has written about thirty books, several concerning Theodore Roosevelt.

811.5
R659H

Edwin Arlington Robinson. 1938. B.R.D. 8+, 3- Macmillan. $3.   **117**

"If the book is not the final word on Robinson, it is in all probability the standard life, which future biographers must always use."—*Boston Transcript.*

"Mr. Hagedorn's portrait of the rebellious Puritan, who remained a Puritan at heart, is convincing and readable."—*Commonweal.*

"The peculiar value of the book lies in the fact that it is a source book of the environment out of which Robinson wrote his poetry."—*Books.*

Hahn, Emily (Mrs. Charles Boxer)   1905-

Born in St. Louis, Miss Hahn was educated at the University of Wisconsin, at Columbia and at Oxford. She has spent many years in foreign travel and journalism, notably in China, 1935-41.

Soong Sisters. 1941. B.R.D. 8+, 3– Doubleday. $3.
110

A lively book about the famous sisters, Mme. Sun Yat-sen, Mme. Chiang Kai-shek and Mme. Kung Hsiang-hsi, whose husband is China's financial wizard.

"A delightful and well-written book. The author has handled a delicate subject with much skill."—*Nation.*

Halsey, Margaret (Mrs. M. R. Stern)   1910-

Miss Halsey was born at Yonkers, New York, and educated at Skidmore, and at Teachers' College, Columbia.

With Malice Toward Some. 1938. B.R.D. 9+, 2–
Simon. $2.   117

*914.2
H19w*

"Miss Halsey gives the reader a rare treat in her simple yet accurate and pointed descriptions of the English landed gentry; their manners, their customs, their food, their clothes and their class society."—*Boston Transcript.*

"A definitive work on the British art of annoying Americans."—*Forum.*

"The English-Speaking Union will probably never recommend this book."—*New York Times.*

"Accepted in the right spirit of give and take, her vivacious jesting should be thoroughly enjoyed, her criticisms not at all resented. England is ready to welcome her again, as she, apparently, to return to it."—*Times* (London).

Hargrove, Marion   1919-

This young newspaperman, born at Mount Olive, North Carolina, had been two years on the staff of the *Charlotte News* when he joined the army in 1941, and continued to contribute to his paper a column called "In the Army Now." He served in the China-Burma-India theater, 1942-44, on the staff of *Yank.*

SEE HERE, PRIVATE HARGROVE. 1942. B.R.D. 8+, 3–
Holt. $2.   189

These sketches about the rookie of World War II
were called "the laugh sensation of the war." Two million copies were sold during the first year after publication. Its bookstore sale was the sixth largest in fifty years.

"Nothing in Private Hargrove's book could bring comfort to the enemy, but almost every line in it could contribute to his confusion. For a book like this, with its
cheerful impudences, couldn't come out of a New Order or
a Greater Co-Prosperity Sphere."—*New York Times.*

370.973
H338

Harvard University

GENERAL EDUCATION IN A FREE SOCIETY. 1945. B.R.D.
6+, 0– Harvard. $2.   120

The field studied includes education in schools—and
most emphatically in high schools— as well as in colleges.

"Required reading for everyone in the teaching profession, and of value to the intelligent layman."—*Library
Journal.*

"If its sensible suggestions are followed, American education can regain direction, discard the bickering and confusion of recent years and help maintain a dynamic democracy."—*New York Times.*

Hayek, Friedrich August von   1899-

Mr. Hayek was born in Austria and educated at the
University of Vienna. He moved to England in 1931 to
teach in the London School of Economics, became a British
subject, and seven years later came to the United States to
lecture and speak on the radio.

330.1
H41R

ROAD TO SERFDOM. 1944. B.R.D. 8+, 1– University
of Chicago. $2.75.   127

This rebuttal of socialism has been widely quoted by
conservatives who still believe in the beneficence of com-
petition and remain calm even when *laissez-faire* is men-

tioned. After a first-hand acquaintance with totalitarianism, the author prefers freedom even to economic security. TVA is all very well, he would say, but it is fatally easy to get too much of many of a good thing.

"It restates for our time the issue between liberty and authority with the power and rigor of reasoning that John Stuart Mill stated the issue for his own generation in his great essay 'On Liberty.'"—Henry Hazlitt, in *New York Times*.

"Its social proposals will do much to remove evils which made the older individualism so burdensome to many of the workers."—*Times* (London).

Heiser, Victor G.   1873-

This eminent hygienist was born at Johnstown, Pennsylvania, and earned his medical degree at Jefferson Medical College, Philadelphia. He was director of Health of the Philippine Islands, 1903-15; Associate Chairman, International Health Division, Rockefeller Foundation, 1915-34. The widest experience was his and many honors in the fields of tropical and international medicine.

AMERICAN DOCTOR'S ODYSSEY; ADVENTURES IN FORTY-FIVE
    COUNTRIES. 1936. B.R.D. 11+, 0- Norton.
    $3.50.   **240**

"Once in a very long time there comes a book so wholly remarkable, alluring, so wide and deep in its appeal, that one wants to rush to an international broadcasting station to shout, 'Read it!' This is such a book."—*Books*.

"It might be Dr. Heiser talking. . . . He is one of those rare individuals whom the printed word does not scare into stilted phrases and carefully worded reservations."—Theodore Roosevelt, Jr., in *Saturday Review of Literature*.

"The romance of medicine from Johnstown, Pennsylvania, to the mouth of the Pei Ho. It should . . . be passed from hand to hand in every printed language."—*Survey Graphic*.

Hemingway, Ernest   1898-

American novelist. Born in Oak Park, Illinois. Educated by World War I, in which he served as a volunteer, first with an American ambulance unit and later on the Italian front, where he was seriously wounded. Virile, athletic, "hard-boiled," well known on the Left Bank and Montmartre, he is the most generally recognized spokesman of the American postwar generation and has been imitated *ad nauseam*.

FIFTH COLUMN, AND THE FIRST FORTY-NINE STORIES. 1938. B.R.D. 3+, 1– Scribner. $2.75.   **135**

"The Fifth Column is hardly a great play." But here are also forty-nine short stories—four of them never before printed, and one of these superb. Clifton Fadiman says of them, "I don't see how you can go through this book without being convinced that Hemingway is the best short story writer now using English."

FOR WHOM THE BELL TOLLS. 1940. B.R.D. 9+, 2– Scribner. $2.75.   **680**

This book's "score" is the highest on record.

A ruf-and-tuf, but deeply serious and sincere story of an American volunteer in the Spanish Civil War—four days of love and danger which ended in death.

"Ernest Hemingway is an artist and his new novel is a rare and beautiful piece of work. . . . It proves that this fine writer, unlike some other fine American writers, is capable of self-criticism and self-development."—R. E. Sherwood, in *Atlantic*.

"A true essay on the real belief in liberty, equality and fraternity."—John Chamberlain, in *Books*.

"This is the best book Ernest Hemingway has written, the fullest, the deepest, the truest. It will, I think, be one of the major novels in American literature."—J. D. Adams, in *New York Times*.

Henderson, Sir Nevile   1882-1942

A graduate of Eton, Sir Nevile began his diplomatic career in 1905 as Third Secretary at St. Petersburg. Thereafter he served at Tokyo, Rome, Paris, Constantinople, Cairo, Belgrade and Rio de Janeiro. He was the British Ambassador to Berlin from 1937 to 1939, the days of Chamberlain's appeasement.

FAILURE OF A MISSION. 1940. B.R.D. 9+, 0– Putnam. $3.   120

940.532
H49f

"The author is at his best in sketching the personalities of Hitler and his associates."—*American Political Science Review.*

"A convincing picture of a conscientious, if limited, British diplomat attempting the impossible. He wanted a compromise peace. Hitler didn't. And Hitler was the stronger man."—Lewis Gannett, in *Boston Transcript.*

"Indispensable to the historian as the sincere and businesslike record of an important eye-witness of this sinister tragedy."—*Spectator.*

Hendrick, Burton J.   1870-

Journalist, historian, biographer. Born at New Haven, Connecticut, and educated at Yale, Mr. Hendrick was editor of the *New Haven Morning News,* 1896-98, and thereafter on the editorial staffs of the *New York Evening Post, McClure's Magazine* and *World's Work.* He is a member of the National Institute of Arts and Letters and thrice a Pulitzer prize winner.

BULWARK OF THE REPUBLIC: A BIOGRAPHY OF THE CONSTITUTION. 1937. B.R.D. 6+, 5– Little. $3.50.   136

342.73
H49

"It moves with breathless rapidity from episode to episode; it is studded with brilliant character sketches of jurists and statesmen; and it exploits to the fullest the dramatic possibilities of doubt and struggle."—H. S. Commager, in *Yale Review.*

923.7
H49s

STATESMEN OF THE LOST CAUSE: JEFFERSON DAVIS AND
    HIS CABINET. 1939. B.R.D. 10+, 6- Little.
    $3.75.   161

"The book as a whole is a splendidly executed succession of fascinating studies."—D. S. Freeman, in *Saturday
Review of Literature.*

"Mr. Hendrick . . . is a fine biographer and well deserves the reputation he has both for thorough research
and for his ability to bring the dead to life. . . . [His book]
does not allow its fine scholarship to be a burden. It is
readable, informative and provocative."—*Atlantic.*

Herndon, William Henry   1818-1891

Herndon, born in Greensburg, Kentucky, was Lincoln's
law partner in 1844. He became an anti-slavery enthusiast
and a great admirer of Lincoln. For thirty years he zeal-
ously collected Lincolniana which others used. His own
book, *Herndon's Lincoln* was not published till 1889. His
flair for romance is probably responsible for the Ann
Rutledge legend.

923.7
L73h5

THE HIDDEN LINCOLN, FROM THE LETTERS AND PAPERS OF
    THE AUTHOR; edited by Emanuel Hertz. 1938.
    B.R.D. 4+, 1- Viking. $5.   117

"A notable contribution to the Lincoln bibliography.
Must be considered by those studying Lincoln or Herndon
hereafter from any angle."—*Nation.*

Hersey, John   1914-

He was born in Tientsin, China, where his parents were
American missionaries. He spoke Chinese before he spoke
English. He was educated in the United States and England. During the summer of 1937 he acted as secretary to
Sinclair Lewis. For some years he was on the editorial
staff of *Life* and *Time,* and he still writes for *Life* and
the *New Yorker.* He observed World War II in Asia
and Europe as a correspondent of *Time.*

Bell for Adano. 1944. B.R.D. 15+, 7– Knopf. $2.50.
472

A story about the troubles of Joppolo, an AMG officer in Italy, during the occupation.

"A study of 'what America can and cannot do in Europe.' As such it is very interesting and very good. . . . Its credo—that government, whatever its professions, can only be as good as the men who govern."—M. Hindus, in *Atlantic*.

"The foreseeable future depends on the Joppolos—the men who can help the liberated peoples get on their feet and help themselves."—*Commonweal*.

Hicks, Granville (1901-) and Stuart, John   1912-

Hicks was born at Exeter, New Hampshire, and educated at Harvard. He taught at Smith and Rensselaer Polytechnic Institute, 1915-35. Became interested in Marxism in the thirties and was a member of the editorial staff of the *New Masses*, 1934-39. He was a Guggenheim Fellow, 1936-37. Still a socialist, he is no longer a Communist. Since 1935 he has lived on a farm at Grafton, New York.

John Reed: the Making of a Revolutionary. 1936.
B.R.D. 9+, 3– Macmillan. $3.50.   112

Born in a wealthy home in Portland, Oregon, Reed died thirty-three years later in Russia, of typhus, and was buried beside the Kremlin in Moscow, mourned by thousands of workers.

"Wrong-headed and socially dangerous as he may have been, there was one of the most brilliant minds, one of the most unselfish hearts, one of the spirits most devoted to the cause of suffering humanity that our time has seen. . . . It would be hard for anyone to write a dull book about John Reed."—*Christian Century*.

Hitler, Adolf   1889-1945

Born at Braunau, Austria, he served as a corporal in the German army in World War I. Some time after the abortive Beer Hall Putsch he became Chancellor of Germany in 1932—also Dictator. When the aged Hindenburg died in 1934 Hitler was named Reichsführer.

MEIN KAMPF. 1939. 994p. Reynal. $3; 669p. Stackpole. $3.   247

Both these editions of the Nazis' Bible are unabridged. (The Houghton edition of 1933 contained less than half the original text.) The Reynal edition has the better and ampler notes. Both translations bear evidence of hasty preparation and can only be described as fairly good.

"Devoid of intellectual content or any pretense of rationality . . . *Mein Kampf* differs from most holy writ in that it is vicious, vulgar and violent."—*Nation*.

"These new translations will give the American public new insight into the mind and character of Europe's latest Napoleon. They contain all the torrential verbiage, the race nonsense, the egocentric emotionalism and the surprising shrewdness that were lacking in the abbreviated version. . . . In page after page, frankly expounding techniques and propaganda and party organization, Adolf Hitler becomes unquestionably the Machiavelli of our age."— *Saturday Review of Literature*.

Hogben, Lancelot   1895-

Born in Portsmouth, England, and educated at Cambridge, Hogben has taught at the Universities of London and Edinburgh, at McGill University, Canada, and at Cape Town University, South Africa. He is a Fellow of the Royal Society. "In many ways Professor Hogben is the *enfant terrible* of the academic world." (*New Statesman*).

MATHEMATICS FOR THE MILLION. 1937. B.R.D. 9+, 1– Norton. $3.75.   204

"For the million," this book emphasizes the historical and social aspects of mathematics.

"A book for fascinated browsing by any serious student, and one to delight any amateur who wishes to see what mathematics is about, and what it can do for human beings."—*Saturday Review of Literature*.

SCIENCE FOR THE CITIZEN; a Self-Educator Based on the
  Social Background of Scientific Discovery. 1938.
  B.R.D. 13+, 5– Knopf. $5.   **135**

This has been called "the outstanding work on general science." It has inspired J. G. Crowther to declare in the *Manchester Guardian* that Hogben seems destined to succeed Shaw and Wells as the leading British popularizer of thought.

"A great and fascinating book—one to rejoice the heart of every citizen who values civilization and enlightenment." —*Times* (London).

"A clearly organized and fascinating account of the most significant facts and hypotheses in the various fields of the sciences, and at the same time a history of European thought and culture from the standpoint of progress in the sciences. But the correlation of this progress with the social background and economic needs of contemporary society is the outstanding feature of this book."—*New Republic*.

Holmes, Oliver Wendell   (1841-1935) and Pollock, Sir Frederick   1845-1937

Holmes the jurist was, of course, born in Boston, for he was the son of the witty and beloved "Autocrat." After years of active service in the Civil War during which he was three times wounded, he resumed his legal studies and practice and rose rapidly to be Chief Justice of the Massachusetts Supreme Court, whence he was called to become an Associate Justice of the United States Supreme Court, 1882-99, and Chief Justice, 1899-1932.

Pollock was born in London and educated at Eton, Trinity College, Cambridge, and Lincoln's Inn. He was Judge of the Admiralty Court, 1914-36.

THE HOLMES-POLLOCK LETTERS: THEIR CORRESPONDENCE,
    1874-1932; edited by M. A. DeW. Howe. 2 vol.
    1941. B.R.D. 9+, 0– Harvard. $7.50.   **140**

"The correspondence for nearly sixty years between
two men of profound learning and highest culture is without parallel. . . . Reading the letters consecutively one
realizes the truth of what Pollock said: 'There was no stage
of acquaintance ripening into friendship; we understood
one another and were friends without more ado.' "—*Books*.

"Holmes is the more human and has the lighter touch.
He relished frivolities that had little temptation for Pollock. Yet both swapped views on life's ultimates."—*Nation*.

"They confirm the conviction that Justice Holmes was
not only the most distinguished jurist, but the most distinguished citizen of his generation."—H. S. Commager, in
New York Times.

Holt, Rackham (pseudonym of Margaret Van Vechten Saunders Holt)   1899-

Born in Denver; married Guy Holt, editor and publisher, in 1923 (he died in 1934); lives at Mt. Sinai, Long
Island.

GEORGE WASHINGTON CARVER. 1943. B.R.D. 11+, 1–
    Doubleday. $3.50.   **231**

The life of Dr. Carver of Tuskegee, pioneer of scientific
agriculture, leader of his race and revered citizen.

"Not only the story of a great American and a great
scientist but, indirectly, the record of the progress made by
a whole race."—*Yale Review*.

"She has created a complete picture—the multiplicity
of interests and the cheerful, kind, simple dignity of a great-
hearted and great-minded man."—*Scientific Book Club*.

Horton, Philip   1911-

Born in Providence, R.I. Educated at Princeton University and at the Universities of Aix-Marseilles and Berlin. Has taught English at Harvard, and served with the O.S.S. during the war.

HART CRANE, THE LIFE OF AN AMERICAN POET. 1937. B.R.D. 10+, 1– Norton. $3.   **102**

811.9
C89B

Critical appraisal of his work as well as biography of a neurotic who wrote admirable poetry. A tragic and sordid story of frustration, in the telling of which the author has skillfully combined tact with candor.

"With a central character who by no conceivable stretch of the imagination can be called sympathetic, he has written an admirable and very moving biography."—Conrad Aiken, in *Atlantic*.

"Mr. Horton keeps his head, does not criticize, does not adore, does not, we feel sure, distort."—*Boston Transcript*.

Household, Geoffrey   1903-

English novelist. Educated at Oxford, he has lived much in Spain, also in Rumania, the United States, the Near East and South America.

ROGUE MALE. 1939. B.R.D. 7+, 3– Little. $2.   **114**

Story of an English sportsman's adventures during and after his attempt to shoot an unnamed European dictator.

"The reader feels . . . a breath-taking uninterrupted concentration. As a work of the imagination *Rogue Male* is an almost overpowering *tour de force*. And in its spare, tense, desperately alive narrative it will keep, long after the last page is finished, its hold from the first page upon the reader's mind."—*New York Times*.

Housman, A. E.   1859-1936

English poet and classical scholar. Born in Worcestershire with Shropshire hard by. Educated at Oxford, he was a clerk in the Patent Office, 1882-92, and thereafter professor of Latin, first at University College, London, and later at Trinity College, Cambridge.

COLLECTED POEMS. 1940. B.R.D. 5+, 1– Holt. $3.   **150**

Contains "Shropshire Lad," "Last Poems," "More Last Poems," and some additional poems and translations.

"It may be, for all I know, the last perfection of its kind; it may quite likely be, as the young men say, that Housman's lovely lines are no more than a melancholy echo of the past and a prescience of the death of all of us."—P. M. Jack, in *New York Times*.

Hutchinson, Ray Coryton   1907-

English novelist; born in London and educated at Oxford.

FIRE AND THE WOOD. 1940. B.R.D. 4+, 2– Farrar. $2.50.   **130**

"Story of a young German-Jew doctor in the years just before and after the Nazis rose to power."—*Book Review Digest*.

"The excitement of violent emotions and reactions, the transforming power of love, make very dramatic this serious novel, well worth reading, although extremely painful to the reader at times."—*Churchman*.

Huxley, Aldous   1894-

English novelist. Educated at Eton and Oxford. Grandson of Thomas Huxley; grand-nephew of Matthew Arnold; nephew of Mrs. Humphrey Ward; brother of Julian Huxley. Serious eye trouble interrupted his education and prevented active participation in World War I. The author of some thirty or more books, he was awarded the James Tait Black Memorial Prize. He married Maria Nys, a Belgian refugee, in 1919, and has lived much in Italy and France. Between 1930 and 1935 he turned, partially at least, from cynicism to mysticism. He has lived in California since 1938.

After Many a Summer Dies the Swan. 1939. B.R.D.
    5+, 5– Harper. $2.50.   **100**

A weird tale, with involved philosophic and religious
side lines, of an American millionaire who is afraid of
death.

"Mr. Huxley may be disappointed in his search after
the good life, but is that any reason for disappointing readers in search of the good novel?"—*Boston Transcript*.

Ends and Means; an Inquiry into the Nature of
    Ideals and into the Methods Employed for
    Their Realization. 1937. B.R.D. 4+, 3– Har-
    per. $3.50.   **144**

"A complete statement of a philosophy of living by a
novelist in whose novels the ideas have always seemed as
important as the action."—H. S. Canby, in *Saturday Review of Literature*.

"A remarkable volume in its own right, its interest is
heightened by the extraordinary transformation it reveals
in Mr. Huxley's mental attitude."—Henry Hazlitt, in *New
York Times*.

Eyeless in Gaza. 1936. B.R.D. 10+, 6– Harper. $2.50.
                                                  104

Beset by doubts and vacillations, an intellectual youth
grows to manhood in a period of war and economic turmoil.
This has been called "the author's most serious novel" as
well as "the year's most important British novel."

"Mr. Huxley's finest novel. . . . *Eyeless in Gaza* is a delight; but on the whole the plan of popping about in time
is a mistake."—David Garnett, in *New Statesman*.

"In this book Aldous Huxley emerges a moralist, a
believer in the efficacy of the spiritual life, in the necessity
that one demand of oneself the achievement of the impossible."—J. D. Adams, in *New York Times*.

"There is a serious danger that . . . those of its readers
who have not the very strongest stomachs will put it aside
in disgust before they realize the seriousness of its purpose."—*Spectator*.

GREY EMINENCE: A STUDY IN RELIGION AND POLITICS.
    1941. B.R.D. 6+, 4– Harper. $3.50.   **120**

A life of Father Joseph, Cardinal Richelieu's mysterious aide.

"Unfolds a convincing argument concerning the legitimate roles of politics, morals and mysticism."—*Commonweal.*

"Mr. Huxley now tries to carry his convictions into practice, and he begins to deserve the respect one accords to a man whose ambition is a sort, even if a mistaken sort, of sainthood."—Malcolm Cowley, in *New Republic.*

"This will hardly attract the audience that waits eagerly for his novels, but it should interest those to whom Huxley's own personality, with its curious shifts and cold agonies, is more interesting than his books."—Clifton Fadiman, in *New Yorker.*

TIME MUST HAVE A STOP. 1944. B.R.D. 6+, 8– Harper. $2.75.   **115**

"Cut from the same die as its predecessor—is the same wonderful and disappointing mixture of horror, erudition and farce."—*New York Times.*

"It is difficult . . . for Huxley to celebrate convincingly in a novel his present ideals of abnegation and withdrawal from the things of the world."—Edmund Wilson, in *New Yorker.*

"The mixture of deplorable characters and homiletic essays is deliberately artificial, packed with wit, rarely dull. Its basic theme is the Huxleyan conviction that world reform must begin in the individual soul."—*Time.*

Ickes, Harold L.   1874-

Born in Blair County, Pennsylvania, and educated at the University of Chicago, he early became interested in Chicago reform politics, working first as a reporter and later as a lawyer. He was on the staff of the Y.M.C.A. with the A.E.F. in France, 1918-19. Long a Republican, he switched to the New Deal in 1932 and was Secretary of the Interior in Roosevelt's cabinet, 1932-46.

AUTOBIOGRAPHY OF A CURMUDGEON.   1943.   B.R.D.   2+, 1– Reynal. $3.   **121**

"The chief value of Mr. Ickes' book resides in the picture it presents of city politics and politicians, both machine and reformist, over a considerable period of time."—*Commonweal.*

"The self-flagellations of a contemporary Jonathan Edwards.   This is the key-note of the tome."—*Yale Review.*

"Perhaps in the eventual sequel we will learn . . . that he never was a curmudgeon at all, but just a kindly, gentle crusader who talked gruffly when his eyes were moist with unshed tears, pitying human frailty.   Somehow the author seems to hint that such should be the ultimate judgment."—D. R. Richberg, in *Survey Graphic.*

Ingersoll, Ralph   1900-

Editor and author.   Born in New Haven, Connecticut, he was educated at Hotchkiss, Yale and Columbia. He worked as a miner, 1921-23, and on the staff of the *New Yorker*, 1925-1930.   He edited *Fortune*, 1930-35; was vice president of *Time*, 1935-39; and an editor of *PM*, 1940-46.   A war correspondent on several fronts, 1940-41, he was in military service in Europe, 1942-45. He resigned his editorship of *PM* in 1946, protesting their acceptance of advertising.

BATTLE IS THE PAY-OFF.   1943.   B.R.D.   12+, 1– Harcourt. $2.   **154**

The detailed description of a battle as it appeared to an intelligent American soldier who was a combatant in Tunisia.

"War reporting at its best."—*Nation.*

"The thing that has been badly needed in this war is a primer that tells how an army works in the field, how it is set up into various compartments and why, and what a battle really looks like. This book is that primer."— *Churchman*.

"No one with any interest in our combat soldiers or in the mechanics of the new American army in battle action can help reading it with avidity."—Walter Millis, in *Weekly Book Review*.

Jackson, Charles   1903-

Born in Summit, New Jersey. After a year at Syracuse University he was ill with tuberculosis, 1927-33. Then came several years as a writer for the radio and as a teacher of radio writing at New York University. He became a teetotaler on realizing that alcohol was interfering with his writing.

Lost Weekend. 1944. B.R.D. 8+, 2– Farrar. $2.50.
                                                    115

Psychological study of a sensitive, refined young man who finds himself a pitiful drunkard on a five-day binge, and not for the first time.

"There has never, to my knowledge, been a book like this. Its frankness is sometimes shocking but never aimed to shock. The aim, and it is unerring, is always for accuracy and the complete truth."—A. C. Spectorsky, in *Book Week*.

Jaffe, Bernard   1896-

Born in New York City; educated at City College and Columbia University. Served with the A.E.F. in France in 1918. Has taught science in the high schools of New York City since 1924 and has written much on scientific subjects.

Men of Science in America. 1944. B.R.D. 1+, 0–
          Simon. $3.75.   **104**

In the lives of nineteen eminent scientists this book summarizes the role of science in the progress of America.

James, Marquis   1891-

American author. Born, Springfield, Missouri; educated at Phillips University, Enid, Oklahoma. Engaged in newspaper work, 1909-16; with the A.E.F. in France, 1917-19; national director of publicity, American Legion, 1919-23; on editorial staff, American Legion Monthly, 1923-32. He has twice won the Pulitzer Prize for biography.

ANDREW JACKSON, PORTRAIT OF A PRESIDENT. 1937.
B.R.D. 7+, 1– Bobbs. $5.   221

This book is a sequel to *Andrew Jackson, the Border Captain*, 1933. A study of conditions that were to lead eventually to the Civil War, it covers the years from 1824 to his death in 1845. It is interesting and enjoyable throughout. A living, breathing Jackson steps out of these pages.

"His Jackson is alive, an 'Old Hickory' of pulsing sap, a man who broke heads while shielding his own heartbreak."—*Saturday Review of Literature*.

CHEROKEE STRIP; A TALE OF AN OKLAHOMA BOYHOOD.
1945. B.R.D. 8+, 1– Viking. $3.   132

"Mr. James's recollections . . . are superb. No other book of childhood reminiscences published in recent years, with the possible exception of H. L. Mencken's *Happy Days*, is comparable to it."—*Weekly Book Review*.

"Written with delightful charm and skillful simplicity . . . an epic of the last cattle kingdom."—*Commonweal*.

Jeffers, Robinson   1887-

A member of the American Academy of Arts and Letters. Generally regarded as one of the major poets of America, Mr. Jeffers was born in Pittsburgh and educated at several Western colleges (including one of medicine and one of forestry) and at the University of Zurich, Switzerland. He lives near Carmel, California, in a stone hermitage by the sea built with his own hands. He inaugurated in 1941 a series of poets' readings in the Library of Congress at Washington.

SELECTED POETRY. 1938. Random. $3.50.　　171

One hundred and twenty-five poems selected by the author and his wife from the ten or a dozen volumes of his published writings. It has been pronounced the best poetry of its year.

Jessup, Philip Caryl　1897-

Born in New York City and educated at Hamilton College, Yale Law School and Columbia, Mr. Jessup served with the A.E.F. in World War I. He has taught international law at Columbia since 1925 and has also been employed on assignments for the State Department, UNRRA, etc.

ELIHU ROOT. 2 vol. 1938. B.R.D. 5+, 0- Dodd. $7.50.　　144

Elihu Root (1845-1937) was long revered first as a protagonist and later as an elder statesman in the American legal and political arena. A great corporation lawyer, he was entrusted with many important political assignments. Among these were two cabinet positions: Secretary of War in McKinley's, and Secretary of State in Theodore Roosevelt's cabinet.

"A sympathetic but not extravagantly sentimental biography, detailed but never dull . . . it is just about what a good biography should be."—*Boston Transcript*

"A miracle, . . . an official biography written with conscience unfettered and utter loyalty to the facts."—*Saturday Review of Literature*.

Johnson, Gerald White　1890-

Journalist and author. Born at Riverton, North Carolina, and educated at Wake Forest College, Mr. Johnson served in World War I, 1917-19, and was an editorial writer on the Baltimore "Sun-Papers," 1926-43. He is the author of about fifteen books (1925-44), mostly on American public men and affairs.

AMERICAN HEROES AND HERO-WORSHIP. 1943. B.R.D. 4+, 1– Harper. $3. **121**

He considers Washington, Hamilton, Jefferson, Van Buren, Clay, Jackson, DuPont, Watson, Theodore Roosevelt and Wilson; and paints a convincing background of the history which formed them.

"Brilliant prose, penetrating comment, the true historian's detachment and sound scholarship make this volume a highly stimulating and profitable experience." —*Christian Science Monitor*.

Johnson, Osa Helen (Mrs. Martin Johnson, now Mrs. C. G. Getts) 1894-

Born in Chanute, Kansas, she eloped with another young Kansan, Martin Johnson. She accompanied her husband on his many expeditions to take movies of savages and wild animals in African jungles and Pacific islands.

I MARRIED ADVENTURE. 1940. B.R.D. 11+, 1– Lippincott. $3.50. **150**

Splendidly illustrated.

"A fine book on many counts. It is a good travel book, a good adventure book, a good book about animals, a good book on photography, and, best of all, it is a good human story about two extremely likable people, told by one of them with simplicity, humor, warmth and complete lack of 'side.'"—*Books*.

"It belongs on any list of Americana, for the Johnsons were as American as David Crockett."—J. W. Krutch, in *Nation*.

Josephson, Matthew 1899-

Born in Brooklyn, New York; educated at Columbia with Lewis Mumford and Edmund Wilson. Edited the magazine *Broom* successively in Rome, Paris and New York, before he invaded Wall Street, where he was successful—for a time. In his late twenties he turned decisively to literature. He was also American editor of *Transition* and a Guggenheim Fellow, 1933-34.

POLITICOS: 1865-96. 1938. B.R.D. 6+, 1– Harcourt. $4.50.   121

Here are all the tin heroes of our politics who flourished in the last third of the nineteenth century, from Ben Butler to William J. Bryan. In retrospect they were certainly not an inspiring lot, but the author seems unnecessarily hard upon them. It's a dreary story, sometimes rather drearily told.

"It is a scholarly work. It stands up, a true picture of the times. It is written with the clarity that arises from a sense of truth."—W. A. White, in *Saturday Review of Literature*.

PRESIDENT MAKERS; THE CULTURE OF POLITICS AND LEADERSHIP IN AN AGE OF ENLIGHTENMENT, 1896-1919. 1940. B.R.D. 4+, 0– Harcourt. $3.75.   160

American politics from McKinley to Wilson. The "President Makers" are Mark Hanna, Theodore Roosevelt, Colonel House and George Harvey; the Presidents made are also considered, particularly Theodore Roosevelt and Woodrow Wilson.

"The book is worth reading and worth owning."— J. T. Adams, in *Saturday Review of Literature*.

"A clear picture of democracy at work, and on the whole a pretty encouraging picture."—*Survey Graphic*.

Joyce, James   1882-1941

Born in a suburb of Dublin, Ireland, Joyce was a graduate (1902) of University College, Dublin, a Jesuit institution. During most of the years from 1902 to 1941 he lived in Paris, Switzerland or Austria. He knew seventeen languages. For many of his last years he was nearly blind. His early work, *Dubliners*, was burned in a public square in Dublin. *Ulysses*, first published in Paris in 1922, was promptly banned in Great Britain, Ireland and the United States, though the ban here was lifted in 1933.

In most of his writing he has played games with words. If one doesn't know the rules or is not good at puzzles the books are unintelligible unless one holds a big guide-book in the left hand and studies it diligently. Those who should know tell us that Joyce was a great genius. Clifton Fadiman in the *New Yorker* likens his lucubrations to those of a god talking in his sleep. This is the highbrow view. To lowbrows his outgivings may suggest rather a learned fool talking through his hat.

FINNEGAN'S WAKE. 1939. B.R.D. 2+, 2– Viking. $5.
133

An excursion to Cloud Cuckoo-Land upon which the author was engaged for sixteen years. (Part of it was earlier published under the title "Work in Progress.") Some critic has called it without fear of contradiction "much the most difficult novel of the year." Of the dozen reviews of the book summarized in the *Book Review Digest* not one can be said to be either definitely favorable or unfavorable, though two are indicated as being both! In very truth it's the sort of book which does strange things to reviewers—sensible fellows after all, who like to keep both feet on the ground as much as they dislike being caught in an embarrassing position.

Kazin, Alfred   1915-

Born in Brooklyn; educated at City College and Columbia. He has taught at City College and Queens College and at the New School of Social Research, all in New York. The high quality of this work has been recognized by a Guggenheim Fellowship and a grant-in-aid from the Carnegie Corporation. On the editorial staff of the *Oxford Companion to American Literature*, he is also an assistant editor of the *New Republic*.

ON NATIVE GROUNDS; INTERPRETATION OF MODERN AMER-
ICAN PROSE LITERATURE. 1942. B.R.D. 6+, 2–
Reynal. $3.75.   **242**

"History of the relation between American prose
writers and our developing society in the years between
1890 and the present." The book has three parts: the
search for reality, 1890-1917; the great liberation, 1918-
29; the literature of crisis, 1930-40.

"Here is a writer patently learned and luminous, a
critic of high moral seriousness and cool fastidious discernment. . . . This book . . . is the signal of a new
force in American criticism."—Irwin Edman, in *Books*.

"Mr. Kazin believes, and he is right, that the common estimation of our literature has been too lenient,
that we still judge our literary past with the pleased
surprise that we have any books at all."—*Nation*.

"One has pleasure in the intelligence of his judgments, even if one occasionally wishes to disclaim them."
—*Saturday Review of Literature*.

Keith, Agnes Newton (Mrs. Harry G. Keith)

The American wife of an English official in North
Borneo. Formerly a San Francisco journalist.

LAND BELOW THE WIND; Sketches by the Author. 1939.
B.R.D. 7+, 2– Little. $3.   **133**

An informal, amusing account of home life and jungle
travel in Borneo before World War II. Since this book
was published the author, her husband and little son
have spent three years as Japanese prisoners of war.
On publication the book won the *Atlantic* Non-fiction
Award of $5,000.

"Eminently readable on every page."—Pearl S. Buck,
in *Atlantic*.

Kimbrough, Emily. *See* Skinner, Cornelia Otis, jt. auth.

Kipling, Rudyard   1865-1936

"The interpreter of the English-speaking race."—*Spectator* (1906.)

"His books vary in interest: they may be different, as 'Stalky' is different from 'Recessional;' but in each and all there is magic that starts somewhere, if not everywhere, in everything signed Rudyard Kipling."—C. Lewis Hind, in *Authors and I*, 1921.

SOMETHING OF MYSELF: FOR MY FRIENDS KNOWN AND UNKNOWN. 1937. B.R.D. 10+, 4— Doubleday. $2.50.   **102**

Generally regarded as a somewhat disappointing book. The *New Statesman* calls attention to the fact that "thirty years and more remain uncovered except by passing allusion."

"One of the most revealing of all writers' records of what made them writers and why and how they worked."— *Chicago Daily Tribune*.

"This book is the cornerstone of that complete biography which awaits some Anglo-American architect."— Edward Weeks, in *Atlantic*.

Knight, Eric   1897-1943

This English novelist came to the United States in 1912; he served with the Canadians in World War I. Thereafter he engaged in journalism in the United States. He died a major in the U. S. Army, in an air accident in Surinam. He was the author of *Lassie, Come Home* and of *The Flying Yorkshireman*—books strangely different, both from each other and from *This Above All*.

THIS ABOVE ALL. 1941. B.R.D. 9+, 3— Harper. $2.50.
                                                            100

A war novel of England in 1940. An English soldier, his valor already proved in battle, is home on leave. Preparing to go back into it, he begins to wonder whether after all the game (England) is worth the candle. But that is only the beginning of the story.

"You can't say, any longer, that no great novel has come out of the second World War. Eric Knight has written one."—*Boston Transcript*.

"A challenging book, which in itself is a tribute to the continued liberty of thought and speech that makes its appearance possible."—*Times* (London) *Literary Supplement*.

Koestler, Arthur   1905-

Novelist. Editors call him "the best of the émigrés." Born in Budapest, Hungary, and educated in Vienna, he was a journalist and foreign correspondent, 1926-31, and became a Communist during the latter year. While a correspondent in Spain during the Spanish war, he was taken prisoner and narrowly escaped execution by Franco. He gave up communism about 1935. When World War II came he soon found himself a prisoner of war in France. He escaped, managed to get to England and into the British army.

ARRIVAL AND DEPARTURE. 1943. B.R.D. 9+, 2– Macmillan. $2.   165

A psychological novel of a refugee Communist who has escaped from the Nazis after capture and torture.

"I shall not retract what I have said: this is a very great book."—H. A. Reinhold, in *Commonweal*.

"I cannot too strongly urge *Arrival and Departure* upon you. It is a book of force, which is not uncommon, but also of understanding, which is rare. . . . If Koestler develops, he may quite conceivably become the great writer of our generation."—Clifton Fadiman, in *New Yorker*.

"The flawless almost poetic prose style and the dreamlike narrative will attract readers, but the analysis of history and political philosophy will be questioned."—Rice Estes, in *Library Journal*.

F
K78d

DARKNESS AT NOON. 1941. B.R.D. 13+, 4- Macmillan. $2.   **200**

This novel is a psychological study of the strange Moscow trials—a story of the arrest, imprisonment, torture, trial, confession and death of an old Bolshevik who is quite innocent of the incredible crimes charged against him.

"This curious, crushing, absorbing book leaves one with a sense of some collective monster existing only in their common mind, to which men willingly become slaves and immolate themselves."—*Yale Review.*

"Most valuable as an interpretation of the Moscow 'confessions,' by some one with an inner knowledge of totalitarian methods."—George Orwell, in *New Statesman.*

"As an anatomy of totalitarianism *Darkness at Noon*, which appears to have been perfectly translated, goes a lot deeper than most of the books on the subject, novels or other."—*Manchester Guardian.*

SCUM OF THE EARTH. 1941. B.R.D. 11+, 1- Macmillan. $2.50.   **100**

The author's recollections of what happened in France to him and others, between the outbreak of World War II and the fall of France. For himself it involved arrest, along with other Communists—"the scum of the earth"— imprisonment in several concentration camps and eventual escape to England.

"Far the best book to come out of the collapse of France."—*Manchester Guardian.*

"As a psychologist he . . . penetrates under the surface of events . . . so this autobiographical report develops into a moving analysis of our entire time."—*Saturday Review of Literature.*

"To the reader who wishes not simply to know the facts concerning Europe's madness but to know what has brought this madness to pass, Koestler's account of the concentration camps of France can be unreservedly recommended."— *Christian Century.*

940.5
K78y

THE YOGI AND THE COMMISSAR AND OTHER ESSAYS. 1945.
B.R.D. 5+, 2– Macmillan. $2.75.   120

Essays mostly about literature, Russia, communism and the very parlous state of the world. "In this war," he says, "we are fighting a total lie in the name of a half-truth."

"A very tragic book."—H. J. Laski, in *Manchester Guardian*.

"As Koestler goes, so goes the intelligentsia of the honest, decent variety. . . . I don't think educators should miss this book. . . . It is the product of a very superior mind, of a man with a pleasantly rich background and of a character of great integrity."—H. A. Reinhold, in *Commonweal*.

"He is able to write down his *ideas* more interestingly than most authors are able to write down their fiction."—Hamilton Basso, in *New Yorker*.

Krebs, R. J. H. *See* **Valtin, Jan**

824.6
J691K

Krutch, Joseph Wood   1893–

American critic, now Brander Matthews Professor of Dramatic Literature at Columbia. Born in Knoxville, Tennessee. Educated at the University of Tennessee and at Columbia. During World War I he was a member of the Army Psychological Corps. He has traveled abroad on a Columbia fellowship; has taught at the Brooklyn Polytechnic, at Columbia, at the New School for Social Research, and at Vassar; was *The Nation's* dramatic critic till 1932, and became its literary editor in 1933. A Guggenheim Fellow, 1930-31. Author of a dozen books. Member, National Institute of Arts and Letters.

SAMUEL JOHNSON. 1944. B.R.D. 9+, 2– Holt. $3.75.
276

A scholarly, impressive, six-hundred-page biography covering Johnson's whole life, by an admirer who writes *con amore*. Boswell has not been rendered superfluous—far from it—but he has been ably supplemented.

"Mr. Krutch has done well to supply an alternative, large-scale biography, written with full awareness of Boswell but with less dependence on him than offhand one would have supposed possible."—*Weekly Book Review.*

Landon, Margaret (Mrs. K. P. Landon)   1903-

Born in Somers, Wisconsin, and educated at Wheaton (Illinois) College.

Browsing Collection

ANNA AND THE KING OF SIAM. 1944. B.R.D. 7+, 1–
Day. $3.75.   288

Story of Anna Leonowens, a young Welsh widow, who for two years in the 1860's was governess of the king's many daughters.

"Not fiction, but skillfully documented biography."—*Atlantic.*

"A biography of unusual charm, an inviting escape into an unfamiliar, exotic past . . . calculated to transport us instantly to the days when women flushed and paled violently, brushed away a tear or replied with hauteur to the impertinences of strangers. . . . The fascination of the piece lies in the contrast between a splendid Scheherazade background and the tidy-minded Victorian lady period-piece."—*New York Times.*

Langley, Mrs. Adria (Locke)

Born in Iowa, reared in Nebraska, she was educated at Fremont College and Northwestern University. She traveled throughout the South selling a service to department stores. Interested in public affairs, she became a crusader for prohibition, then for the New York dairymen, then for the poor of New York City and then against demagogues.

LION IS IN THE STREETS. 1945. B.R.D. 8+, 3– Mc-
Graw. $3.   108

A story of "Magnolia State"—the share-croppers and fishermen of the bayous.

"Strongly reminiscent of the late Huey Long. . . . It is both an intensely readable tale and a social document, for it reveals how mass ignorance and legalized injustice can become grist for the mill of the clever demagogue."—*Weekly Book Review.*

"There is more to be said for the social and economic ferment that prepares the way for a man such as Hank Martin, but if we are to begin with the man himself we have here, in Martin, a comprehensive study of the American-type dictator, perhaps the best thus far."—*Saturday Review of Literature.*

Laski, Harold   1893-

Born in Manchester, England, and educated at Oxford, he taught history at McGill, Harvard, Yale and Amherst, 1914-20. He returned in the latter year to Europe where he taught at the London School of Economics and London University, at Cambridge, at Moscow and at Dublin. Once a convinced Marxist, he is not a Communist. The study of American history and politics is one of his specialties.

AMERICAN PRESIDENCY, AN INTERPRETATION. 1940. B.R.D. 13+, 2– Harcourt. $2.50.   **100**

"In his opinion eleven American presidents have been extraordinary men."—*Library Journal.*

"It takes its place along with the works of de Tocqueville and Bryce as an acute analysis of American political institutions."—*American Political Science Review.*

"The author shows unusual sympathy with our governmental difficulties, and he is never dull. To an anti-socialist, also, he has been exasperatingly prophetic."—*Boston Transcript.*

Lattimore, Owen E.   1900-

"The best-informed American on Asiatic affairs." Born in Washington, D.C., reared in China, educated in Switzerland and England, he returned to China in 1919, and began his travels in the interior, first for an exporter, then on fellowship assignments, and finally on his own. When the Japanese came he returned (1937) to the United States and became a director of the Page School of International Relations at Johns Hopkins. From 1941 to 1942 he was political adviser to Chiang Kai-shek. Then came three years with the Office of War Information in the United States and China, followed by a government economic mission to Japan, at the conclusion of which he returned to teaching at Johns Hopkins.

SOLUTION IN ASIA. 1945. B.R.D. 12+, 2– Little. $2.
156

"A little book with a large importance."—*Boston Globe*.

"Will be read in foreign offices throughout the world."—*New Republic*.

"No one desiring to understand the political forces in the Far East can afford to ignore this book."—W. O. Eddy, in *Ethics*.

"Owen Lattimore has not only stated the main issues of the Asiatic dilemma lucidly and concisely, but has drawn up a rough blueprint for the future that combines reality with justice."—*Weekly Book Review*.

Lauterbach, Richard E. 1914-

The Moscow correspondent for *Life* and *Time*. He speaks Russian and was in the country a whole year during which W. L. White's briefer visit occurred.

THESE ARE THE RUSSIANS. 1945. B.R.D. 10+, 3– Harper. $3.
108

In a sense this is an answer to W. L. White's *Report on the Russians*, also published in 1945.

"It is certainly the most readable of the many books on the Soviet Union."—W. C. White, in *Saturday Review of Literature*.

"This is, without reservation, one of the better recent books on the Soviets."—*Foreign Affairs*.

"A book by a foreign correspondent which can be warmly commended."—*Nation*.

"The author's firm conviction that we should and can work with the Russians gives his book urgency."—*Horn Book*.

"A book which ought to be widely read, for it gives Americans a sensible understanding of the Russians—of how they feel, what they have been through, what they want; and such an understanding is desperately needed."— John Hersey, in *Book Week*.

Lawson, Capt. Ted W.   1917-

Bomber pilot. Born in Los Angeles, he was educated at the Los Angeles Junior College, where his future wife was librarian.

940.538
L42t

THIRTY SECONDS OVER TOKYO: edited by Robert Considine. 1943. B.R.D. 8+, 0– Random. $2.   143

Describes the Doolittle raid, the preliminary training for it, and its aftermath. The author lost a leg. It is said that this book has earned him a quarter of a million dollars.

"For pure adventure and high excitement this story ranks right at the top of the war books."—*Nation*.

"Certainly the most stirring story of individual heroism that the war has so far produced."—W. L. White, in *New York Times*.

"It's the most exciting and interesting and engrossing book out of this war to date—it surpasses any experience record of the last war."—*Book Week*.

Leech, Margaret (Mrs. Ralph Pulitzer)   1893-

Born in Newburgh, New York, and educated at Vassar, she married Ralph Pulitzer in 1928. (He died in 1939.) She lives in New York City.

973.7453
L48r

REVEILLE IN WASHINGTON, 1860-65. 1941. B.R.D. 11+, 3– Harper. $3.50.   360

This panorama of Washington during the Civil War, the author's fifth book, won the Pulitzer Prize in history.

"It places Miss Leech at once among the foremost contemporary historians of America."—Clifton Fadiman, in *New Yorker*.

"Swarming picture of a people's energies, creating out of next to nothing the greatest armies and armaments the world had then seen."—*Time*.

"A faithful mirror of a great and critical time in our nation's history—and a time that seems nearer to us now than it has for many years."—S. V. Benét, in *Saturday Review of Literature*. (Written in summer of 1941.)

"This is how democracy always fights and usually wins; it is a lesson of encouragement in the midst of our present indecision. Yet to me the book is scarcely reassuring. . . . It would be hard to resist and impossible to defeat a totalitarian Europe by the same policy of muddle."—M. Cowley, in *New Republic*. (Written in August 1941.)

Leonardo da Vinci   1452-1519

Italian painter, sculptor, architect, musician, scientist. Born at Vinci, Italy, the painter of the "Last Supper" in Milan and the "Mona Lisa" in the Louvre, his was "a genius for art and science unparalleled in any other individual in all history."

NOTEBOOKS; arranged, translated and edited by Charles MacCurdy. 2 vol. 1938. B.R.D. 4+, 1— Reynal. $15.   162

"A magnificently produced work of great permanent value."

"A work of supreme importance."—*New Yorker*.

Lewis, Sinclair   1885-

American novelist and satirist. Born in Sauk Center, Minnesota. His father, grandfather, brother and uncle were doctors. Educated at Yale, where he edited the "Lit" in his senior year. An early job was that of janitor of Upton Sinclair's socialist experiment, Helicon Hall. Joke-writing and newspaper work—not very successful—preceded editorial employment with publishers and continued till the increasing success of his own books enabled him to devote all his time to them. *Main Street*, 1920, was his first big success. His *Arrowsmith*, 1925, was chosen in 1944 by *Saturday Review of Literature* as the best American novel in twenty years. He refused the Pulitzer Prize for *Arrowsmith* in 1926, but accepted the Nobel Prize from the Swedish Academy four years later. He married Dorothy Thompson in 1928 but they have since been divorced. His son by an earlier marriage was killed in World War II. Member, American Academy of Arts and Letters.

CASS TIMBERLANE; A NOVEL OF HUSBANDS AND WIVES. 1945. B.R.D. 6+, 6– Random. $2.75.   **252**

"And a shabby lot of husbands and wives they are."— *Catholic World*.

"The one really good novel Sinclair Lewis has written since *Dodsworth*."—*Springfield Republican*.

"The sentimental ending conforms to Hollywood's specifications. . . . It will be popular and only a few will regret that a mellower or perhaps a wiser Lewis is at work."— *Library Journal*.

"Sinclair Lewis has done it again. With that observant, buzz-saw mind of his, he has sliced through the main trunk of American life to lay bare a cross-section more worm-eaten than we like to suppose."—Edward Weeks, in *Atlantic*.

Lin, Yu-tang   1895-

He was born at Chang-chow, Fukien Province, China, and educated at St John's College, Shanghai, and at Harvard, Jena and Leipsig. He taught in Peking, 1916-26, and has edited several Chinese magazines. He is the author of seventeen books in English and several in Chinese.

BETWEEN TEARS AND LAUGHTER. 1943. B.R.D. 4+, 4– Day. $2.50.   **143**

A book of essays on the "most urgent issues of our times— . . . an enduring peace and the future relations between Asia and the Western World."

"Even in disagreement it should be read. Its voice and passion and special pleading are of the reawakened Asia, no longer a princess sleeping and supine."—Edward Weeks, in *Atlantic*.

"We shall just have to write off this book and hope that the author will regain his poise in the future. If he is going to write about politics, he might well study a little political science, however hateful scientific discipline may seem to him."—Reinhold Niebuhr, in *Nation*.

IMPORTANCE OF LIVING. 1937. B.R.D. 6+, 2– Reynal. $3.
                                                                        119

A Chinese philosophy of life, written with a chuckle, for Western readers. He calls it "a personal guide to enjoyment," and it seems to be a distillation of the sly wisdom of centuries of Chinese sages.

"There is real stuff here, as fine a presentation of the case for a present-day, urbane paganism as could be asked." —*Christian Century*.

MOMENT IN PEKING. 1939. B.R.D. 9+, 1– Day. $3.
                                                                        104

A novel of family life in China from 1900 to 1938.

"It is the great good fortune of the West that someone not of it has been able to look at China objectively and to show us its virtues and weaknesses, its beauties and on occasion its sordidness and tragedies, as Lin Yu-tang here gives us his country and his people."—*Books*.

"No other novel about China in English approaches the scope of this one, and probably none surpasses it in authenticity and detail."—*Nation*.

"Read *Moment in Peking* slowly and even if it may seem odd, with relaxed rather than rigid attention. . . . The book is a remarkable panorama; you must sit back in your seat and allow it to flow past your eyes."—Clifton Fadiman, in *New Yorker*.

Lindbergh, Anne Morrow (Mrs. Charles Augustus Lindbergh)   1907-

Author and aviatrix. Born in Englewood, New Jersey, she is the daughter of the late Dwight Morrow, the financier, who was American ambassador to Mexico. She was educated at Smith College, and married Charles Lindbergh in 1929 when he was America's hero. Soon tragedy came to them. This book was written years later.

LISTEN! THE WIND. 1938. B.R.D. 13+, 1− Harcourt. $2.50.   **234**

Account of ten days spent in a survey flight (1933) from Africa to South America.

"One of the finest writers in America is a woman who probably had no intent to become a writer, no torturing ambition to see her name in print or to feel literary laurels on her brow. . . . She is a gallant woman, exquisitely understanding, and she can't keep these qualities out of her book."—*Books*.

"The unconscious beauty of poetry and poetic thinking that runs throughout the book makes it a story that all should read."—*Churchman*.

"Mrs. Lindbergh's books, quite apart from their value as aeronautical history, are small works of art."—*New Yorker*.

Lippmann, Walter   1889-

Member, American Academy of Arts and Letters. Born in New York City; educated at Harvard, where he specialized in philosophy and psychology. The preparation of data for American use at the Peace Conference in 1919 interrupted editorial work on the *New Republic*. He was on the editorial staff of the *New York World* from 1921 till it ceased publication in 1931, at which time he joined the staff of the *Herald Tribune*. His syndicated column now appears in many newspapers. Committed to no cause or party save those of wisdom and righteousness, he is one of the ablest objective thinkers of the day and has the knack of expressing with extraordinary clarity his lucid thought.

UNITED STATES FOREIGN POLICY: SHIELD OF THE REPUB- *327.7391*
LIC. 1943. B.R.D. 10+, 2- Little. $1.50.   264 *L76u*

"A little book . . . bulging with big ideas. Many of its chapters are short enough to read twice, and ought to be read three times."—*Christian Science Monitor*.

"Both the expert and the layman will find in this little volume a great deal of wisdom."—*Foreign Affairs*.

"A definite service to his country. . . . He has undermined all possible arguments either for isolationism or for the imperialism to whose standards the isolationists will repair as soon as they find that they are licked."—Clifton Fadiman, in *New Yorker*.

"He does not ridicule the naivete of his country since comparatively recently, he confesses, he was naive himself." —Raymond Swing, in *Weekly Book Review*.

UNITED STATES WAR AIMS. 1944. B.R.D. 8+, 3- *940.531*
Little. $2.50.   173 *L766u*

Supplements *United States Foreign Policy*, 1943.

"Nothing just like it has been brought forward."—*New York Times*.

"He is the clearest of all writers on international policy. . . . He is a realist who understands that statesmen do, in the long run, what they must do in the light of geographical and economic facts."—*Political Science Quarterly*.

"The book bristles with challenges. It is desirable that it should be read widely, discussed freely and criticised unsparingly."—*Weekly Book Review*.

Llewellyn, Richard   1907(?)-

Born at St. David's, Pembrokeshire, Wales. He left school at sixteen to study hotel management in Italy, where he also studied art and where his long continued interest in the study of cinema technique was born. He served in the British army, 1926-31. It was then, in India, that the first draft of *How Green Was My Valley* was written. His army service was followed by more movie work and writing till, in 1940, he rejoined as Captain of the Welsh Guards.

HOW GREEN WAS MY VALLEY. 1940. B.R.D. 17+, 3–
    Macmillan. $2.75.   **250**

This first novel is about a family of coal miners in South Wales.

"A story as noble as it is simple and strong. It is a beautiful story, too, told in words that have Welsh music in them."—*Atlantic*.

"Without sugar-coating any part of the life he depicts, it leaves a good taste in the mouth. It is a poetic novel from beginning to end."—*Nation*.

Lowell, Mrs. R. T. S., Jr. *See* **Stafford, Jean**

Luce, Mrs. Henry R. *See* **Booth, Clare**

Lynd, Robert S.   (1892-) and Lynd, Helen M.
    1897-

American sociologists. Robert Lynd was born at New Albany, Indiana; educated at Princeton, Union Theological Seminary and Columbia; served in Field Artillery in World War I; editor, *Publishers' Weekly*, 1914-18; has directed research projects in education and sociology. Professor of sociology at Columbia since 1931.

MIDDLETOWN IN TRANSITION; A STUDY IN CULTURAL CON-
    FLICTS. 1937. B.R.D. 12+, 2– Harcourt. $5.
                                               238

"Middletown" is commonly supposed to represent Muncie, Indiana. This book is a sequel to *Middletown*, 1935, which covered 1888 to 1925. Stuart Chase calls this new book better than the first one: "more exciting, acute and profound."

" 'Required reading' for everyone interested in the social landscape of America.   But in this case, 'required reading' will prove to be as interesting as it is enlightening."
—*Science Book Club Review*.

"Like the earlier volume, *Middletown in Transition* is destined to become a classic."—*Commonweal*.

Lyons, Eugene   1898-

Born in Uzlian, Russia, he came to the United States in 1907 and was naturalized in 1919.   He was educated in New York at City College and Columbia; served in the U.S. Army in World War I.   Then came journalism, featured by a crusade for Sacco and Vanzetti, followed by work for Russia's Tass Agency and a United Press assignment in Russia, 1928-34.   He was editor of the *American Mercury*, 1939-44.

ASSIGNMENT IN UTOPIA.   1937.   B.R.D.   8+, 3–   Harcourt. $3.50.   170

"The story of a man's stubborn fight to hold on to ideals, to integrity of conscience, to a perspective that can swallow the present in its glimpse of the future, to a philosophy of social justice strong enough to carry the blows of injustice."
—*Books*.

"A book that any supporter of any dictator system will find it hard to answer. . . . It will strengthen the movement to put life and fighting spirit into an idealistic liberalism."
—R. L. Duffus, in *New York Times*.

MacLeish, Archibald   1892-

American poet.   Born on the shore of Lake Michigan; his father a devout Protestant merchant from Glasgow; his mother (Vassar graduate and teacher) of a sea-faring family of Connecticut Yankees.   Educated at Yale and at Harvard Law School.   Went abroad with a hospital unit in 1917, but shifted to the Field Artillery ("out of shame") and saw active service at the front.   After World War I, he taught at Harvard for a year and practiced law for three.

In 1923 he decided on poetry as a career. He is the author
of a score of books. Was Librarian of Congress, 1939-44;
Assistant Secretary of State, 1944-45, and succeeded to
other posts in Franklin Roosevelt's New Deal.

FALL OF THE CITY; A VERSE PLAY FOR RADIO.   1937.
     B.R.D. 5+, 0- Farrar. 50c.   102

The first play of its kind written in America.

"Contains some of Mr. MacLeish's most persuasive
work to date."—*Christian Science Monitor.*

"This drama, written in thrilling, swift-moving, intense
verse, left the mind tingling with excitement."—*Forum.*

"It is to be hoped that no one will fail to emphasize the
power of this poet's imagination and its magnificent im-
mediacy."—Louis Untermeyer, in *Saturday Review of Literature.*

PUBLIC SPEECH; POEMS. 1936. B.R.D. 8+, 2- Farrar.
     $1.   112

Consists of ten short pieces on current problems, and
ten more love poems which contain some of his finest
imagery. This little book moved the *Herald Tribune Books*
to declare that "he is now, unquestionably, the most important poet writing in America today."

"MacLeish had his period of profound murkiness . . .
but these are better poems."—*New York Times.*

McWilliams, Carey   1905-

Champion of the foreign-born, of racial minorities, of
migratory workers. Born at Steamboat Springs, Colorado,
and educated at the University of Southern California. He
was appointed Commissioner of Immigration and Housing
by California's Governor Olson; he organized the John
Steinbeck Committee and was soon at odds with the state's
powerful Associated Farmers. When Earl Warren became
governor in 1943, his first official act was the dismissal of
Carey McWilliams. He won a Guggenheim Award in 1941.

BROTHERS UNDER THE SKIN. 1943. B.R.D. 6+, 3–
    Little. $3.   **110**

"A discussion of the status of non-white minorities in
the United States."—*Book Review Digest.*

"Mr. McWilliams is not a practical politician. . . . He
will convince the converted, but he may annoy some of the
hesitating."—R. L. Duffus, in *New York Times.*

"When the show-down comes on these racial problems
McWilliams' brave leadership for justice and the right will
be acclaimed as it should be today."—O. G. Villard, in
Saturday Review of Literature.

PREJUDICE, JAPANESE-AMERICANS: SYMBOL OF RACIAL IN-
    TOLERANCE. 1944. B.R.D. 7+, 0– Little. $3.
                                                            115

The story of our Japanese problem and especially of
the so-called relocation centers during World War II.

"A book . . . for all intelligent Americans whose children may be the hostages of another war because we proved
once again to be blind to human realities."—*Book Week.*

Malraux, André   1895–

French novelist, born in Paris. He is interested in
Oriental archaeology and in the world struggle against
Fascist tyranny. He aided the ill-fated struggle in Spain
where he commanded the Loyalist government's International Air Force and flew sixty-five missions over Fascist
territory. Later he toured France and the United States
to raise funds for the Loyalists.

MAN'S HOPE. 1938. B.R.D. 12+, 3– Random. $2.50.
                                                            126

The English title is "Days of Hope."

"It is not only a novel of Loyalist Spain he has written,
but a study of contemporary man on the field of battle."—
A. Kazin, in *Books.*

"There can only be one summing-up. *Man's Hope* is a
great book."—*New Republic.*

"Malraux sets out to give a complete picture of Government Spain. . . . His book is history in its most thrilling form."—*New Statesman.*

Mann, Thomas   1875-

German novelist. Born in Lübeck, of mixed ancestry which included an oriental strain. His people were well-to-do merchants. His formal education, for a German of his class, was unusually casual and meagre. In 1929 he was awarded the Nobel Prize for literature. His American publisher has shyly admitted that Thomas Mann is the world's greatest living author. When the Reichstag burned, a troubled but "non-political" Mann was lecturing in Holland. He never returned to Germany. For a year or more he was deaf to his family's pleas to take a stand against Nazism. But in 1936 he declared himself in such ringing tones they were heard the world around. Since 1938 he has lived in the United States which he regards as the world's citadel of democracy. For several years he made his home in Princeton, New Jersey, but now seems permanently settled in California.

THE BELOVED RETURNS; LOTTE IN WEIMAR. 1940. B.R.D. 11+, 3– Knopf. $2.50.   **130**

Charlotte, the heroine of *The Sorrows of Werther*, was really Lotte, an early love of Goethe. She was so indiscreet as to call upon him forty years later. This long novel was inspired by the story of that indiscretion. The incident gleams like a tiny jewel set in this vast tapestry of the old man's pictured personality.

"There emerges from the pages such a hopeful view of man as master of his own fate that the reader cannot fail to be lifted above himself."—*New York Times.*

"No simpler than a serpent's eye: an eloquent, cold, quietly appalling, enigmatic investigation of genius in its inmost nature and effects."—*Time.*

COMING VICTORY OF DEMOCRACY. 1938. B.R.D. 4+, 0–
    Knopf. $1.   **108**

The text of the lecture Mann delivered on his coast-to-coast trip in the spring of 1938.

"Germany's greatest writer and America's most distinguished new citizen has managed to state in the brief compass of a single lecture the whole case of freedom against despotism."—Simeon Strunsky, in *New York Times*.

"Thomas Mann's magnificent lecture . . . says, I think, the profoundest things that have yet been uttered on the subjects of fascism and democracy—says them classically, says them irrefutably."—Clifton Fadiman, in *New Yorker*.

"The most important book of the year. . . . It gives the believers in democracy the reasoned groundwork of the faith once delivered to their fathers—reasons that the fathers understood even if many of their descendants have forgotten them."—Elmer Davis, in *Saturday Review of Literature*.

THE JOSEPH TETRALOGY

Consists of the following:

1. *Joseph and His Brothers*. 1934. }   See *Best Books of*
2. *Young Joseph*. 1935.   }   *the Decade, 1926-35*.
3. *Joseph in Egypt*. 2 vol. 1938. B.R.D. 10+, 2–
    Knopf. $5.   **144**
4. *Joseph, the Provider*. 1944. B.R.D. 9+, 3– Knopf.
    $3.   **138**

"A literary event of the first magnitude."—*New York Times*.

"A great creative work has been completed. America will read it proudly."—*Book Week*.

"Among the few masterpieces of our time. The word 'great' that is so often misapplied can be used this time without embarrassment."—M. Cowley, in *New Republic*.

"There can remain no doubt . . . that it is one of the great imaginative efforts of our time. . . . It would be but a piece of provincial spite to deny Mann's central place in modern writing."—*Nation*.

"A vast and leisurely fable of the nature, state and destiny of man. The whole constitutes a work which in encyclopedic scholarship, in imaginative power and magnitude of conception can hardly be approached by any other literary product of our time."—*Atlantic*.

Marquand, John P.   1893-

Member National Institute of Arts and Letters. Born in Wilmington, Delaware, and educated at Harvard. After an interval of newspaper work in Boston and New York, he went to "Plattsburg" to prepare for service in France as a first lieutenant in World War I. His first book was published in 1922 and he now has more than a dozen to his credit. He lives at Newburyport, Massachusetts, where as a youth he attended high school after a childhood in Rye, New York. It may be of interest to recall that Margaret Fuller, the mid-Victorian blue-stocking of New England, was his great-aunt.

H. M. Pulham, Esq. 1941. B.R.D. 8+, 2- Little. $2.50.   260

This novel is a supposititious autobiography, satirizing "the best people" of Boston who go to the right school, the right college, and of course belong to the right club—and are slowly bored to death.

"The spectacle of people 'letting "I dare not" wait upon "I would" '—when they really should—is never funny, nor is the spectacle of people boring themselves and one another for years on end in the name of propriety and loyalty."—*Atlantic*.

The Late George Apley; a Novel in the Form of a Memoir. 1937. B.R.D. 13+, 0- Little. $2.50.   272

"Mr. Marquand is as kind as veracity permits and, as far as I am concerned, has done a whacking good job."— C. P. Curtis, in *Atlantic*.

"People who like Boston and take George Apley at his surface value will run blood pressures fit to get them in the Somerset Club."—Lucius Beebe, in *Books*.

"What Mr. Santayana did in philosophic vein in *The Last Puritan* Mr. Marquand has done in crisper and infinitely more amusing style."—*Living Church*.

"In the disguise and labored style of a minor man of letters undertaking to write the life of a friend whom he admired to idolatry, Mr. Marquand manages to be most hilariously funny. All the dreadful little jokes of the pious biographer . . . every ineptitude of an amateur man of letters has been reproduced."—*American Review*.

So LITTLE TIME. 1943. B.R.D. 11+, 4– Little. $2.75.
264

A satiric fictional study of America, not just Boston this time, on the threshold of war, between the German invasion of France and Pearl Harbor (1940-41).

"It is something to be grateful for—having in our generation a novelist as thoroughly readable as John Marquand. *So Little Time* is as good reading as its predecessors."—J. W. Beach, in *New York Times*.

"Mr. Marquand is that rarest of artists, a sympathetic satirist. He satirizes without damning. And it is fitting that the last words of this novel, so far his biggest and his best, should be: 'Forgive us our debts, as we forgive our debtors.' "—*Saturday Review of Literature*.

WICKFORD POINT. 1939. B.R.D. 8+, 3– Little. $2.75.
123

Story of a family run to seed, somewhere near and north of Boston.

"He is a novelist—and a real one—with all that the word implies."—S. V. Benét, in *Saturday Review of Literature*.

"John Marquand . . . is like the king's jester; he dons motley that he may the better tell the truth. The true worth of *Wickford Point* lies below its satiric surface."—*New York Times*.

"Whether he is being sentimental, or brusque, or satirical, or yielding a little to pathos Mr. Marquand bubbles with entertainment. . . . There is not a single dull page in his novel—and that is extraordinary for a Pulitzer Prize winner."—*Books*.

Marshall, Bruce   1899-

British novelist and satirist, chartered accountant, soldier. He lost a leg as second lieutenant in World War I, yet served as captain in World War II. He has lived mostly in Edinburgh, and has published seven books, mostly humorous yet reverent tales with a priestly hero.

WORLD, THE FLESH, AND FATHER SMITH. 1945. B.R.D.
    10+, 2- Houghton. $2.50.   156

"Can be recommended as superior entertainment, even for heretics."—*Nation*.

"He writes with an open heart, a salty understanding of frailty, and with the most delightful, impertinent wit that I have chuckled over this year."—Edward Weeks, in *Atlantic*.

"The best novel of Catholic clerical life that has appeared since the days of Canon Sheehan. . . . It is difficult to conceive of anyone—Catholic, Protestant or unbeliever, who will not enjoy every page of this book."—*Commonweal*.

Marshall, George Catlett   1880-

Born at Uniontown, Pennsylvania, and educated at Virginia Military Institute, he was commissioned second lieutenant in 1901 and major general in 1939. He served with the A.E.F., 1917-19; was aide-de-camp to General Pershing, 1919-24; was successively Deputy, Acting, and Chief-of-Staff with rank of general, 1938-45; Ambassador to China, 1945-47; Secretary of State, 1947- .

WINNING OF THE WAR IN EUROPE AND THE PACIFIC. 1945.
    B.R.D. 5+, 1–   Simon. $2.50.   (Paper edition,
    $1).   **156**

Covers events from the invasion of Italy to the collapse of Japan.

"The greatest state paper of the War. It is required reading for every American citizen. It is required study material for every school and college."—G. F. Eliot, in *Saturday Review of Literature*.

"If the art of prose lies in clear, concise communication of ideas, General Marshall's report is a work of art. Any literate citizen can, in some three or four hours' time, learn from it more about the war in Europe and in the Pacific than he has learned by reading newspapers and periodicals for the last four years."—*Book Week*.

Martin du Gard, Roger   1881-

Born in Neuilly, a suburb of Paris, he graduated in 1906 from L'École des Chartes as archivist-paleographer and published his first novel in 1908. He served in World War I, 1914-19, in charge of a transport division. Worked on *The Thibaults*, 1920-36. After Paris fell in World War II he and his family escaped to Unoccupied France.

THE THIBAULTS; translated by Stuart Gilbert. 1939.
    B.R.D. 11+, 5–   Viking. $3.   **142**

This long French novel is a chronicle of the bourgeois Thibault family in the years before World War I. It won a Nobel Prize in 1937. The present volume contains the first six parts—about one half of the whole. (The complete work appeared in English (1941) in two volumes as *The World of the Thibaults*.)

"It is the perfectly human document of an epoch. . . . Roger Martin du Gard steers his even keel in the broad stream of French Naturalism."—E. Boyd, in *New York Times*.

"We are bound to recognize in *The Thibaults* one of the great novels of our time, a work to be put beside Jules

Romain's *Men of Good Will* and Rolland's *Jean-Christophe.*"—*Books.*

"Martin du Gard, limited as he may be, is so much less limited than all but a very few contemporary English and American writers that it becomes the duty of serious readers to accord him their whole attention."—Clifton Fadiman, in *New Yorker.*

Masefield, John   1874-

Sailor, factory-worker, bar-tender; poet, novelist, dramatist. His father was a seal-cutter, his mother a clergyman's daughter. Many universities have delighted to honor him and he has been England's Laureate since 1930, though he is a graduate only of the "University of Hard Knocks."

IN THE MILL. 1941. B.R.D. 12+, 1– Macmillan. $2.
100

The prose story of the author's two years in a Yonkers, New York, carpet factory.

"An exciting adventure story of self education."—*New York Times.*

"Rabid Left-wingers will not take Mr. Masefield's moralizings seriously."—*Manchester Guardian.*

"In every line and between the lines of this limpid personal record the discerning will find the quality, will take the measure, of him who was presently to be the poet of 'The Everlasting Mercy.'"—Wilson Follett, in *Atlantic.*

Matthiessen, Francis Otto   1902-

Born in Providence, Rhode Island, he was educated at Yale, at Oxford (where he was a Rhodes Scholar) and at Harvard. He has taught history and literature at Yale and then at Harvard, where he is proud of being a charter member of the Teachers' Union.

AMERICAN RENAISSANCE; ART AND EXPRESSION IN THE
AGE OF EMERSON AND WHITMAN. 1941. B.R.D.
8+, 3– Oxford. $5.   **150**

Discusses chiefly Emerson, Thoreau, Hawthorne, Melville and Whitman.

"Perhaps the most profound work of literary criticism on historical principles by any modern American, with the possible exception of Lowes's *Road to Xanadu* (1927)."— R. E. Spiller, in *Saturday Review of Literature.*

"It is a formidable book and has to be studied and mastered with a patience and seriousness equal in some measure to Dr. Matthiessen's own. . . . It is an extraordinarily sound and unusual introduction to our understanding of American character and development."—Alfred Kazin, in *Books.*

Mattingly, Garrett   1900(?)-

Born in Washington, D.C., educated at Harvard; awarded Sheldon fellowship for study and travel in Europe in 1922; and a Guggenheim fellowship in 1937-38 for research on the life of Catherine of Aragon. He edited hitherto unpublished correspondence of Charles V's ambassadors in England during the reign of Henry VIII which the British Public Record Office printed as a Supplement to the series of Calendars of State Papers, Spanish. He teaches history at Long Island University.

CATHERINE OF ARAGON. 1941. B.R.D. 9+, 2– Little. $3.50.   130

"Mr. Mattingly has told the story of Henry VIII's first queen superbly. . . . This is in no sense of the word a popular life; it is an achievement of distinguished and exhaustive scholarship."—*New York Times.*

"This is a living biography. The life that pours through it derives from the strength and depth of its grip upon character. . . . His success is unequivocal."—*New Republic.*

Maugham, W. Somerset   1874-

English novelist, playwright, physician. Born in Paris, where his father was an official in the British Embassy. Educated at King's School, Canterbury; Heidelberg University; St. Thomas's Hospital, London. Author of twenty-five or more books. He is a man of the world with, as some one has said, "a bland contempt for humanity."

RAZOR'S EDGE. 1944. B.R.D. 11+, 8– Doubleday.
$2.75.   **173**

The story has a post-World War I background and describes the rather bewildered world-wanderings of a tired flyer.

"Maugham, with a skill that is almost obscenely spectacular, twists the story's tail and puts it through its paces with a flick of the wrist."—*Book Week*.

"I believe that *The Razor's Edge* will be enthusiastically and politely received. No one else could have written it except Mr. Maugham with that superb and contemptuous arrogance that is displayed by the skilled matador."—Harrison Smith, in *Saturday Review of Literature*.

"If he keeps on writing with his tongue in his cheek, it may well become permanently stuck there."—*New Yorker*.

SUMMING UP. 1938. B.R.D. 8+, 1– Doubleday. $2.50.
153

"It is not often that an author writes an honest book about his own life . . . but in this book Mr. Maugham has done so. . . . *The Summing Up* is not a book about a happy man or a happy life; it is the book of a man wounded and aloof, who has sought consolation in excelling in his profession."—*Christian Science Monitor*.

"Reading has made a full man of Mr. Maugham, writing, an exact one. . . . *The Summing Up* is a report, a summary, the result of a continuous conference that Mr. Maugham has held with himself on the subject of life and letters during the last forty-odd years."—*Saturday Review of Literature*.

"Where the book is of real value is in its analysis of the art of the dramatist and the novelist. . . . No man or woman who hopes to be a professional writer can afford to miss these chapters; they are a veritable course in the art of writing."—*Commonweal*.

"It tells exactly how a considerable contemporary writer
—and furthermore a very successful one—learned his
trade. . . . It is, though not an autobiography of his life,
an autobiography of his mind."—*Forum.*

Mauldin, Bill (William H.)   1921-

Cartoonist. Born in Mountain Park, New Mexico, he
served in World War II (1940-45) in Sicily, Italy, France
and Germany.

UP FRONT. 1945. B.R.D. 9+, 1- World. $3.   **324**

940.53418
M44u

This book was awarded a Pulitzer Prize for cartoons
and was a Book-of-the-Month Club selection.

"A collection of cartoons, nearly all of which are excellent, plus a text, nearly all of which is also excellent,
by the twenty-three-year-old soldier who might perhaps be
called the Ernie Pyle of artists."—*New Yorker.*

"His text has the same biting humor that has gone into
his drawings of wry, unshaven, sardonic dog-faces. It
makes the whole a 'must' book of the war."—W. R. Benét,
in *Saturday Review of Literature.*

Maurois, André   1885-

Born as Emile Herzog, at Elbeuf, France, the son of
mill-owners there. Released from business by World War
I, his mastery of English attached him to the British army
in France as liaison officer, and gave him time to write.
Ariel: the Life of Shelley won him international fame as
author of a new sort of biography. M. Maurois has lectured at many universities including Princeton, Yale and
Cambridge. He served in World War II with the British
army in France, 1939-40, and with the Allies in North
Africa in 1943.

THE TRAGEDY IN FRANCE. 1940. B.R.D. 5+, 1- Har-
    per. $2.   **130**

940.53
M45t

A liaison officer between the French and British forces
in the early months of World War II, M. Maurois tries

to tell us why his country crumbled so easily under the German onslaught.

"Combines the readability of fiction with the authenticity of an acute and first-hand appraisal of one of history's most tragic and most curious disasters."—*Christian Science Monitor*.

Maxwell, William   1908-

American novelist. Born in Illinois, he was for a time an editor of the *New Yorker*. He lives in New York City.

FOLDED LEAF. 1945. B.R.D. 8+, 1- Harper. $2.50.
192

This first novel is a story of the friendship between two modern American boys.

"The best novel to appear in the last decade."—*Springfield Republican*.

"This drama of the immature, with no background more glamorous than middle-class apartments and student fraternity houses, is both more moving and more absorbing than any of the romantic melodramas which have been stimulated by the war."—Edmund Wilson, in *New Yorker*.

"Katherine Anne Porter, it seems to me, is the one American writer who has no reason to envy William Maxwell his gifts; and offhand the only novel I can think of that is at all comparable to *The Folded Leaf* is *The Apple of the Eye*, also a story of adolescence, written by Glenway Wescott twenty years ago."—Charles Jackson, in *Book Week*.

THEY CAME LIKE SWALLOWS. 1937. B.R.D. 7+, 1- Harper. $2. **102**

The story of an American family in the fall of 1918. There was the Armistice—and there was also the epidemic of "flu."

"Commonplace happenings, commonplace conversations . . . woven together by an art that is discriminating and touched to life by sympathy and understanding—that is Mr. Maxwell's book."—*Saturday Review of Literature*

"Its simplicity reveals its distinction. No one who was not a master of his work could have created its authentic pathos and humor; could so have given dignity and individuality and meaning to the everyday life of a family."—*Books*.

Mears, Helen   1900-

Born in New York City and educated at Goucher College, Baltimore, Miss Mears has lived in China and traveled in North Africa, England and the Caribbean. She went to Japan in 1935, spent eight months there and has since written many articles on Japan in addition to this book. She was assistant editor of *Survey*, 1929-34.

YEAR OF THE WILD BOAR; AN AMERICAN WOMAN IN JAPAN. 1942. B.R.D. 7+, 0- Lippincott. $2.75.
137

915.2
M48y

Pictures of the daily life of the middle and lower classes in Japan.

"It is refreshing to find a book about Japan of which not a line has apparently been added or changed because of recent events. . . . Miss Mears has given, without malice and without sentimentality an excellent portrait of Japan and the Japanese."—*New York Times*.

"Miss Mears is not out to make us like or dislike the Japanese. She does succeed in making us understand them at least roughly."—*New Yorker*.

Mencken, Henry L.   1880-

Born in Baltimore and educated at the Baltimore Polytechnic, Mr. Mencken has worked on Baltimore newspapers, 1899-1941; on the *Smart Set*, 1908-23; on the *American Mercury*, 1924-33; on the *Nation*, 1921-32; and has written dozens of books. He is not a college graduate, and has no honorary degrees. That would not be cricket—for Mencken.

420
M53ac

AMERICAN LANGUAGE; AN INQUIRY INTO THE DEVELOP-
    MENT OF ENGLISH IN THE UNITED STATES: Supple-
    ment 1. 1945. B.R.D. 7+, 1– Knopf. $5.   **216**

Like the original work, published in 1919 and several
times revised and enlarged, this is a book on the American
use of the English language.

"For anyone with an interest in words, the new volume
is absolutely fascinating."—Edmund Wilson, in *New
Yorker*.

"One of the most delightful books imaginable. . . . I
found myself dropping everything else and devoting two
days to devouring its pages, footnotes and all. For sheer
fun of reading it is the treat of the season."—R. Watts, in
New Republic.

HAPPY DAYS, 1880-1892. 1940. B.R.D. 11+, 0– Knopf.
    $2.75.   **190**

Twenty essays on his boyhood in Baltimore, up to the
age of twelve.

"A very happy and amusing book."—*Catholic World*.

"He has written a chronicle of childhood for which
truth and a sense of balance have long been clamoring. To
say that it is a readable book is almost an impertinence
in the case of Mr. Mencken."—Simeon Strunsky, in *New
York Times*.

HEATHEN DAYS. 1943. B.R.D. 5+, 0– Knopf. $3.
    121

Random recollections of humorous experiences from
1890 to 1936.

"This is an anecdotal book, full of humor, full of the
old rip-snorting rhetoric, full of comic exaggerations, and
above all else full of gusto."—Allan Nevins, in *Saturday
Review of Literature*.

"Time has served to perfect a style which was always
robust and exuberant, but which has grown with the years
better balanced and better integrated until it has now
achieved an almost classical perfection without losing its
individuality."—J. W. Krutch, in *Nation*.

NEWSPAPER DAYS, 1899-1906.   1941.   B.R.D.   6+, 0–
   Knopf. $3.   **230**

A continuation of *Happy Days*, 1940.

"I would call Mencken a peculiarly American article. . . . His book is a treasury of fact and fable without
dull stretches, a genial book and full of life."—O. Ferguson,
in *New Republic.*

"Here is Henry Mencken at his delightful best, gay,
extremely amusing, ever exposing hypocrisy and shams with
his brilliant lance of complete honesty and good-natured,
but often devastating frankness and humor."—O. G. Villard, in *Saturday Review of Literature.*

Millay, Edna St. Vincent   1892-

American poet.   Member, American Academy of Arts
and Letters.   Born at Rockland, Maine, and educated at
Barnard and Vassar Colleges.   Early adventures included
a period of hack-writing in Greenwich Village and service
as actress and playwright with the Provincetown Players.
In 1923 she married Eugen Jan Boissevain.   The Columbia
poetry prize was awarded to her in 1921; the Pulitzer
Prize, in 1923.

COLLECTED SONNETS.   1941.   B.R.D.   3+, 1– Harper. $5.
                                                                    120

One hundred and sixty-one sonnets are here but only
two are new ones.

"She was very good to begin with; if the emotion has
cooled and passion at times is mimicked rather than felt,
nevertheless, the manner remains original, the contrivance
adroit, the epithet nice, the music clear."—*Nation.*

CONVERSATION AT MIDNIGHT.   1937.   B.R.D.   9+, 10–
   Harper. $2.   **153**

Semi-play in verse, consisting of an after-dinner talk on
many problems of modern life by seven diverse individuals.

"Prose is the only medium for talk of this kind."—
Manchester Guardian.

"The poet most applauded for her unaffected lyricism has written a book that is as prosy as it is pretentious."—Louis Untermeyer, in *Saturday Review of Literature*.

HUNTSMAN, WHAT QUARRY? 1939. B.R.D. 7+, 5—
    Harper. $2.   **114**

Lyrics and sonnets. One group is about Czechoslovakia, China and Spain; another in memory of her friend, Elinor Wylie.

"I think the reader will see a great adventure in these new songs. And it ought to discourage those critics who keep warning us that Edna Millay will outgrow her essentially youthful subjects of love and the worshipfulness of the moment."—R. P. T. Coffin, in *Books*.

Miller, Mrs. Alice Duer   1874-1942

Born in New York City, Mrs. Miller was educated at Barnard College. She lived in Costa Rica, Scotland, London, the Riviera and Lake Bomoseen, Vermont, and wrote more than a score of books, mostly fiction, besides many motion picture scenarios.

WHITE CLIFFS. 1940. B.R.D. 4+, 0— Coward. $1.
                                                                  170

This short novel in verse is the story of an American woman—married to an Englishman, widowed, and living in England—against the background of two world wars. It is the most popular book of poetry in many years.

"I should think that even a Hottentot, provided he had a reasonable knowledge of the English language, could not fail to be impressed and touched by the sincerity, quality and charm of this book; but I am an Englishman and as such obviously prejudiced, very prejudiced indeed, and very grateful."—Noel Coward, in *Books*.

Miller, Douglas   1892-

Born at Fayette, Indiana; educated at the University of Denver, and at Oxford, where he was a Rhodes Scholar.

He was in non-combatant service in World War I and its aftermath, in England, Mesopotamia, Siberia and Germany. He taught economics and was in U.S. government service, 1921-45. For some years, just before World War II, he was a commercial attaché in our Embassy in Berlin.

You Can't Do Business with Hitler. 1941. B.R.D. 7+, 0- Little. $1.50.   **100**

At the Berlin Embassy Mr. Miller tried hard to do business with Hitler. It just couldn't be done, though Lindbergh thought otherwise. Mr. Miller found out the hard way. The book is absorbing reading, even in postwar days. Let's not forget it.

"In this volume an analytical mind has given us a simple yet profound understanding of what Hitler and Hitlerism mean, and, more important, what the Nazis intend to do about the United States."—*New York Times* (in 1941).

Miller, John Chester   1907-

Professor of history at Bryn Mawr. Born in Santa Barbara, California, and educated at Harvard.

Origins of the American Revolution. 1943. B.R.D. 8+, 4- Little. $3.50.   **100**

Reviews the background from George III's accession to the Declaration of Independence.

"There was a time when a volume with such a title would have been regarded as of interest only to the scholars and students of history. Yet here is a thoroughly scholarly piece of work, precisely documented, and still lively and spirited enough for a best seller list."—*Saturday Review of Literature.*

Millis, Walter   1899-

American journalist. Born in Atlanta, Georgia; educated at Yale; on editorial staff of *Baltimore News*, New York *Sun, Globe* and *Herald Tribune* since 1924. Second lieutenant, Field Artillery, 1918.

WHY EUROPE FIGHTS. 1940. B.R.D. 9+, 0– Morrow.
$2.50.   **100**

Resume of Europe's economic and political history during the long armistice between World Wars I and II.
The viewpoint is not that of either a pacifist or an isola-
tionist.

"I know no better primer of the background of this war
[World War II]."—Lewis Gannett, in *Boston Transcript*.

"The best short history of the two decades between the
two World Wars that has yet appeared."—*Nation*.

Mitchell, Margaret (Mrs. John Robert Marsh)   1900-

Born in Atlanta, Georgia. She was educated at Washington Seminary, Atlanta, 1914-18, and at Smith College,
1918-19; and was married in 1925. Contributed many special articles to the Atlanta newspapers.

GONE WITH THE WIND. 1936. B.R.D. 18+, 7– Mac-
millan. $3.   **312**

The most phenominally successful book of the century.
One million copies had been sold six months after publication. It topped the best-seller lists throughout both 1936
and 1937. Two million copies had been sold by 1939, and
three million six hundred and twenty-five thousand by 1945.
In American book stores its sale was the largest ever
reached throughout the fifty years during which records
have been kept. As one bookseller remarked, "Mrs. Mitchell must feel sometimes a little like Frankenstein."

It is a thrilling story throughout its thousand and more
pages, but is not generally regarded as a *great* book.

"The best Civil War novel that has yet been written."—
J. D. Adams, in *New York Times*.

"A solid and vividly interesting story of war and reconstruction, realistic in detail and told from an original point
of view."—S. V. Benét, in *Saturday Review of Literature*.

Moley, Raymond   1886-

Born at Berea, Ohio, and educated at Baldwin-Wallace College, Oberlin and Columbia. He has taught political science at Western Reserve and Columbia during most of the years since 1916. He was Assistant Secretary of State in 1933; editor of *Today*, 1933-37; and thereafter an associate editor on *Newsweek*. He has written a dozen books and served on many government surveys and commissions. One of the original Brain Trusters of the New Deal, he is said to have been Mr. Roosevelt's leading "ghost-writer" for five years.

AFTER SEVEN YEARS. 1939. B.R.D. 5+, 4− Harper. $3.   104

Recollections of his experiences as a member of the New Deal's inner circle. "There is no reason to doubt the essential accuracy of the accounts. They are an important and rare contribution to our knowledge of the times. But it must be remembered that the color and shadings are all Professor Moley's."—*Christian Science Monitor*.

"A historical document that the well-informed can ill afford to miss, a document which requires . . . an answer from the present administration."—*Forum* (in 1939).

"No historian of these times, no student of the many-faceted prism which is the personality of Franklin Roosevelt can possibly make a just appraisal of the New Deal without it."—A. Krock, in *New York Times*.

"A book which is replete with interesting quotations and is at the same time fascinating, informative and revolting."—*Survey Graphic*.

"An invaluable contribution to the proper understanding of American history. Mr. Moley has filled in the details with the ruthless reality of the candid camera. Mr. Roosevelt and his friends may well resent it bitterly."—Nicholas Roosevelt, in *Books*.

Morgenthau, Henry, Jr.   1891-

Born in New York City, Mr. Morgenthau studied for two years at Cornell and served in the navy in World War I. He was publisher of the *American Agriculturist*, 1922-33, and Secretary of the Treasury, 1934-45. His New Deal diary runs to some hundreds of unpublished volumes.

GERMANY IS OUR PROBLEM. 1945. B.R.D. 3+, 1– Harper. $2.   120

This is the basis of the "Morgenthau Plan" for turning Germany into an agricultural nation.

"The Morgenthau plan *in toto* will never be adopted. It can be, however, a yardstick to measure our flagging will to render Germany impotent for war."—Leon Henderson, in *Nation*.

"No book since *Mein Kampf* has offered the American people information so important for their survival. . . . If we read and profit by Mr. Morgenthau's warning we should be able to prevent that third World War."—*New York Times*.

Morison, Samuel Eliot   1887-

Born in Boston and educated chiefly at Harvard and Oxford. He served as an infantry private in World War I. He has taught history at Harvard during most of the years since 1915, and at Oxford, 1922-25. He has been named by the navy to write its official history of World War II.

ADMIRAL OF THE OCEAN SEA; A LIFE OF CHRISTOPHER COLUMBUS. 1942. B.R.D. 11+, 1– Little. $3.50.
                                                284

Won Pulitzer Prize for biography in 1943.

Himself a sailor as well as a historian, it seems fitting that even as Parkman in preparation for writing his *Pioneers of France* series followed their footsteps in journeys through the northern forests, so Morison before writing this book followed faithfully all the routes of Columbus's ships, in sailing craft of about the same tonnage as his caravels.

"It is a must book of course for all those interested in history as well . . . as for those interested in the sea."—*Books*.

"Professor Morison's scholarly, unpedantic prose is, to use an expression dear to British seamen, a fair treat. . . . It is certainly pleasant to read."—William McFee, in *Nation*.

"There is no danger at all in saying that it is the best book about Columbus so far printed."—G. Mattingly, in *New Republic*.

Morley, Christopher   1890-

American author. Born in Haverford, Pennsylvania, of distinguished English parentage. Educated at Haverford College and (as a Rhodes Scholar) at New College, Oxford. Years of book editorial work at Garden City were followed by other years as a columnist on Philadelphia and New York papers, till the success of his many books enabled him to forsake journalism for literature and for a zestful experience as an impresario of antique melodrama in Hoboken. He has written fifty or more books which he would be the first to admit is far too many. Member of the National Institute of Arts and Letters.

KITTY FOYLE. 1939. B.R.D. 5+, 2- Lippincott. $2.50.
133

An autobiographical novel about a modern Philadelphia working girl which carries her into her late twenties.

"As a woman, we take the liberty of congratulating Mr. Morley on his expert knowledge of our thoughts and emotions."—Rose Feld, in *Boston Transcript*.

"A portrait of the American girl that is as real as anything in your family album. With this difference: the family portraits give you the bone and muscle structure and the features of your sisters, your cousins and your aunts; *Kitty Foyle* gives you the heart and spirit which lie beneath them."—*Books*.

"Those who have been afraid of Mr. Morley because they figure his whimsy will come off on them should not on that account steer clear of *Kitty Foyle*. It has the Morley touch, all right, but the fancifulness is restrained and somehow the book seems pretty close to certain realities of the twenties and early thirties."—Clifton Fadiman, in *New Yorker*.

Mumford, Lewis   1895-

American critic and sociological planner. Member, National Institute of Arts and Letters. Born at Flushing, Long Island; educated in the New York public schools, City College, Columbia, New York University, and the New School for Social Research. He served in the navy in 1918, and was a Guggenheim Fellow in 1932. Author of some fifteen books, he has been an enthusiastic disciple of the late Patrick Geddes, British apostle of city planning.

CULTURE OF CITIES. 1938. B.R.D. 9+, 0- Harcourt.
 $5.   180

This historic study of cities from the Middle Ages to the present, with proposals for their betterment, has been described as "a plea for the spiritual regeneration of America."

"Worthy of the greatness of its subject."—*Books*.

"One of the most distinguished books of many years."— M. M. Colum, in *Forum*.

"Here is a book of the decade. Dramatic, scholarly and exciting."—*Social Forces*.

"Nobody can read this book without finding his public interest heightened in potential. And what more can ever be said for a book."—Alvin Johnson, in *Yale Review*.

Myrdal, Gunnar Karl   (1898-) and others

Swedish professor of economics. Born at Gustafs, Sweden, Mr. Myrdal graduated from the law school of the University of Stockholm and spent the years from 1925 to 1929 in European travel. He studied in the United States on a Rockefeller Fellowship, 1929-30; was director of a study of the American Negro problem for the Carnegie Corporation, 1938-42. He has been active in Swedish public affairs since 1933.

AMERICAN DILEMMA; THE NEGRO PROBLEM AND MODERN DEMOCRACY. 2 vol. 1944. B.R.D. 9+, 2- Harper. $7.50.   **110**

"Frank and not always pleasant reading, this study is a real contribution towards more rational understanding of race relations and of discrimination in its cumulative effect. Recommended to all who take their 'American creed' seriously; especially noteworthy is Chapter I, 'American Ideals.' "—Rudolph Hirsch, in *Library Journal*.

Nash, Ogden   1902-

Writer of humorous verse. Born in Rye, New York, he studied at Harvard, 1920-21, and worked for publishers until they began to publish his own books. He lives in Baltimore.

I'M A STRANGER HERE MYSELF. 1938. B.R.D. 3+, 1- Little. $2.   **108**

The most popular book of verse of its year.

"His verse always makes good reading; often it is the best light verse written in America today."—Louis Untermeyer, in *Saturday Review of Literature*.

"Mr. Nash . . . is as funny an essayist in verse as G. K. Chesterton in prose, or Mark Twain, or Saki, or P. G. Wodehouse; or, to come nearer to his habitat, Mr. Nash is as infectious and genuinely inimitable in his poetic homilies as was Ring Lardner in his short stories."—P. M. Jack, in *New York Times*.

Nehru, Jawaharlal   1889-

Born in Allahabad, son of a Kashmiri Brahmin, he was educated at Harrow and Cambridge and joined the Nationalist movement on returning to India. Soon he became a follower of Gandhi and an enthusiastic Congress-wallah.

He declared for immediate independence and for socialism, going beyond Gandhi's policy of patient non-resistance. During World War II he was active in opposing the British raj and has been imprisoned many times. He is the political leader of the Hindus today.

954
N39

TOWARD FREEDOM; Autobiography. 1941. B.R.D. 12+, 1- Day. $4. **140**

This is really the revised edition of *Autobiography; with Musings on Recent Events in England*, published in England in 1936.

"One of the most absorbing personal histories of modern times."—*Nation.*

"This book presents more effectively than any other the Indian point of view in the long, strained relations with the government of London."—*Christian Science Monitor.*

"A book which possesses the high, clear unity of a work of art. The category into which it goes is one of the smallest in all literature—books which tell the tale of great historical developments from the point of view of men greatly and intimately concerned."—Vincent Sheean, in *Books.*

Nevins, Allan   1890-

American publicist. Born at Camp Point, Illinois; educated at the University of Illinois and at Columbia. He taught English for a while at Illinois before becoming an editorial writer on New York daily and weekly newspapers, 1913-27. He has been teaching history at Cornell since 1927, and at Columbia since 1931. He was Harmsworth Professor of American History at Oxford, 1940-41. Author of a score of volumes on history and biography and editor of as many more. He has twice received the Pulitzer Prize for biography and is a member of the National Institute of Arts and Letters.

901
N52

GATEWAY TO HISTORY. 1938. B.R.D. 4+, 0- Appleton. $3. **100**

"A helpful discussion of historiography and methods of research."—*Social Studies.*

"Whether Mr. Nevins is discussing the falsified tyranny and immorality of Tiberius Caesar, . . . whether he is demonstrating once again that it was Jefferson and not Washington who definitely warned America of 'entangling alliances,' or whether he is submitting to a critical *ad hoc* analysis the relative impartiality of newspapers such as *The New York Times* and *The Herald Tribune*, Mr. Nevins is always interesting."—*New York Times*.

HAMILTON FISH; THE INNER HISTORY OF THE GRANT ADMINISTRATION. 1936. B.R.D. 7+, 0− Dodd. $5.
153

Mr. Fish was President Grant's Secretary of State.

"One of the best of the author's works, and that in itself is the highest praise."—*Saturday Review of Literature*.

"An illuminating and impressive biography which meets with distinction every test of thoroughness, understanding and candor that criticism can apply."—*Books*.

"Fish has hitherto been the 'most obscure of the really eminent leaders of the nineteenth century.' At last he is revealed, at full length, and he is fortunate in his biographer."—*New York Times*.

JOHN D. ROCKEFELLER; THE HEROIC AGE OF AMERICAN ENTERPRISE. 2 vol. 1940. B.R.D. 6+, 0− Scribner. $7.50.
240

Declared the year's most important biography.

"A rich record of a unique American life history, and one of its most charming features are the photographs."—Lewis Gannett, in *Boston Transcript*.

"It has stronger claims to consideration as a work of art than either his Cleveland or his Hamilton Fish, although they both won Pulitzer prizes."—*Books*.

"An admirable biography of a remarkable man. Gracious and entertaining in style, critical and yet sympathetic in judgment, it is documented according to the best tradition of historical writing. It is neither partisan nor apologetic."—F. L. D. Goodrich, in *Library Journal*.

Nock, Albert J.   1873(?)-1945

American publicist, essayist and iconoclast. Once a clergyman, he was a graduate of St. Stephen's College, New York, now a part of Columbia, and did graduate work in other institutions. He was associate editor of the *Nation* and of the old *Freeman* and conducted an anti-New Deal column, "The State of the Nation," in the *American Mercury*. For many years a convinced Single Taxer, his works include a book on Henry George. He died in Wakefield, Rhode Island.

MEMOIRS OF A SUPERFLUOUS MAN. 1943. B.R.D. 4+, 0– Harper. $3.   **110**

These "Memoirs" are really essays expounding the author's "philosophy of informed common sense."

"I have not since the days of the early Mencken read a more eloquently written blast against democracy or enjoyed more fully a display of crusted prejudices. Mr. Nock is a highly civilized man who does not like our civilization and will have no part in it. He is a rare bird, one of an almost extinct species, and, as he very properly puts it, a superfluous one. We are not apt to see his like again." —Clifton Fadiman, in *New Yorker*.

Norris, George W.   1861-1944

Born on a farm in Sandusky County, Ohio; educated at Baldwin University, Ohio, Northern Indiana Normal School and Valparaiso University. He moved to Nebraska in 1885 and served successively as prosecuting attorney, judge, congressman and for five terms (1913-43) as United States Senator.

FIGHTING LIBERAL; the Autobiography of George W. Norris. 1945. B.R.D. 13+, 3– Macmillan. $3.50.   **108**

"This humanitarian who wrote 'My religion and my politics are one and the same' has composed here his own tribute."—*Commonweal*.

"Bare alike of literary graces and the nursed rancors which are the chief attractions of so many memoirs, this life story holds you by its unconscious revelation of a magnificent human being; strong, incredibly honest, growing and learning until he died at eighty-three."—*Springfield Republican.*

Ottley, Roi   1906-

Born in Harlem, New York City, studied at St. Bonaventure College, University of Michigan, Columbia, New York University, and St. John's University Law School. He was editor, columnist and reporter on the *Amsterdam Star News*, 1930-37. The Rosenwald Foundation sponsored a round-the-world tour for him and he was a foreign correspondent for *Liberty Magazine.*

New World A-Coming; Inside Black America. 1943.
B.R.D. 8+, 2– Houghton. $3.   143

The book tells what the Harlem Negro is thinking, feeling, doing, saying and expecting.

"In depicting the color and rhythm of Harlem Roi Ottley is at his best. . . . He faithfully reflects the mood of the people, voicing their militant demand for a full share of 'democracy—cleansed and refreshed,' and expressing their faith in the ultimate realization of this demand."— *New Republic.*

Page, Elizabeth   1889-

Born in Castleton, Vermont, and educated at Vassar and Columbia, she has lived in Brooklyn, Oklahoma, Wyoming and California. During World War I she was with the Y.M.C.A. in France and later with Dr. Grenfell in Labrador. A member of the Religious Society of Friends, she now lives in Manchester, Vermont.

The Tree of Liberty. 1939. B.R.D. 6+, 4– Farrar.
$3.   152

A long historical novel which displays the life and times of this our America from 1754 to 1806. Jefferson appears prominently and successfully. The consensus of critical opinion seems to be that the author is a rather better historian than novelist. Yet H. S. Commager says "The story itself—clear, straightforward , skillfully contrived and gracefully told, has a vitality that sustains it to the end."

Papashvily, George   (1895?-)   and Papashvily, Helen (Waite)   1906-

George Papashvily was born in Kobiankari, Georgia, in 1895. He spent six years in the Czar's army in World War I and came to America in 1923. Helen Waite was born and educated in California, an American of English ancestry. They now live on a farm in Allentown, Pennsylvania, where he is a machinist and sculptor, and she runs a book shop.

ANYTHING CAN HAPPEN. 1945. B.R.D. 10+, 2– Harper. $2.   120

Another tasty dish of propaganda for the melting-pot. Mr. Papashvily reads and speaks but does not write English. He "told" the book to Mrs. Papashvily.

"*Anything Can Happen*, with its charming violence to English and its ridiculous adventures, can be read for sheer entertainment. . . . But it is also a deeply satisfying American document which can teach while it delights us."—*Springfield Republican*.

"The humor proves contagious; it communicates itself to the reader and leaves him smiling at the happy ending of this tale of tribulation and bewilderment."—*Saturday Review of Literature*.

Parran, Thomas   1892-

American hygienist. Born at St. Leonard's, Maryland, he was educated at the University of Maryland and Georgetown University, Washington, D. C. He was Health Commissioner of New York State, 1930-36, and Surgeon-General of the United States, 1936-48.

SHADOW ON THE LAND: SYPHILIS. 1937. B.R.D. 11+, *614.5*
  1– Reynal. $2.50.   119 *P25*

History of syphilis and its treatment in America and Europe, with a program for its elimination in the United States.

"Dr. Parran's book will be a blessing indeed if it accomplishes even half of the purpose that he has in mind."—*Catholic World*.

"Sound and honest in every line, it has the clarity and the vividness of an immediate human problem, presented by a scientist and a statesman."—*Yale Review*.

Partridge, Bellamy

Lawyer, literary critic, author. Born in Phelps, New York, and educated at Hobart College and Union University, he was a foreign correspondent in World War I and at the Versailles Conference.

COUNTRY LAWYER; THE STORY OF MY FATHER. 1939. *340.069*
  B.R.D. 9+, 1– McGraw. $2.75.   133 *P29P*

This humorous narrative of a life in old-time (1870-1920) up-state New York has been pronounced its year's most popular book of non-fiction.

"A work of atmospheric color, a Currier and Ives series, rich, humorous and of historic verity."—*Saturday Review of Literature*.

"*Country Lawyer* is grand reading and grand documentation. Here is Main Street and the cross streets and the furtive alleys and the little lanes that slide out into the country. Here are both sides of the tracks."—John T. Winterich, in *New York Times*.

Paul, Elliott Harold   1891-

American journalist, novelist and musician. Born in Malden, Massachusetts, he studied at the University of Maine, 1908-09. He was a sergeant in the A.E.F. in

World War I, and was an editor, successively, of the Paris editions of the *Chicago Tribune* and the *New York Herald*, 1925-30.

LAST TIME I SAW PARIS. 1942. B.R.D. 14+, 7– Random. $2.75.   **168**

An American expatriate's nostalgic picture of the Paris that was.

"*Must* reading for anyone who has ever lived in France —or wanted to."—Edward Weeks, in *Atlantic*.

"It is an obituary and an epitaph, carved with clear writing and sculptured with many humble figures of France's tragic Third Republic, now dead."—*Books*.

"Always it gets along with the job in hand. That job is to record the natural history of a Paris street, to tell how its people lived, and to describe the great events of our time as they were mirrored in their lives."—*New Republic*.

"For all who knew Paris and loved her—and those who did not love her did not know her—this is an intolerably heart-breaking book."—*Saturday Review of Literature*.

LIFE AND DEATH OF A SPANISH TOWN. 1937. B.R.D. 8+, 0– Random. $2.50.   **238**

The first half of the book describes the idyllic life of the little Spanish town of Santa Eulalia in the Balearic Islands, where the author spent five happy years. Then came war (July 1936) and the spirit of the book changes. The author escaped with his family in September, knowing that their dearly loved dwelling place was doomed to almost certain death and destruction.

"Elliot Paul can write. For sheer literary flavor [this book] has not even been approached by any other non-fiction book this year."—N. B. Cousins, in *Current History*.

"The predicament of a human being in society today is all the more convincing here because it is included within the unit of a village. But the threat abroad in the world does not stop at Santa Eulalia."—*Nation*.

Pearson, Hesketh   1887-

Born at Hawford, Worcestershire, England, and educated at Bedford Grammar School, where perhaps the spirit of Bunyan interested him in biography. After trying out the life of a clerk he went on the stage in 1911. His career as an actor was interrupted by military service in Mesopotamia and Persia. After World War I he returned to the theater and remained on the boards till 1931 when his real career began as an author of biographies.

G. B. S., A FULL LENGTH PORTRAIT. 1942. B.R.D. 9+,
        2- Harper. $3.75.   **168**

"A book both of uncommon importance and uncommon delight."—*Saturday Review of Literature*.

"The portrait of Shaw is the more convincing since the author is robustly critical of Shavian inconsistency and sheer perversity when these must be faced."—*Manchester Guardian*.

"Mr. Pearson's biography is immensely amusing and will, if you are given that way, make you rock with laughter. And it is something more than that. It contains 'revelations' it tells everything!"—*New Statesman*.

Peattie, Donald Culross   1898-

Nature writer, born in Chicago. Both his father and mother were writers and so is his wife. He was educated at the Universityy of Chicago and Harvard and has written about twenty-five books. He was a Guggenheim Fellow, 1936-38, and is a member of the National Institute of Arts and Letters.

GREEN LAURELS: THE LIVES AND ACHIEVEMENTS OF THE
        GREAT NATURALISTS. 1936. B.R.D. 13+, 4- Simon.
        $3.75.   **121**

"He has read and digested what is known about [his subjects] and has then in the most excellent and smooth language given them vivid consideration."—William Beebe, in *Saturday Review of Literature*.

"There is not a line which is not dramatically vivid and entertaining."—*Nation.*

"The book is as good as one of the sentences about John Bartram: 'With him nature was a personal affair, a direct impact like weather on a bird.' "—Mark Van Doren, in *Books.*

"So interesting, so fresh, and so informed with an original sensibility as to disarm even the second thoughts of watchful critics."—J. W. Krutch, in *Nation.*

580, 069
P36

ROAD OF A NATURALIST, illustrated with woodcuts by Paul Landacre. 1941. B.R.D. 8+, 0– Houghton. $3.
110

Autobiographical essays, strung on the thread of an auto trip throughout the Southwest during which the author discusses natural beauty and the quiet pleasures of the botanist and zoologist. The book justifies his wife's statement that he has both the truly trained eye of the scientist and the vision of the poet.

"With all his erudition and his art, Peattie brings to his contemplation of nature the open-eyed wonder of a child. And he brings to his comments on nature a gusto which perhaps more than any other quality has enabled him to make us aware of beauties which we have been too busy or too blind to see."—*Yale Review.*

Pederson, Mrs. A. *See* Field, Rachel

Pennell, Joseph Stanley   1908–

Journalist, teacher, actor, second lieutenant in World War II. He was born in Junction City, Missouri, and educated at the University of Kansas and at Oxford.

F
P413h

HISTORY OF ROME HANKS AND KINDRED MATTERS. 1944. B.R.D. 8+, 4– Scribner. $2.75.   **150**

A first novel about the Civil War. It provokes the critics to a spate of adjectives like terrific, frenzied, violent, ribald, modern, chaotic, irritating and wild. Most of them, in discussing it, find that allusions to Thomas Wolfe are helpful and more than one also mentions William Faulkner.

"[In a sense] the book is the story of our nation. In this reviewer's opinion, it has been handled with a sweep and scope and awareness that has not been equalled since Stephen Vincent Benét's *John Brown's Body*. This is Pennell's first novel, but on any basis it is a superb achievement, both in plan and execution."—N. K. Burger, in *New York Times*.

"A work of unusual talent, and among other things, the best novel about the Civil War I have read, with the natural exception of *The Red Badge of Courage*."—Hamilton Basso, in *New Yorker*.

Percy, William Alexander   1885-1942

Lawyer and poet. The son of a U. S. Senator, he was born at Greenville, Mississippi, and educated at the University of the South and at Harvard. He served in World War I, 1917-19, as first lieutenant and captain.

LANTERNS ON THE LEVEE; RECOLLECTIONS OF A PLANTER'S
    SON. 1941. B.R.D. 9+, 2– Knopf. $3.   **110**

This autobiography might be described as a Southern aristocrat's quiet assertion of his stoic faith.

"You may not agree with all that Mr. Percy says, but you have rarely heard his side stated with so much wisdom, gentleness and wit. Since the regime he lived for and by is a passing one, set this down as a very creditable swansong."—*New Republic*.

"A volume delightfully conceived and very well written, a remarkable achievement, worthy of recommendation to any and all readers. It is full of authentic information, it reflects a rich experience, and above all it is wholly free from the neurosthenic drivel which afflicts so many of the current sentimental outpourings about the Old South."—A. J. Nock, in *Atlantic*.

Pertinax (pseudonym of André Géraud)   1882-

French journalist. He was born at St. Louis de Mont-ferrand, and educated at the University of Bordeaux. He fled to America on the fall of France in 1940 after a most successful career of many years as a Paris journalist. He has long specialized in French foreign affairs and has been an enthusiastic advocate of an Anglo-French alliance.

940.5344
G358

GRAVEDIGGERS OF FRANCE. 1944. B.R.D. 11+, 3– Dou-bleday. $6.   **104**

"Detailed analysis of the men and forces responsible for the fall of France."—*Library Journal.*

"Though the author does not pretend that this is defini-tive history it is inevitably going to be one of the prime sources on which future historians will rely, for the author's wide knowledge of the events and persons he describes is unsurpassed."—*Foreign Affairs.*

"Far and away the most authoritative and informative account of the French military and political collapse and of the establishment of the feeble Vichy dictatorship."— W. H. Chamberlin, in *Atlantic.*

Phelps, William Lyon   1865-1943

Professor Phelps was born and died in New Haven, Connecticut, and was educated at Yale. He taught English at Yale from 1892 until his retirement in 1933. He was the first teacher in an American university to sponsor courses on the Russian novelists and on contemporary fiction. He was member of the American Academy of Arts and Letters.

370.923
P54

AUTOBIOGRAPHY WITH LETTERS. 1939. B.R.D. 8+, 0– Oxford. $3.75.   **152**

Though this Baptist deacon's story of his life runs to about a thousand pages (the same length as that other giant, *Gone with the Wind*), it has been extremely popular.

"As the pages roll on, the wonder grows that any one human being should have been able to do so many different things and get such fun out of all of them. . . . Few men since Samuel Pepys have had such unflagging zest for life." —S. V. Benét, in *Books*.

"Professor Phelps has never been a rigorous critic, and nobody will find much reasoned criticism in this book. There is almost no reference to the outspoken and controversial writers who have made a new American literature within the past two decades."—Carl Van Doren, in *Saturday Review of Literature*.

"This book, though picturing many personalities in the academic world, in the theater and in literature, is mostly 'Billy' Phelps. There are only a thousand pages of it and of him—and none too much."—*Springfield Republican*.

Pinckney, Josephine   1895-
Poet and novelist. Born in Charleston, South Carolina; educated at Charleston College, Radcliffe and Columbia.

THREE O'CLOCK DINNER. 1945. B.R.D. 8+ 3– Viking. $2.50.   **120**

A novel about two families in Charleston; one had money, the other breeding. But these facts were but trifles to Dan Cupid.

"A thoroughly satisfying novel. . . . Miss Pinckney's success with an old formula shows how good old formulas can be when they are processed by a knowing hand. . . . All in all, it is a complete tour of Charleston, and a beautifully planned *tour de force* as well."—*New York Times*.

"Miss Pinckney arranges all with quiet competence. I got a certain pleasure out of watching her tactics, and admired the way she moved her major pieces at times; but she never convinced me that she was doing anything more than playing a game."—Hamilton Basso, in *New Yorker*.

Pollock, Sir F. *See* Holmes, O. W. jt. auth.

Porter, Katherine Anne   1894-

A great-great-great-granddaughter of Daniel Boone, she was born at Indian Creek, Texas, and "educated in small Southern convent schools." From 1920 to 1937 she lived in New York or abroad, in Europe or Mexico. She now lives at Ballston Spa, New York.

LEANING TOWER AND OTHER STORIES. 1944. B.R.D.
        10+, 0-   Harcourt. $2.50.   **288**

"Miss Porter is absolutely a first rate artist."—Edmund Wilson, in *New Yorker.*

"A collection of nine short stories by one of the most exquisite stylists and subtle and penetrating writers of our time."—*Yale Review.*

"Miss Porter's style is, so to speak, perfection. . . . We have no American fiction as good as what her twenty-two sketches, stories and novelettes indicate she might give us with good luck and a long life. Given a good plot, I can imagine her writing, a sort of *War and Peace* for us . . . in her styleless style which is rather like translation by an angel."—Glenway Wescott, in *New York Times.*

Pringle, Henry Fowles   1897-

American journalist and biographer. Born, New York City; educated at Cornell. Reporter on New York *Sun, Globe* and *World,* 1920-27; editor, *The Outlook,* 1929-31; has taught journalism at Columbia, 1932-43. He held a Guggenheim Fellowship, 1944-45.

LIFE AND TIMES OF WILLIAM H. TAFT. 2 vol. 1939.
        B.R.D.   6+, 1-   Farrar. $7.50.   **218**

"Mr. Pringle has written a most important book. It is a scholarly job, but his scholarship never runs to seed in mere erudition."—William Allen White, in *Saturday Review of Literature.*

"Mr. Pringle has done his work with admirable fidelity, spirit and skill. He has served Taft well. He has served history better."—Ellery Sedgwick, in *Atlantic.*

"Mr. Pringle has written a truly admirable biography of Taft, a more important book, probably, than his excellent life of Theodore Roosevelt. Taken together the two works present an extraordinarily effective picture of recent American history."—M. A. De W. Howe, in *Harvard Law Review*.

"Mr. Pringle's notable achievement is to bring Taft to life . . . and to make him irresistibly attractive. He has given us a full length biography. He is not full dress."—H. S. Commager, in *Books*.

Pulitzer, Mrs. Ralph. *See* Leech, Margaret

Pyle, Ernie (Ernest Taylor Pyle)   1900-1945

Born in Dana, Indiana, and educated at Indiana University. He worked as a more or less undistinguished newspaperman from 1923 to 1935. Thereafter until killed in action on Ie, a Pacific island, in 1945, he wrote a daily syndicated column which appeared in two hundred newspapers. He was the most widely beloved correspondent of World War II.

The flag-waving Spanish War had its glamorous storyteller in Richard Harding Davis; the first World War had its competent, blustering Floyd Gibbons; and the second World War had frightened, honest little Ernie Pyle, who wore his nobility inside, as though ashamed of it. Thinking of these three men, it would seem that we have come quite a distance in fifty years, and perhaps, for a democracy, we are headed in the right direction.

BRAVE MEN. 1944. B.R.D. 11+, 0−   Holt. $3.   **299**

Describes the fighting of our army in Europe from the landing on Sicily, June 1943, to the liberation of Paris, September 1944.

"It reads like a rambling series of letters to the folks back home."—*New York Times*.

"For a long time, and in homes where not many books are bought, *Brave Men* will be read with pangs and with American pride."—*Springfield Republican.*

"He was doing a job which he hated but felt he had to do; and that was exactly how most of the soldiers felt about it. In fact, Ernie is the G.I. soldier—with the gift of expression added—the typical doughboy, wired for sound."—*Nation.*

HERE IS YOUR WAR. 1943. B.R.D. 10+, 0– Holt. $3.
165

He describes the campaign in North Africa, emphasizing as always the human qualities of the American infantryman.

"The main reason soldiers and civilians like what Ernie writes is Ernie's own participation in all he sees."—J. L. Greene, in *Book Week.*

"It was written behind rocks scored by snipers' bullets, in pup-tents, foxholes and dugouts, in freezing cold and cruel heat, in the midst of dust and dirt and unnamed crawling things."—Edward Streeter, in *New York Times.*

Rauschning, Hermann   1887-
Born in East Prussia and educated at the University of Berlin, he served in the German army and was wounded in World War I. He joined the Nazi regime in 1931 and was active in it for three years, being president of the Danzig senate, 1933-34. After a disagreement with Hitler he fled to America, where he applied for citizenship in 1942.

REVOLUTION OF NIHILISM; A WARNING TO THE WEST. 1939. B.R.D. 4+, 0– Alliance. $3.   **190**
The English title of this indictment by the former Nazi is "Germany's Revolution of Destruction." His warning is to the effect that Hitler aimed at world dominion. It is called "the most important book on National Socialism since Hitler's *Mein Kampf.*"

"Realizing that it may well be too late, I commend it to Mussolini and Stalin."—Clifton Fadiman, in *New Yorker* (September 1939).

Rawlings, Marjorie Kinnan (Mrs. N. S. Baskin) 1896-

Born in Washington, D.C., and educated at the University of Wisconsin, she engaged in publicity work for the Y.W.C.A. in World War I and thereafter in journalism till 1931. For many years she has owned and managed an orange grove in Cross Creek, Florida. Member, National Institute of Arts and Letters.

CROSS CREEK. 1942. B.R.D. 10+, 0– Scribner. $2.50.
                                                        189

Describes the life and people of the tiny and remote Florida hamlet where for a long time Mrs. Rawlings has lived and raised oranges and stories.

"Luminous descriptions of the lush vegetation, the exotic birds, the animals and reptiles; the sounds and scents of the subtropics; the changes which take place even there as the four seasons turn."—*Christian Science Monitor*.

"All of her sketches and ruminations and local bits and pieces are firmly mortised with the cement of her own temperament, clear-eyed, humorous and reverent."—*New Yorker*.

YEARLING. 1938. B.R.D. 11+, 1– Scribner. $2.50. **306**

This story won the Pulitzer Prize for fiction in 1939. It tells the tale of one year in the life of a Florida boy and his beloved fawn—a year that ended in tragedy. As Jody said, "Life knocks you down but you stand up again."

"Within the terms of its intention, this is as nearly perfect a work of art as American fiction can display."—*North American*.

"As Mrs. Rawlings writes we are all there in the scrub; and beyond the sanctuary of boyhood and the sesurity of the clearing, struggle and burdens, fear and weariness await us all."—Jonathan Daniels, in *Saturday Review of Literature*.

"*The Yearling* is a distinguished book. . . . Mrs. Rawlings . . . has captured a child's time sense in which everything lasts forever and the change of season takes him almost unawares."—*Atlantic*.

Riasanovsky, A. *See* Fedorova, N.

Richter, Conrad   1890-

Born at Pine Grove, Pennsylvania, a succession of miscellaneous jobs preceded for Mr. Richter journalism and the conduct of a small business. As a side line he began writing in 1914, and it has been his vocation since 1933. He now lives in New Mexico.

THE TREES. 1940. B.R.D. 8+, 0– Knopf. $2.50.   110

A historical novel showing what happened during the first act of our great national drama of pioneering. Time, the closing years of the eighteenth century; place, the trek westward from Pennsylvania over the Alleghanies to Ohio. Unlike those in so many historical novels his characters are real flesh-and-blood men and women, never mere puppets tricked out in strange garb and speaking an artificial, archaic lingo.

"We close the book convinced that this is how the woodsmen in the great forests of the Northwest Territory really lived."—*Saturday Review of Literature*.

"So vivid is his description of the land, so real his characters and their problems that one forgets he is painting a picture of an early American epoch."—*New York Times*.

Roberts, Elizabeth Madox   1886-1941

Novelist and poet. Born at Perryville, Kentucky, of an old Kentucky family, she studied and wrote poetry at the University of Chicago, 1917-21. She lived in Colorado, New York and California, returned later to her native state, and died in Florida.

BLACK IS MY TRUE LOVE'S HAIR. 1938. B.R.D. 7+, 0–
Viking. $2.50.   **100**

Most of the reviewers say that this tale of the Kentucky countryside is more enjoyable on a second reading than on the first. Not that the book is hard to understand, but there are depths of significance in it that do not yield all their treasure at first glance.

"The book is rewarding chiefly for its excellent language wrought from the quaintness and rhythm of Kentucky speech."—*Christian Science Monitor*.

"A simple story . . . but deep in its reading of the human heart, sure and skillful in its psychology, with never a false or jarring note."—J. D. Adams, in *New York Times*.

"Combining, as the title suggests, the directness and pure feeling of the English ballad, with the lyricism of the great romantic novels, Miss Roberts' latest book calls to mind *The Ordeal of Richard Feverel, The Return of the Native,* and *Far from the Madding Crowd*."—*Nation*.

Roberts, Kenneth Lewis   1885-

American author. Member, National Institute of Arts and Letters. Born, Kennebunk, Maine; educated at Cornell; engaged in the journalism of humor, 1905-18; captain in Intelligence Section, Siberian Expeditionary Force, 1918-19; Staff correspondent of *Saturday Evening Post,* 1919-37. Kennebunkport is still his home.

NORTHWEST PASSAGE. 1937. B.R.D. 11+, 4– Doubleday. $2.75.   **323**

Historical novel about Major Robert Rogers and his Rangers and the Indians they fought two hundred years ago —a straightforward, romantic tale of derring-do, till he comes to the middle of his story. Thenceforward he lets it wobble strangely.

"He does not get far inside his characters. But he does introduce us to their company, makes us see them, hear them and even smell them, and that is almost all one ought to ask of historical romance."—R. L. Duffus, in *New York Times*.

"The hunger and desire of the nation just about to break westward into the untrodden lands, the tangle of cupidities and venalities and stupidities that in great part conditioned them—they are in *Northwest Passage* as they have not been in our fiction before."—B. DeVoto, in *Saturday Review of Literature*.

OLIVER WISWELL. 1940. B.R.D. 9+, 5– Doubleday. $3.

210

The historical novel of its year—a tale of the Revolutionary War, with—strange!—a Tory hero.

"In sustained interest this is the best piece of work Kenneth Roberts has done."—*Christian Science Monitor*.

"I believe that *Oliver Wiswell* will reach countless readers, and will revise the opinions held by almost every one of them about the Revolution. It is also an absorbing narrative in itself without benefit of history."—Carl Van Doren, in *Atlantic*.

Romains, Jules (Louis Farigoule)   1885-

French novelist. Born at Saint Julien-Chapteuil, Haute-Loire, France; educated at the Lycée Condorcet, the École Normale Supérieure and the Sorbonne; specialized in the natural sciences and philosophy; has taught at Laon, Brest, Nice and Paris. He has also written poetry, drama and philosophy.

MEN OF GOOD WILL. 12 vol. 1933-45. Knopf $3 each.

190

This novel is a vast sequence, still (1947) in course of composition. In it the philosopher-novelist hopes to present us with another *Comédie Humaine*, a survey of *all* sections of Parisian life in the twentieth century; this ambitious project being intended to exemplify his philosophy of "unanism."

"*Men of Good Will* is without doubt the considerable literary enterprise of our time. It is almost incredible that a single hand should dare to commit itself to such an immense task."—*Spectator*.

"It is increasingly evident that M. Romains can go on like this as long as his health and the paper-supply hold out. He is a competent craftsman and his books are always readable. Often they reflect admirably the treacherous currents of European life—but so do the files of any major newspaper."—*Saturday Review of Literature.*

Roosevelt, Franklin Delano   1882-1945

American statesman. Born at Hyde Park, New York; educated at Harvard and at Columbia Law School. Practiced law in New York City, 1907-10. Member, New York Senate, 1910-13. Assistant Secretary of the Navy, 1913-20. Practiced law, 1924-29. Governor of New York, 1929-33. President of the United States, 1933-45.

PUBLIC PAPERS AND ADDRESSES; compiled and collated by Samuel I. Rosenman. 5 vol. 1938. B.R.D. 2+, 0– Random. $3 each.   **142**

The set includes his public statements from 1928 to 1936. Twenty-five hundred were sold in the year of publication.

"A source book indispensable to any student of the history of the recent past or of the near future."—Elmer Davis, in *Saturday Review of Literature.*

"It is for posterity to decide whether Mr. Roosevelt is a *great* man; but, contemplating this record no one can deny that his is a personality of remarkable breadth and enormous power."—Walter Millis, in *Books.*

The needs and hungers and aspirations of the ordinary man and woman speak, in all their confusion. through these volumes as they have never spoken before in the state papers of an American president since Lincoln."—Max Lerner, in *Nation.*

Ross, Leonard Q. (pseudonym of Leo C. Rosten) 1908-

American economist and humorist. Born in Lodz, Poland, he came to America as a small child; was educated at the University of Chicago and the London School of

Economics. He has held various Federal positions. For the Carnegie Corporation he has studied movies and for the Rockefeller Foundation, the movie makers. Fellow of the Social Science Research Council.

EDUCATION OF HYMAN KAPLAN. 1937. B.R.D. 5+, 0–
    Harcourt. $2.   **170**

The education took place in the "American Night Preparatory School for Adults," and this book about it has been described as "the funniest and kindest book of the year."

"All men," says Mr. Kaplan, slightly paraphrasing the Emancipation Proclamation, "are created in the same way."

"Mr. Kaplan has achieved that high place for which his soul secretly yearned. He now belongs to the ages."—*Books*.

"This reviewer can do no better than echo the last line of Hyman's final composition: 'ps, I don't care if I don't pass, I love the class'."—Helen McAfee, in *Yale Review*.

Rosten, Leo C. *See* Ross, Leonard Q.

Rourke, Constance M.   **1885-1941**

Biographer of Americans. Born in Cleveland, Ohio; educated at Vassar and the Sorbonne, and by study in the British Museum and the Bibliothéque Nationale. Taught English at Vassar, 1910-15. For many years her home was in Grand Rapids, Michigan, where she died.

Her great-great-uncle when a baby was stolen by Indians. He knew Davy Crockett well. No wonder Miss Rourke was one of the first to write on the pioneers' folk-hero, Paul Bunyan.

AUDUBON. 1936. B.R.D. 19+, 2– Harcourt. $3.   **152**

Superbly illustrated by twelve colored reproductions from Audubon's *Birds of America*, and by black and white drawings by James MacDonald.

"Intended for young readers, it is of equal interest to adults."—*Book Review Digest*.

"This is not a book of the year, but one of a lifetime." —*Atlantic*.

"In this life, Miss Rourke has done for Audubon what he did for the birds of his new country. She has painted him in his habitat, and alive."—S. V. Benét, in *Books*.

Roussy de Sales, R. J. J. F. de   1896-1943

French journalist. Educated in Paris and England. A champion of General de Gaulle and the Fighting French. After 1932 he was a resident of the United States.

MAKING OF TOMORROW. 1942. B.R.D. 10+, 3– Reynal. $3.   **105**

"An attempt . . . to analyze the elements of the world situation that is fundamentally new."—Wilson Follett, in *Atlantic*.

"It is most valuable in its searching analysis of the historical roots and the present problems of the world catastrophe."—Reinhold Niebuhr, in *Nation*.

"Of the what's-it-all-about books I recommend, as one of the most lucid that has come my way, *The Making of Tomorrow*."—Clifton Fadiman, in *New Yorker*.

"One of the important books about World War II. Reason: it brings into the open some of the fears that are secretly gnawing at democratic minds. . . . Its theoretic value is great, for the democracies are bedeviled by fear."— *Time*.

Rukeyser, Muriel   1913-

Left-wing poet and biographer. Born in New York City, she studied for two years at Vassar College. Then came crusades for the Scottsboro boys in Alabama and for the war in Spain.

Willard Gibbs: American Genius. 1942. B.R.D. 8+
1– Doubleday. $3.50.   105

A biography of the little known American physicist,
called by his colleagues of a later generation "the father of
physical chemistry," and thought by some to have been the
greatest scientific genius America has produced. He was
born in 1839 and taught at Yale for thirty years. Clifton
Fadiman hails him as "the greatest intellect in our country's
history." Miss Rukeyser's biography won an award of
$1,000 in 1942 from the American Academy of Arts and
Letters.

"Her biography is bound to remain the standard for
years to come."—Waldemar Kaempffert.

"The definitive biography of an American genius done
with the pen of a distinguished poet in the tradition of Par-
ington's *Main Currents of American Thought*."—B. Jaffe,
in *Books*.

"Praiseworthy attempt to make the general public aware
of the personality and lasting merits of her hero, whom she
ranks with Lincoln, Melville and Whitman among the great
men of his time."—*Library Journal*.

Russell, Countess. *See* "Elizabeth"

Russell, Bertrand (The third Earl Russell)   1872-

English mathematician and philosopher—a critic of
Bergson. Santayana calls his doctrine "a new scholasti-
cism." A pacifist in World War I, he ardently supported
the democracies in World War II. New York City's Board
of Higher Education was forced by public opinion to rescind
his appointment as lecturer at City College because of his
radical opinions on marriage. During World War II he
purchased a farm in Chester County, Pennsylvania, but his
permanent address is still Trinity College, Cambridge. He
is the author of about thirty-five published works.

POWER; A NEW SOCIAL ANALYSIS. 1938. B.R.D. 5+,
1− Norton. $3.   **108**

"Discussion of the part played by man's 'will-to-power' in the world's political and economic affairs."—*Book Review Digest.*

"A brilliant book, one of the most stimulating, as well as one of the most horrifying that I have read for some time. The horror is in the subject matter; the stimulus is in its treatment."—C. E. M. Joad, in *New Statesman.*

St. Exupéry, Captain Antoine de   1900-1944

French essayist, novelist and aviator. Educated at Jesuit schools in France and the Collège de Fribourg in Switzerland. He served in the infantry in World War I. After the Armistice he joined the French Foreign Legion and was trained in Morocco in military aviation. Soon he became a commercial flyer and was a pioneer in establishing routes across Africa and South America. On the outbreak of World War II he was commissioned a captain in the Air Corps reserve. He has been missing since a mission over southern France in August 1944.

FLIGHT TO ARRAS. 1942. B.R.D. 8+, 1− Reynal. $2.75.
                                                   137

A story of his last reconnaissance flight during the final days of French resistance. Both the translation and the illustrations deserve the high praise they receive when declared worthy of the original text.

"A vibrant and lasting contribution to civilization from France's tragic battle-front."—*New York Times.*

"A truly noble attempt to think out his war experiences as a philosopher would, not as a soldier would, or a mere writer. *Flight to Arras* is a credo, the credo of a fighting man to whom the ordinary reasons for fighting have proved unsatisfactory."—Clifton Fadiman, in *New Yorker.*

629.13
S13

WIND, SAND AND STARS. 1939. B.R.D. 8+, 0– Reynal. $2.75.   247

A book about his flights over Spain in wartime and over deserts and waste places in Africa and South America —what happened to the flyer and, more important to him, what he thought about as he flew and now and again beheld Death coming up to meet him.

"To read it is to forget that we are earth-bound."— Edward Weeks, in *Atlantic*.

"This is a great, a beautiful and a permanent book."— *Christian Century*.

"St. Exupéry is a poet and a philosopher by virtue of experience and thought. He has found, for himself at least, a meaning in life, and he sees all things and evaluates all happenings within the frame of that meaning."—*Books*.

Sandburg, Carl   1878-

American poet and biographer. Born in Galesburg, Illinois, of Swedish immigrant parents originally named Johnson. He worked all over the West as a casual laborer, with little schooling, till his enlistment in the Spanish-American War. On returning to Galesburg he decided to work his way through Lombard College. This he accomplished with distinguished success. Then came journalism as the gateway to literature. Established as a poet, he has traveled much about the country, lecturing, reading his poetry, singing and collecting folksongs. He now lives in Flat Rock, North Carolina. Member American Academy of Arts and Letters.

973.7
L7352

ABRAHAM LINCOLN; THE WAR YEARS. 4 vol. 1939. B.R.D. 11+, 1– Harcourt. $20.   484

Sequel to *Lincoln; the Prairie Years*, 1926.

The rules of the Pulitzer Committee preclude the awarding of the biography prize for any life of Lincoln; so they gave him instead the history prize. A poll conducted by the *Saturday Review of Literature* declared that he should receive for the present book Pulitzer Prizes in *both* history and biography.

"A book that every American should read."—S. V. Benét, in *Atlantic*.

"It is all here. As detailed as Dostoievsky, as American as Mark Twain."—*Books*.

"No United States biography surpasses it in wealth of documentation and fidelity to fact, . . . none can compare with it in strength, scope and beauty."—*Time*.

"The greatest of all Lincoln biographies; one of the great biographies of our literature."—H. S. Commager, in *Yale Review*.

"*The War Years* follows *The Prairie Years* into the treasure house which belongs, like Lincoln himself, to the whole human family. It has been a monumental undertaking. It is grandly realized."—R. E. Sherwood, in *New York Times*.

"It contains the finest collection of Lincoln illustrations ever put between book covers. Of this there can be no question."—*New Yorker*.

THE PEOPLE, YES. 1936. B.R.D. 6+, 1– Harcourt. $2.50. **176**

A poem in which the American idiom is used with great success.

"Portrait of the American people, through an accumulation of bits of folklore, legends, tall tales, slang, wise and foolish sayings; with the poet's own philosophy as the binding thread."—*Book Review Digest*.

"At its best, when it is almost a phonographic recording of the barbaric yawps, the pinched wisdom, the rough laughter, the warm heart of these United States. . . . This may not be folk-poetry, but it is folk-wisdom and folkspeech."—Lewis Gannett, in *New York Herald Tribune*.

Santayana, George 1863-

Anglo-American philosopher, poet and novelist. Of Spanish birth and parentage, he lives now in Rome.

LAST PURITAN; A MEMOIR IN THE FORM OF A NOVEL.
   1936. B.R.D. 16+, 5− Scribner. $2.75.   **200**

This first novel, published when the author was seventy-three years old, is said to have been the second greatest success of its year.

"Nowhere else in fiction has the latter-day puritan New England been so profoundly plumbed, so unsparingly dissected. . . . Since Henry James there has been no American novel so rich in thought and analysis."—Henry Hazlitt, in *Nation*.

"[The hero] convinced himself, on puritan grounds, that it was wrong to be a puritan. . . . He thought it his clear duty to give up puritanism, but couldn't."—*New Republic*.

"Here at last is a Book—a book worth attacking, worth defending, worth digesting, a book which may become a controversy in American literature like *The Education of Henry Adams*, like *Moby Dick*, to both of which it is subtly related by resemblance and contrast."—H. S. Canby, in *Saturday Review of Literature*.

PERSONS AND PLACES; THE BACKGROUND OF MY LIFE.
   1944. B.R.D. 11+, 3− Scribner. $2.50.   **184**

Book closes with his graduation from Harvard.

"It gives us something that the author had not got into his other works; not merely the facts of his career but a searching and subtle study of the meaning for him of his experience."—Edmund Wilson, in *New Yorker*.

"*Persons and Places* has the expected qualities of Santayana; the impeccable phrase, the lyric distinction, the intellectual acuteness. It has also the detachment mixed with malice and the homeless nostalgia of the cosmopolitan bred in two cultures and disdainful of both and of all things."—Irwin Edman, in *Yale Review*.

MIDDLE SPAN. 1945. B.R.D. 5+, 2− Scribner. $2.50
   132

Called also Volume 2 of *Persons and Places*, it is the continuation of his autobiography and covers his graduate study, his travels and his thirty years of teaching at Harvard.

"Written with the self-satisfaction of egotism and the cool breeze of serenity. It is also written with a command of English which would be preeminent at any time. . . . It is the exaltation of the private life, the classic isolation of the ivory tower."—Edward Weeks, in *Atlantic*.

"An autobiography with a metaphysical plot; it stands somewhere between Proust's great novel and *The Education of Henry Adams*, less dramatic and intense than the former but much richer in wisdom than the latter and with more of humanity in it. . . ."—Edmund Wilson, in *New Yorker*.

REALM OF TRUTH. 1938. B.R.D. 3+, 1– Scribner. $2.75. 108

The third volume of his *Realms of Being*.

"This book will hardly be completely intelligible to the general reader who has not read its predecessors in the *Realms of Being*. But whether truth is actually described or defined, the book itself on every page will yield treasures of that poetry which for Santayana is itself a form of truth."—Irwin Edman, in *Books*.

"It would be superfluous to extoll the rich variety and controlled fire of Mr. Santayana's prose. Apart perhaps from Bradley at certain moments, no one since Hume and Berkeley has married English philosophy to such stately measures."—*Times* (London) *Literary Supplement*.

Saroyan, William 1908-

American author of stories and plays. Born at Fresno, California, of Armenian parentage. He nibbled for some years at high school and at many small jobs till his growing literary success enabled him to cast them aside. He served from 1942 to 1945 as a private in World War II. He was awarded the Pulitzer Prize for drama in 1939 but refused to accept it. Someone has described him as a quarrelsome but seldom tiresome genius. Member, National Institute of Arts and Letters.

HUMAN COMEDY. 1942. B.R.D. 9+, 6— Harcourt. $2.75.   **121**

A tender tale of a California family—developed from the movie script.

"A glowing, original and heart-warming story. George Jean Nathan was right after all: if there's anybody remotely resembling a genius in American letters today his name is Saroyan."—Bennett Cerf, in *Weekly Book Review*.

"The sentiment . . . is Epworth League with a strong admixture of swami. With this book he passes beyond mere authorship and becomes àn influence, a potential West Coast Father Divine."—Clifton Fadiman, in *New Yorker*.

"*The Human Comedy* seems to me a book which answers all questions of childhood in terms of beauty and wisdom and so I give it a place on my shelf."—Annie Carroll Moore, in *Horn Book*.

MY NAME IS ARAM. 1940. B.R.D. 5+, 2— Harcourt. $2.50.   **110**

The boyhood of Aram in the Armenian colony at Fresno, California.

"These Armenian memories are honest and simple and very real. They were written with that combination of bravado and humility that is Saroyan's best charm, and with tenderness for small boyhood's turbulent mistakes and poor people's difficulties."—*Commonweal*.

"The events in this little book are all boys' events. . . . They are all trivial in themselves, and perfectly delightful. . . . I should vote, indeed, for this story of an Armenian boyhood as the most truly American book of the year."—H. S. Canby, in *Saturday Review of Literature*.

"I regret that I cannot see in any of these sketches the 'grown and many-colored artist, the genuine poet in prose, and spokesman for the youth of the world' that Mr. Christopher Morley, for example, sees."—Clifton Fadiman, in *New Yorker*.

Schlesinger, Arthur Meyer, Jr.   1918-

Son of the veteran professor of history at Harvard, who published the first of his many books on American history in 1918, the same year in which the author of *The Age of Jackson* was born. The wife and mother in this historiographical family was born Elizabeth Bancroft.

AGE OF JACKSON. 1945. B.R.D. 11+, 1– Little. $5.
408

973.56
534a

"A thoughtful and scholarly book, substantially documented, but not for popular reading."—*Kirkus.*

"A remarkable piece of analytical history, full of vitality, rich in insights and new facts, and casting a broad shaft of illumination over one of the most interesting periods of our national life."—Allan Nevins, in *New York Times.*

"At a time when such a heavy proportion of second-rate or downright shoddy historical writing is being widely praised and widely read, it is a pleasure to report on a book like this and find oneself part of a general chorus of approval. Mr. Schlesinger's book is a major contribution to American historiography."—*New Republic.*

Schuster, M. Lincoln, compiler   1897-

He was born at Kalusz, Austria, to parents who were American citizens and who brought him to the United States when he was six weeks old. He was educated at the Columbia School of Journalism and engaged in newspaper and publicity work for several years after his graduation. In 1924 he became a founder and partner of the publishing house of Simon and Schuster.

TREASURY OF THE WORLD'S GREAT LETTERS. 1940. B.R.D.
3+, 0– Simon. $3.75.   **130**

808.86
T78

"A fine collection and a perfect bedside book for the week-end guest."—*New Yorker.*

"A delectable bundle, and I have no criticism to pass upon what Mr. Schuster has put in or left out. In following his own zestful bent he has made an absorbingly readable collection of letters."—Roy Cortissoz, in *Books*.

Scott, Robert Lee, Jr.   1908-

Born in Waynesbore, Georgia, and educated at Mercer University and the United States Military Academy. On his graduation in 1932 he was assigned to flight duty. In January 1943, came his assignment to combat duty in the Pacific theater. He is now a colonel.

GOD IS MY CO-PILOT. 1943. B.R.D. 7+, 0– Scribner. $2.50.   **132**

The title, though striking, somewhat misrepresents this true tale of hazardous duty with the Flying Tigers in China.

"Primarily to be recommended to those who like stories of adventure, resourcefulness, raw courage and sudden death."—*New York Times*.

"*Life* magazine calls Scott the 'greatest of all pursuit men.' And critics will call this book the best writing to come from any flyer with the exception of St. Exupéry."— *Book Week*.

Seagrave, Gordon Stifler   1897-

Born in Rangoon, Burma, and educated at Denison University and at Johns Hopkins Medical School. He practiced medicine on the Chinese border of Burma for nearly twenty years before joining General Stilwell's army as a surgeon in 1942. After the Burma adventure he served in the Medical Corps of the British army.

BURMA SURGEON. 1943. B.R.D. 11+, 0– Norton. $3.   **176**

Experiences of a medical missionary turned army surgeon. Covers the twenty years in Burma before the Japanese explosion and the famous retreat through the jungles to India.

"Epitomizes a life of extreme service, a life in which religion became a practical demonstration of efficiency and devotion."—*Science Book Club*.

"He can make you see, smell and feel the jungle; he can dramatize the building of a great road, the horror of war and the agony of retreat. . . . You will not forget Dr. Seagrave and his little nurses if you live to be ninety. He gives the word courage a new and deeper meaning."—*Book Week*.

Seghers, Anna   1900-

German novelist. Born in Mainz, Germany, she won her doctor's degree at Heidelberg University in 1923. As a Jewish refugee she fled to Paris with her family in 1933. Her husband was sent to a concentration camp soon after the beginning of World War II. When Paris fell he escaped to Unoccupied France. Later the family was able to reach Mexico City which is now the author's home.

SEVENTH CROSS; translated from the German by James A. Galston. 1942. B.R.D. 11+, 3- Little. $2.50.   179

"It is more than a compelling story of a man's escape from a German concentration camp; it is a testament to the grandeur and nobility of the human soul. . . . Those of us who read it comfortably, safely, are strangely humbled."—Rose Feld, in *Books*.

"In this reviewer's opinion, it is not only the most compelling contribution to world literature made, so far, by any exiled German author, but also one of the most remarkable books to come out of these times of chaos and mortal danger."—Robert Pick, in *Saturday Review of Literature*.

Seversky, Major Alexander P. de   1894-

Airplane designer, inventor, industrialist. Born in Tiflis, Russia; educated at the Russian Imperial Naval Academy and Military School of Aeronautics. He lost a leg in 1915 while flying with the Russians in World War I. Came to the United States in 1918 and was a test pilot and designer for the U. S. Army, 1918-21. Later he established his own business as a designer and manufacurer of airplanes, and became a citizen of the United States in 1927.

VICTORY THROUGH AIR POWER. 1943. B.R.D. 9+, 4–
    Simon. $2.50.   137

"Whether one believes that his forecast of events five years ahead will come to pass then [1947], or not for some years after, the fact remains that Major Seversky has made a most thought-provoking contribution to the study of aviaion in its relation to world war."—*Times* (London) *Literary Supplement.*

"Perhaps no airman today has a more devoted following and a more bitter opposition than Major de Seversky. Like the late Billy Mitchell, to whom this book is dedicated, the Major has talked and written himself into such disfavor at the War Department, that his very great abilities are being shamefully neglected, despite the fact that some of America's best planes are directly traceable to Seversky designs. Be that it may, his book is interesting, provocative and instructive reading."—*New Republic.*

Shapiro, Karl Jay   1913-

American poet. Born in Baltimore and educated at the University of Virginia and Johns Hopkins University. In World War II he saw service as a sergeant in the Medical Corps, mostly in Australia. He has received two awards from *Poetry Magazine.*

ESSAY ON RIME. 1945. B.R.D. 8+ 4– Reynal. $2. 108
    "A brilliant critique in verse of the present state of poetry."—*Kirkus.*

"This book may very well be the most remarkable contribution of American art yet to have come out of the war." F. O. Matthiesen, in *New York Times.*

"Apart from its wit, its gusto, and its technical ingenuity, Shapiro's *Essay on Rime* is of vital importance to any lover of poetry today, for it is essentially and first of all a work of belief, a resonant affirmation of faith."—Louis Untermeyer, in *Yale Review.*

Sharp, Margery (Mrs. Geoffrey Castle)   1905-

English novelist. Educated at Bedford College and London University.

CLUNY BROWN. 1944. B.R.D. 12+, 2– Little. $2.50.
115

The droll young witch, Cluny, is not only the heroine but also a plumber's niece, and very competent she is in both roles.

"Miss Sharp's characters are always amusing and whimsically drawn, but Cluny is probably the most startling of them all. Wherever Cluny appears life takes on an Alice-in-Wonderland quality, people and things behave in the strangest fashion, and through it all Cluny moves unself-consciously, unaware of the disorderly fairy tale she is making of life."—*New York Times.*

"Miss Sharp's admirers will know exactly what they are getting, and will probably find it very suitable bed-time reading for these nights in which some part of our attention must inevitably be reserved for noises off, in the sky."—*Spectator* (London), in July 1944.

Shaw, George Bernard   1856-

Irish dramatist. Born in Dublin, Shaw says he is an educated man because he escaped from school at fourteen. At twenty-three, after a casual job or two, he was in London writing novels, book reviews, musical criticism. His first play was produced in 1892. Soon after Shaw was firmly established as a popular and fashionable irritant. Only in his still voluble old age did the knowing ones begin to tire of him and his japes.

EVERYBODY'S POLITICAL WHAT'S WHAT.   1944.   B.R.D.
    5+, 2– Dodd. $3.   **104**

"Shaw might have called his book 'The Statesman,' because its subject is the education of the ideal statesman of the future. . . . Even where his thinking fails somewhat in coherence, there is a kind of general wisdom that soaks through the cracks of his argument."—Edmund Wilson, in *New Yorker*.

"The four hundred pages of the 'Political What's What' bring together in a new, simplified and up-to-date form the entire Shavian system, the word and thought of half a century, not only of criticism but of what amounts to constitution-making."—J. Barzun, in *Weekly Book Review*.

"I solemnly testify that this book is unreadable. I have worked through it because I have been paid to do so."—Walter Elliot, in *Spectator*.

Sheean, Vincent   1899-

Journalist, novelist, essayist. Born in Christian County, Illinois; educated at the University of Chicago. He has adventured all over Europe and in Morocco, Persia, China and Palestine. His wife was Diana Forbes-Robertson.

NOT PEACE BUT A SWORD.   1939.   B.R.D.   6+, 1–
    Doubleday. $2.75.   **123**

English title: *The Eleventh Hour*.

The book describes the tragic background of World War II when, from March 1938, to March 1939, Sheean watched the growth of fascism in visits to Spain, Vienna and Prague.

"There is little that is personal, except as Mr. Sheean, naturally enough, finds it difficult to tell what he saw without telling how he felt. His emotions, however, are always under control. He has achieved a mastery that makes literature of the horror and indignation which swept over him with much of what he saw, the admiration for human courage that some other spectacles inspired in him."—R. L. Duffus, in *New York Times*.

Shepard, Odell   1884-

Born in Sterling, Illinois, and educated at Northwestern University, University of Chicago and Harvard. He has taught English at the University of Southern California, at Harvard, at Radcliffe and at Trinity College. He was a Guggenheim Fellow, 1927-28, and Lieutenant Governor of Connecticut, 1940-41.

PEDLAR'S PROGRESS: THE LIFE OF BRONSON ALCOTT. 1937. *818.4*
    B.R.D. 11+, 3– Little. $3.75.   153 *A355S*

Won the Pulitzer Prize in biography, 1938.

Bronson Alcott was a rustic Yankee pedlar who became the philosopher and teacher whom Emerson called "the most refined and the most advanced soul we have had in New England." Fortunately for him he was also the father of the author of *Little Women*.

"Readers whose memories go back to the nineteenth century will find delightful this full-flavored account of a pattern of life which the machine age has pretty thoroughly destroyed."—*Springfield Republican*.

"Mr. Shepard's book reflects faithfully the Arcadian innocence of this transcendental pedlar who had the heart of a child and the mind of a seer. . . . It explains the past and the present in terms of a man, the invulnerable integrity, the shining symmetry of whose life epitomized a whole society."—H. S. Commager, in *New York Times*.

"Alcott was probably as perfect a teacher as any man can be who lacks an abundance of sense, and Mr. Shepard has done his memory a signal service by saying so. For that matter Mr. Shepard has done all that can be done for Alcott with respect to any phase of his activity throughout eighty-eight years."—Mark Van Doren, in *Books*.

Sherrod, Robert Lee   1909-

Journalist and war correspondent. He was born in Thomas County, Georgia, and educated at the University of Georgia. A *Time* reporter, he was in the Pacific theater from 1942 to 1945 and "landed with the fifth wave" on

Tarawa beach in November 1943. He was officially commended by the U. S. Marine Corps for "brave and efficient service under extraordinaryy conditions of combat."

TARAWA, THE STORY OF A BATTLE. 1944 . B.R.D. 6+, 0–
    Duell. $2.   **138**

"An eye-witness, minute-to-minute account of the capture of Tarawa by our Marines—thoroughly authentic and vivid to the point of ghastliness."—*Catholic World*.

"This is about as near as you can get in an arm-chair to being in the midst of battle. . . . Mr. Sherrod tells what war is really like."—*Nation*.

"Perhaps the best first-hand description of action that has yet come out of the war."—Edmund Wilson, in *New Yorker*.

Sherwood, Robert Emmet   1896-

Dramatist. Born in New Rochelle, New York, and educated at Harvard. He served with the Canadians in World War I, 1917-19, and was gassed and wounded. He did editorial work on *Vanity Fair*, the old *Life*, *New York Herald Tribune* and *Scribner's Magazine*, 1919-27, and has written much for the movies. He was Director of the Overseas Branch of OWI in World War II till 1944. He has won three times the Pulitzer Prize for drama.

ABE LINCOLN IN ILLINOIS; a Play in Twelve Scenes; with a foreword by Carl Sandburg. 1939. B.R.D. 5+, 0– Scribner. $2.   **123**

Describes Lincoln in New Salem in the thirties and to the day in 1861 that he set out from Springfield for Washington.

"To show Lincoln becoming a great man because of (and in spite of) internal stresses and to show it in scenes and with characters of pioneer simplicity, is a difficult and fine achievement."—W. P. Eaton, in *Books*.

"Mr. Sherwood is one of a few who have grasped and held firm the elusive personality which is Lincoln's. He has achieved something which very few others have achieved. Lincoln's soul speaks in these lines."—*Saturday Review of Literature*.

THERE SHALL BE NO NIGHT. 1940. B.R.D. 4+, 1–
    Scribner. $2.   **110**

813.5
S55t

Pulitzer Prize play about the Russian invasion of Finland in 1939.

"The play is rich in wisdom and pity because it deals honestly with the elementals of life. Here are not the discussions of one family, or of Finland, but of us all, revealed in a pattern deep enough to include the words of Goethe and St. Paul."—*Survey Graphic*.

Shiber, Etta (Mrs. William Noyes Shiber)   1878–

Mrs. Shiber was born in New York City. After her husband's death in 1936 she went to live in Paris with an English woman friend. They harbored successively many British soldiers after Dunkirk and during the Nazi occupation. At last they were caught and jailed. The friend was sentenced to death, but Mrs. Shiber to only three years of imprisonment, from which she was released after a time in exchange for a German woman spy.

PARIS UNDERGROUND; in Collaboration with Anne and Paul
    Dupré. 1943. B.R.D. 6+, 0– Scribner. $2.50.
                                                     100

940.538
S55p

"Mrs. Shiber's story is a thriller better than any spy fiction, because it is true. It is authentic; probably the best picture we have yet had of France under the Occupation."—*Saturday Review of Literature*.

"To the readers of her story should come an invigorated impulse toward the kind of personal sacrifice which these two women so quietly offered to the common cause." —V. Sapieha, in *Weekly Book Review*.

Shirer, William Lawrence   1904–

War correspondent. Born in Chicago and educated at Coe College, Cedar Rapids, Iowa.

940.53943
S556

BERLIN DIARY; THE JOURNAL OF A FOREIGN CORRESPOND-
    ENT, 1934-41. 1941. B.R.D. 17+, 2− Knopf. $3.
                                                    380

"He doesn't deal in venom. He lets the evidence speak
and his stark quotation of the German headlines is one of
his most skillful strokes."—Edward Weeks, in *Atlantic*.

"[There is] no brooding over political tactics and no
querulous speculations about the worth of democracy.
Nazism is a macabre indecency. It is good to read such a
book."—*Nation*.

"I have yet to find anyone who picked the book up who
was able to put it down unfinished. . . . *Berlin Diary* is
the most important non-fiction book of the season; probably of the year."—W. L. White, in *Saturday Review of
Literature*.

Silone, Ignazio   1900-

A radical Italian novelist. Born in Pescina, Italy, a
town which has since been destroyed by flood and earthquake. Educated in Catholic schools, he was a pacifist during World War I. An anti-Fascist from the first, he was
forced to leave Italy after the March on Rome. He became a Communist and was imprisoned several times.
Finally he foreswore the party. Free Switzerland has been
his home since 1930.

F
S585

BREAD AND WINE; translated from the Italian. 1937.
    B.R.D. 7+, 1− Harper. $2.50.   119

"This novel is not a tract and offers no solution. It is
a picture, extraordinarily sympathetic from an exile like
Silone, of a great country in the grasp of a ruthless will."—
H. S. Canby, in *Saturday Review of Literature*.

"Reveals Silone's full stature; he must now be recognized as one of the most truly contemporary and significant
writers of our time."—*Nation*.

"A quiet, shrewd, humorous and bitter book about the
Italian peasantry under fascism."—P. M. Jack, in *New
York Times*.

"Here is the voice of Italy's Sinclair Lewis, repeating more subtly, more poetically—'It *has* happened here.'"— *Forum.*

Simonov, Konstantin M.   1905-

Soviet journalist, playwright, novelist. He was war correspondent for *Red Star* and *Pravda.*

DAYS AND NIGHTS; translated from the Russian by Joseph Barnes. 1945. B.R.D. 11+, 2– Simon. $2.75.
190

891.7
S59d

Novel about the siege of Stalingrad in World War II. Excellently translated and unspoiled by propaganda.

"The truest book we have yet had on the Russian war." —John Hersey, in *New Yorker.*

"The superb merit of the book is its series of portraits of men in battle. That they happen to be Russians is incidental; they are first of all human and after that brave; such men lived before Agamemnon and just such men came from Iowa and Alabama to follow Eisenhower."—*New York Times.*

Sinclair, Upton   1878-

American novelist and reformer. Born in Baltimore, of an old Southern family, and educated at City College and Columbia, New York City. His first success was *The Jungle* (1906), a novel which attacked the Chicago meat industry. He invested his royalties in founding a socialist colony, Helicon Hall, at Englewood, New Jersey. It burned down. (Was it because Sinclair Lewis was the furnaceman?) He lives at Pasadena, where he advocates his EPIC (End Poverty in California) scheme, and ran for governor. His books are said to have been translated into forty-seven languages. In foreign lands his books are read more, perhaps, than those of any other American.

WORLD'S END. 1940. B.R.D. 8+, 5– Viking. $3. **100**

A long novel about Europe and Americans in Europe, 1913-19. One gathers from it that corruption in high society and finance causes world wars.

"It is Upton Sinclair's biggest and most successful volume."—*Books*.

"It has a range and perspective attained in no other of his novels."—Lewis Gannett, in *Boston Transcript*.

"On its own level *World's End* is a job it would be hard to beat."—Granville Hicks, in *New Republic*.

"Surprisingly free of Mr. Sinclair's usual didactic touch."—*New Yorker*.

"Mr. Sinclair emerges as the successful painter of an epoch, as a first-class mingler of fiction with historic fact, even, after all these years, as a humorist."—R. L. Duffus, in *New York Times*.

BETWEEN TWO WORLDS. 1941. B.R.D. 8+, 6– Viking.
   $2.50.   100

The even longer sequel to his long novel *World's End*, 1940. The present book is a vast panorama of world events in the period beginning with the Versailles Treaty and ending with the financial crash of 1929.

"If Mr. Sinclair is not quite a great novelist, if he is sometimes absurd, he nevertheless handles a crowd of characters, a score of locales, and dozens of events with remarkable skill, insight and moral courage."—*New Yorker*.

"He has become a novelist—a novelist with about as many faults as a reviewer could shake a stick at, but still a novelist of considerable power and significance."—R. L. Duffus, in *New York Times*.

Skinner, Cornelia Otis (Mrs. Alden S. Blodget) (1901-   ) and Kimbrough, Emily (Mrs. John Wrench)   1899-

Miss Skinner is actress, humorist and the daughter of Otis Skinner, the actor. She was born in Chicago and educated at Bryn Mawr and the Sorbonne. Miss Kimbrough was also educated at Bryn Mawr and the Sorbonne, and from 1927 to 1929 was managing editor of the *Ladies' Home Journal*.

OUR HEARTS WERE YOUNG AND GAY. 1942. B.R.D. 5+,
 0– Dodd. $2.50. 143

Reminiscences of their hilarious trip to Europe just after World War I.

"A joyous chronicle from beginning to end."—*Books*.

"The book is compact of little nothings, made electric by the irresistible delight of youth in life and adventure. We defy anyone to read it without laughter or recall it without a smile."—*Saturday Review of Literature*.

Smith, Betty (Mrs. Joseph Piper Jones) 1904-

Actress, playwright, novelist. Born in Brooklyn, she was educated at the University of Michigan and at the Yale Drama School. She has written and published over seventy one-act plays.

TREE GROWS IN BROOKLYN. 1943. B.R.D. 8+, 2– Harper. $2.75. 297

The story of a German-Irish-American family of the tenements in the Williamsburg section of Brooklyn during the first years of the twentieth century. Two million copies were sold. This sale equals that of the phenomenally successful *Boston Cooking School Cook Book*, which was published in 1896.

"A first novel of uncommon skill, an almost uncontrollable vitality and zest for life, the work of a fresh, original and highly gifted talent."—*Yale Review*.

"If ever a sensitive, expressive young woman offered you a fragment from the very heart and fiber of her being, that is Betty Smith writing *A Tree Grows in Brooklyn*.—*Weekly Book Review*.

"Betty Smith has written her book out of a deep nostalgia which colors every page. . . . Writing like this is rare. It establishes an intimacy between reader and book which is to be cherished for many a day."—*Springfield Republican*.

Smith, Howard K.   1914-

Foreign correspondent and news commentator. Born in Ferriday, Louisiana, and educated at Tulane University, he was a Rhodes Scholar in 1937.

LAST TRAIN FROM BERLIN. 1942. B.R.D. 7+, 2- Knopf. $2.75.   **137**

After six years in Berlin, he was the last American correspondent to leave the city before the United States declared war. Just before his departure all his notes for the book were either burned by himself or confiscated by the Gestapo. The book describes conditions in Germany just before and during the early part of World War II and suggests a method of hastening the defeat of the Nazis.

"A true successor and companion-piece to [Shirer's] *Berlin Diary.*"—*Books.*

"While recording the signs of deterioration . . . he insists that the overthrow of Hitler must come through military means."—*Times* (London) *Literary Supplement.*

Smith, Lillian   1897-

Born at Jasper, Florida, and educated at Piedmont College, Peabody Conservatory and Teachers' College, Columbia. She taught for a time at Virginia School, Hachow, China, and in 1936 became co-editor of *The South Today.*

STRANGE FRUIT; a Novel. 1944. B.R.D. 14+, 4- Reynal. $2.75.   **368**

Realistic story of white and black and miscegination in the deep South. It ends with a lynching. The book was banned in Boston.

"The tragedy of the South is explicit in every line."—*New York Times.*

"At the speed things are moving today, I suspect we shall be needing a new *Uncle Tom's Cabin* for each decade. This one comes from the South and this time New England seems afraid of it."—Edward Weeks, in *Atlantic.*

"It is written honestly and with a fine bitterness against the inhumanity of Southern whites to blacks, and it rings some interesting changes on a theme which one might have thought had been worn threadbare. Edifying and saddening reading."—*New Yorker*.

Smith, Robert Aura   1899-

Born in Denver, Colorado, and educated at Ohio Wesleyan University and at Oxford as a Rhodes Scholar. He served as a private in the Field Hospital Service of the A.E.F., 1917-19. He taught college English, 1920-25; was foreign correspondent of *Christian Science Monitor*, 1926-30; was editor of the *Manila Daily Bulletin* and correspondent of the *New York Times*, 1930-37. From 1942 to 1945 he directed the OWI in Indiana and New York.

OUR FUTURE IN ASIA. 1940. B.R.D. 6+, 1- Viking. $3.   **100**

"An extraordinarily careful and thoughtful survey of America's place in the Far East."—*Nation* (in October, 1940).

"Smith, *New York Times* correspondent in the Orient, has anticipated today's headlines with an accuracy that is bound to arouse the admiration of newspapermen everywhere."—Norman Cousins, in *Current History* (in October, 1940).

"Should be read by every American before venturing opinions on whatever action our government may take with reference to our interests in the Western Pacific."—*New York Times* (in October, 1940).

Smyth, Henry DeWolf   1898-

Physicist and associate editor (1927-30) of *Physical Review*. Born in Clinton, New York, and educated at Lawrenceville School and Princeton and Cambridge Universities, he has taught physics at Princeton since 1924. He was a Guggenheim Fellow, 1931-32, and has been consultant on war research projects for the National Research Council since 1940. He was also consultant for the Monkton District projects of the U. S. Engineers, 1943-45.

541.2
S66ab

ATOMIC ENERGY FOR MILITARY PURPOSES; THE OFFICIAL REPORT ON THE DEVELOPMENT OF THE ATOMIC BOMB UNDER THE AUSPICES OF THE UNITED STATES GOVERNMENT, 1940-45. 1945. B.R.D. 4+, 0- Princeton. $2.   **132**

"Can be understood by any person who has had a high school or college education in physics and who is willing to read patiently and attentively."—Waldemar Kaempffert, in *New York Times.*

"Virtually a text book on nuclear physics which traces the history of radioactivity, the efforts to break down the atom by bombardment, the organization of the greatest research team in scientific history to develop the bomb, and an account of how success was achieved in three years."— *New York Times.*

Snow, Edgar Parks   1905-

Foreign correspondent. Born in Kansas City, Missouri, and educated at Kansas City Junior College, the University of Missouri and Columbia University. He was editor and correspondent in the Far East, 1929-45.

327.47
S67p

PATTERN OF SOVIET POWER. 1945. B.R.D. 8+, 3- Random. $2.75.   **120**

"Lucid, frank and authentic appraisal of the new Russia."—*Book Week.*

"Honest, informed and objective report on the Russians in 1944."—*Weekly Book Review.*

"He relates the by now familiar story of the revival of 'traditionalism' in Soviet Russia."—*New York Times.*

"A thread through the maze of world politics and a sane corrective to the flood of tendentious anti-Soviet literature now current."—*Saturday Review of Literature.*

"His attitude of friendly understanding, if not necessarily complete approval, for what the Soviets are trying to achieve in international politics is a corrective to what appears to be an increasingly hostile tone on the part of many other writers on Russia."—*Commonweal*.

PEOPLE ON OUR SIDE. 1944. B.R.D. 7+, 0– Random. $3.50.   **196**

Russia and China are described as they are under the pressure of war.

"His reflective passages, especially those on China, make very good sense."—*New Yorker*.

"It is good, because it is lucid, readable and honest, and because it helps us, as few recent books do, to understand the people on our side"—*Saturday Review of Literature*.

"Anybody who is interested in exercising his rights as an American citizen to voice his say in United States postwar policies should read it. *People on Our Side* will certainly make you think."—C. L. Sulzberger, in *New York Times*.

By far the most comprehensive and objective job of bringing our Eastern allies closer to our understanding that has yet been done. It will go a long way to clarify the many phases of the war which until now have puzzled most Americans."—*Book Week*.

RED STAR OVER CHINA. 1938. B.R.D. 15+, 5– Random. $3. New revised edition with epilogue. 1944. Modern Library. 95c.   **135**

Valuable as a book of travel in almost unknown territory; exciting as a book of dangerous adventure; important as a significant study of politics and history—including the kidnapping of Chiang Kai-shek.

"Undoubtedly the best job of reporting on China that has appeared in English or any other language."—*Boston Transcript*.

"A piece of brilliant and unique reporting. Edgar Snow is the first foreigner to have penetrated to the Chinese-

Soviet regions, to have lived with the Red armies, and to have made a thorough study of every phase of life in Soviet China."—*New Statesman.*

Stafford, Jean (Mrs. R. T. S. Lowell, Jr.)   1915-

Novelist. Born at Covina, California, and educated at Colorado University. She spent a year in Germany and thereafter was on the staff of *The Southern Review* in Louisiana.

BOSTON ADVENTURE. 1944. B.R.D. 11+, 8- Harcourt. $2.75.   **173**

Character study of Sonia Marburg, daughter of a German father and a flighty Russian mother. The story begins with Sonia's poverty-stricken childhood in a Massachusetts fishing village, and closes with the girl established as a protege of a wealthy Boston woman."—*Book Review Digest.*

"Undoubtedly the most interesting novel of the season."—*Commonweal.*

"Miss Stafford is not Proust and her method has many suggestive limitations. . . . But she is an extraordinarily talented novelist, and her book will give great pleasure to sensitive readers."—Alfred Kazin, in *New Republic.*

"Miss Stafford is a commanding talent, who writes in the great tradition of the English novel; and unless her work is a flash in the pan (and Heaven send it be not), American letters have been enriched by a unique, brilliant and remarkable artist."—*Saturday Review of Literature.*

Steffens, Lincoln   1866-1936

American publicist. Born, San Francisco; educated at Universities of California, Berlin, Heidelberg, Leipsig, the Sorbonne. Engaged in newspaper work in New York, 1892-1906; was managing editor, *McClure's*, 1902-06; and assistant editor, *American* and *Everybody's*, 1906-11. He was the leader of the useful group of Muckrakers. He was a member of the secret Bullitt Mission to Russia in 1919 and in his last years he was sympathetic to communism. His *Autobiography* (1931) was a best-seller.

LETTERS; edited by Ella Winter and Granville Hicks. 2 vol. 1938. B.R.D. 6+, 1- Harcourt. $10.   **100**

The letters were written to his family and friends between 1889 and 1936.

"Steffens was a reporter, and a good one. Here he reports not on his own progress to a certain goal but the conditions which drove him relentlessly onward."—*Boston Transcript.*

"I can hear his voice in these letters as clearly as if he were in the room. . . . For Steffens wrote as he spoke. There was no effort to be polished, no desire to be the man of letters. He was just his own self."—O. G. Villard, in *Nation.*

Stegner, Wallace Earle   1909-

Born at Lake Mills, Iowa, he was educated at the Universities of Utah, Iowa and California. He taught English at Augustana College and at the Universities of Iowa, Utah and Wisconsin and at Harvard. Son of a restless pioneer, he has lived in many regions of the Northwest.

BIG ROCK CANDY MOUNTAIN. 1943. B.R.D. 8+, 2- Duell. $3.   **132**

The story of wandering Bo Mason's life-long search for the rainbow's end.

"A fictional footnote to the era that saw the end of the American dream."—*Weekly Book Review.*

"Well-written story of a footloose family. . . . The life of the household is a misery of continual cruelty and often crushing poverty, alternating with occasional scenes of simple family happiness which stand out beautifully and unforgettably."—*New Yorker.*

Steinbeck, John   1902-

Born in Salinas, California, of German, Irish and old New England descent. He graduated from Salinas High School in 1918, and studied at Stanford University in 1919, specializing in science. For some years after leaving Stanford he worked at odd jobs. His first book was published in 1929. He has written about a dozen books, many of which are hard-boiled fiction about proletarians. He might be described as an anti-puritan and something of a mystic. In 1943 he was a war columnist overseas.

GRAPES OF WRATH. 1939. B.R.D. 13+, 4— Viking.
    $2.75.   589

Won the Pulitzer Prize for fiction in 1940. Has the second highest score of the books of the decade.

A story of the "Okies" driven to California by the dust storms of 1934 and by the pressure of the big corporate farms.

"It is the book for which everything else Steinbeck has written was an exercise in preparation. . . . This is the full symphony, Steinbeck's declaration of faith."—*Books*.

"*The Grapes of Wrath* is the summation of eighteen years of realism. . . . The book is profane and sometimes shocking in its detail. So is that segment of America which Steinbeck describes with such truth. This is no book for the timid."—Edward Weeks, in *Atlantic*.

"One salutes it as a fiery document of protest and compassion, as a story that had to be told, as a book that must be read. It is, I think, one of those books—there are not very many—which really do some good."—L. Kronenberger, in *Nation*.

"It belongs very high in the category of the great angry books like *Uncle Tom's Cabin* that have roused a people to fight against intolerable wrongs."—*New Republic*.

"What sticks with me is that here is a book, non-political, non-dogmatic, which dramatizes so that you can't forget it the terrible facts of a wholesale injustice committed by society. Here is a book about a people of old American stock, not Reds, or rebels of any kind."—*New Yorker*.

"It is great in the way *Uncle Tom's Cabin* was great—because it is inspired propaganda, half tract, half human interest story, emotionalizing a great theme. . . . Readers will find it one of the most impassioned and exciting books of the year."—*Time*.

LONG VALLEY. 1938. B.R.D. 5+, 1– Viking. $2.50. 117

Consists of fifteen short stories. It includes *Red Pony* —"a heart-breakingly true picture of boyhood." "I think it's a masterpiece," says Clifton Fadiman.

"*The Long Valley* leaves Steinbeck still a bright prospect in American letters."—Elmer Davis, in *Saturday Review of Literature*.

"A remarkable collection by a writer who so far has neither repeated himself nor allowed himself a single careless sentence."—*New Yorker*.

"He is writing about people, beautiful or nauseating, as they come. He knows his people and his scene without being bogged down by realistic detail. Beyond that he has a tremendous and abiding sympathy for human beings on all levels of experience."—*New York Times*.

THE MOON IS DOWN. 1942. B.R.D. 13+, 5– Viking. $2. 116

Story of the German occupation of Norway—the resistance of the inhabitants of an occupied village.

"The best novel yet produced by this war."—*New Statesman*.

"Both first class fiction and a valuable document and, one is inclined to think, a little masterpiece."—*Current History*.

"The lesson this book carries should be known to every American. It is one of the best short novels I have ever read."—John Gunther, in *Books*.

"A novel, a stage play, a moving picture, a radio drama. It is all these things, and merits being all of them."—R. L. Duffus, in *New York Times*.

"This is not history; it is prophecy. It is the affirmation of a high faith in humanity—which is the same thing as faith in the ultimate triumph of freedom over force. That faith has not been more beautifully stated than in this novel."—*Christian Century.*

OF MICE AND MEN.; a Novel. 1937. B.R.D. 6+, 4– Covici. $2.   **246**

Story about two proletarians, one of them a Hercules, who is one of "God's fools."

"This is a work of art so nearly perfect that it is a work of supererogation to heap up adjectives about it."— *North American.*

"A thriller, a gripping tale running to novelette length, that you will not set down until it is finished. It is more than that; but it is that."—*New York Times.*

"Each of them follows some instinct as a bull follows the chain which runs through a hole in his nose, or as a crab moves toward its prey. The scene is a ranch in California, and the bunk-house talk is terrific."—Mark Van Doren, in *Nation.*

"Its style is right for its subject-matter, and that subject-matter is deeply felt, richly conceived and perfectly ordered. That is praise enough for a book."—H. S. Canby, in *Saturday Review of Literature.*

Stern, Mrs. M. R. *See* Halsey, Margaret

Stewart, George Rippey   1895-

Born at Sewickley, Pennsylvania, and educated at Princeton, the University of California and Columbia. He has taught English since 1920 at the University of Michigan and Columbia and at the University of California since 1923. He served in World War I, 1917-19, and as a civilian in the Navy in 1944.

NAMES ON THE LAND; A HISTORICAL ACCOUNT OF PLACE-NAMING IN THE UNITED STATES. 1945. B.R.D. 13+, 0– Random. $3.   **192**

"In every way an interesting and important book. Mr. Stewart writes well out of full knowledge."—*Christian Science Monitor.*

"A valuable reference book, made more so by the inclusion of a good index."—*Library Journal.*

"A sort of informal history of America written around his central theme. The result is highly readable."—*Nation.*

"A sort of prolegomenon to the subject. . . . Mr. Stewart has performed a useful job in a very competent manner."—H. L. Mencken, in *Weekly Book Review.*

STORM. 1941. B.R.D. 10+, 3– Random. $2.50.   **200**

Something new in fiction—an autobiographical novel about a storm named Maria.

"The book for the layman who wishes to know how meteorology impinges upon human consciousness."—*Scientific Book Club.*

"The freshness and vividness of Mr. Stewart's background give it novelty and the storm gives the individual characters something to fight. The individual lives are well sketched . . . and Maria herself is a very decided character."—S. V. Benét, in *Books.*

"With remarkable skill of suggestion the incidents move along, and interest is sustained. After all, there is material enough. Lovers do get caught in mountain snowstorms, linemen perish at their duty, the maintenance of traffic does demand action, even heroism."—*Saturday Review of Literature.*

Stone, Mrs. Grace Zaring. *See* Vance, Ethel, pseud.

Stone, Irving   1903-

Born in San Francisco; educated at the University of California and at the University of Southern California where he later taught economics till 1926. Then came ten years of play-writing in New York and Europe. With the success of *Lust for Life*, 1934, he realized that biography was his métier.

SAILOR ON HORSEBACK. 1938. B.R.D. 9+, 4– Houghton. $3.   **126**

A life of Jack London.

"A vivid and exciting history of a vivid and exciting personality."—*Times* (London) *Literary Supplement.*

"It is not only true but it sounds true. Jack London lives again in this book."—Floyd Dell, in *Books*.

"A full, lively, perhaps over-lively biography of Jack London. Mr. Stone puffs up an interesting but mediocre writer to unnatural proportions and makes the most of the cinema romance of London's life."—*New Yorker*.

"Mr. Stone apparently gave no hostages in exchange for important material; he is uncompromisingly objective in his attitude toward all the principles in the story, whether living or dead."—John Chamberlain, in *New Republic*.

Stowe, Leland   1899

Born at Southbury, Connecticut; educated at Wesleyan University. He has been a newspaperman since 1921; a foreign and war correspondent from all over the world since 1926.

THEY SHALL NOT SLEEP. 1944. B.R.D. 6+, 0– Knopf. $3.   **219**

Written with complete candor from notes in his war diary between July 1941, and December 1942—observations in China, Burma, India and Soviet Russia.

"A powerful blow to smugness."—*Springfield Republican*.

"His pages read like mature journalism and not like a crossing between Frank Merriwell and Richard Harding Davis."—*New Yorker*.

"His book is remarkably accurate, considering its scope, and it is one in which this writer, having himself lately visited every country Stowe describes, finds no major contention not born out by facts."—E. Snow, in *Nation*.

Streit, Clarence   1896-

American journalist and publicist. Born at California, Missouri, and reared in Montana where he was graduated from the State University. He served in France during World War I and at the Versailles Conference, being at one time Woodrow Wilson's bodyguard. Then came a Rhodes Scholarship at Oxford, followed by many years as a foreign correspondent.

UNION NOW, A PROPOSAL FOR THE FEDERAL UNION OF THE DEMOCRACIES OF THE NORTH ATLANTIC. 1939. B.R.D. 7+, 3– Harper. $3.   **161**

"I believe this to be the most important book published thus far [1939] in this dark twentieth century."— E. H. Wilkins, in *Christian Century*.

"It may constitute seed for a future and more hopeful drive toward international sanity."—Leland Stowe, in *Books*.

"Its great value lies in the fact that it will prepare public opinion for what must ultimately be the solution of the problem of peace."—Robert Dell, in *Nation*.

Strode, Hudson   1893-

Teacher, lecturer, author—especially of books about foreign countries. Born at Cairo, Illinois, to Southern parents, he was educated at the University of Alabama, Harvard and Columbia. He has taught English since 1916 at the University of Alabama, save for a sojourn in Bermuda from 1929 to 1932 for reasons of health. He has traveled much in Europe and South America and has lectured all over the United States.

TIMELESS MEXICO. 1944. B.R.D. 8+, 3– Harcourt. $3.50.   **104**

A history of Mexico from Montezuma to 1944.

"One of the three or four best books I know on the subject."—Stark Young, in *New Republic*.

"When you have finished the book, you are aware of having had a very pleasant time while really finding out something that you should have known all along about Mexico."—*Book Week*.

"His book is scholarly without being pedantic, factual without being dull, and readable without being superficial. In short an excellent one-volume survey of Mexico."—*New Yorker*.

Struther, Jan (pseudonym of Mrs. Joyce Anstruther Maxtone Graham)   1901-

Poet and novelist. Born in England and privately educated in London, she had published five books of poems and sketches before her great success. In 1940 she brought her children to New York City "for the duration."

Mrs. Miniver. 1940. B.R.D. 11+, 0- Harcourt. $2. **240**

Story sketches of small domestic matters in upper middle-class England.

"This is mandarin writing, beautifully selected with hardly a superfluous phrase. Anglophobes won't care for it."—Edward Weeks, in *Atlantic*.

"The book wasn't written for America; there isn't a word of propaganda in it. Yet reading it, you understand why the poets have written so many of their loveliest lines about 'this England.'"—Lewis Gannett, in *Boston Transcript*.

"Jan Struther's *Mrs. Miniver* is a small book of sketches about very small things. But it is not trivial. She is sentimental, playful, domestic, as was Charles Lamb. . . . Mrs. Miniver, like Charles Lamb, will place a gentle hand on your elbow and bid you stop to observe something quite insignificant, and lo! it is not insignificant at all."—Clifton Fadiman, in *New Yorker*.

Tate, Allen   1899-

Poet and novelist. Born at Winchester, Clarke County, Kentucky, he was educated at Vanderbilt University where he graduated *magna cum laude*. He was a Guggenheim Fellow, 1928-30, and taught English, 1934-39, at Southwestern College, at Women's College of the University of North

Caroline and at Columbia. He was a resident fellow in poetry at Princeton, 1939-42, the incumbent of the chair of poetry at the Library of Congress, 1942-44, and professor of English at the University of the South since 1944. He is the author of a score of books.

THE FATHERS. 1938. B.R.D. 4+, 1− Putnam. $2.50.
117

This first novel is a psychological horror story about conflicting loyalties to state and nation in the Virginia of 1861.

"Mr. Tate has a man-sized subject; his characters are drawn with warmth and unusual understanding. A fine novel, in short, by a fine poet."—*New Yorker*.

Tregaskis, Richard   1916-
American war correspondent. Born in Elizabeth, New Jersey, and educated at Harvard, he engaged in newspaper work, 1937-42, and was a correspondent with the Pacific Fleet, 1942-43. After Guadalcanal he was assigned to the Mediterranean theater till wounded. Thereafter he covered the European Theater and the battles on the Western Front in 1944.

GUADALCANAL DIARY. 1943. B.R.D. 7+, 1− Random. $2.50.   **110**

"An artless, rough diary, but it has a first-hand, on-the-spot quality that partly atones for its total lack of literary finish."—*New Yorker*.

"Marines with whom I have talked have only good to say of *Guadalcanal Diary*. There are pages in this book which are not pretty. But it is well that we back home should know what our men are up against as they jump from foothold to foothold."—*Atlantic*.

Trumbull, Robert
City editor of the *Honolulu Advertiser*.

THE RAFT. 1942. B.R.D. 11+, 3− Holt. $2.50.   **158**

The book is the story of three navy flyers who made a forced landing in the Pacific and spent thirty-four days on an eight-by-four-foot raft which finally drifted ashore on an atoll. The story was told to the author by Aviation Chief Machinist's Mate Harold Dixon, the Petty Officer who was in command of the "vessel." He was forty-one years of age while his shipmates were in their early twenties.

"The story which Americans will be telling their children for generations. It illustrates man's ability to master any fate."—H. A. Wallace, in his "Free World Victory Speech."

"The special quality of this book is that it restores and documents by deed something that has long been lacking from man's books and minds—the sense of the therapeutic goodness of the unflagging will to live."—*Time*.

"This is a far greater epic than Bligh's voyage, as the three Americans who performed this feat are better men than Bligh. Told in plain prose by a journalist who gets everything out of the tale there is to get and puts nothing in."—*New Yorker*.

Tweedsmuir, Lord. *See* Buchan, J.

Ullman, James Ramsey   1907-

Born in New York City and educated at Phillips Academy, Andover, Massachusetts, and at Princeton. He was a journalist, 1929-33; a playwright, 1930-35; a producer, 1933-37; and a first lieutenant in World War II, 1942-43. He has been a free lance writer since 1939 and is the author of five books.

BROWSING COLLECTION

THE WHITE TOWER. 1945. B.R.D. 8+, 5− Lippincott. $3.   **180**

A novel about the near conquest of a virgin mountain in Switzerland by five men and one woman, while World War II, in which they had all been involved, was rumbling not far away. The characters are American, English, German, Austrian, French and Swiss.

Skim over and forget, if you wish, the allegory and the mysticism. There remains a fine, absorbing tale of adventure, toil, hardship and danger. The hero, to our satisfaction, is a brave American flyer with nerves of steel. Tired and cynical on the surface, he has a noble heart.

"If Mr. Ullman falls short of the summit, even as Martin Ordway, he still climbs impressively."—*Saturday Review of Literature.*

Untermeyer, Louis   1885-

Anthologist and poet. Born in New York City, he left high school at fifteen "because of his failure to understand geometry." And having found that little talent went with his passion for music, he entered dutifully upon a business career with his father which soon came to be mitigated by an increasing addiction to literature. He has written or compiled forty or more books and has lectured on poetry in many colleges. Member of the National Institute of Arts and Letters.

Heinrich Heine: Paradox and Poet: the Life.   1937.
          B.R.D.   3+, 1− Harcourt. $3.75.   119

"Louis Untermeyer has done a definitive piece of work."—Percy Hutchison, in *New York Times.*

"Written with understanding and sympathy, the result of a lifetime of study."—*Book Review Digest.*

"The biography exhibits critical insight and felicity of phrase. . . . It embodies the result of sound historical research which has brought into the picture some new factual material in regard to Heine's irregular and unquiet life."—*Christian Century.*

Vagts, Mrs. A. *See* Beard, Miriam

Valtin, Jan (pseudonym of Richard Julius Herman Krebs)   1905 (or 1904)-

Born at Darmstadt (or near Mainz), Germany. His youth was spent mostly in foreign lands. He returned to Germany in 1923, became a Communist "activist" and traveled over the world for three years as a mischief-maker. Three more years were then spent reading and studying in San Quentin Prison, California, to which he was sentenced for slugging. He was back again in Germany between 1929 and 1933 working for the Comintern. In the latter year he was captured by the Gestapo and spent four years in Nazi prison camps. The Comintern then ordered him to pretend to work for the Gestapo. He did so and was sent to spy in Russia. The Ogpu, having lost faith in him, he fled back to Germany and was soon arrested again by the Gestapo. Finally he escaped to America, its editors and publishers.

OUT OF THE NIGHT. 1941. B.R.D. 13+, 0– Alliance. $3.50.   **100**

Narrative describes the author's adventures in the underground conflict of Gestapo and Ogpu.

"You will be the wiser for the reading, but you will not be happier."—*Survey Graphic*.

"I believe his story to be, in the main, true, and as pitiful a confession as these tragic years have produced." —Vincent Sheean, in *Books*.

"There is no better picture of the life of a secret agent flitting about the Communist underworld of the twenties."— *Manchester Guardian*.

" 'Jan Valtin' is certainly one of the finest story tellers I have ever encountered, and I must confess that his book cost me many hours of sleep."—R. A. Reinhold, in *Commonweal*.

"Not only a unique study of Communist psychology, but an important documentary account of the inner workings of the Comintern and of its activities all over the globe."— Frieda Utley, in *Saturday Review of Literature*.

"Valtin's story casts a flood of light on the international underworld that has grown up in the shadow of the totalitarian dictatorships."—W. H. Chamberlin, in *New York Times*.

"Its sincerity is manifested by the utter cynicism with which the author acknowledges his crimes, and by the tone in which he tells, without shame and without pride, of the various frauds, falsifications and even assassinations which were everyday routine in his trade."—*Current History.*

"This vicarious experience of Communists and Fascists gained at expense of another man can be of great usefulness to the reader [who leans toward totalitarianism]."—*Yale Review.*

"No one has told in such circumstantial detail the story of the Communist agitators in foreign lands; and it is a story that is immensely worth telling."—John Chamberlin, in *Atlantic.*

"Before you start to read it you had better plan to take three days off. Its suspense is such that you will not be good for anything else until you have turned the last page. And then you will need time to think and to remember."—*Nation.*

Vance, Ethel (pseudonym of Mrs. Grace Zaring Stone) 1896-

Born in New York City and educated in convents and by foreign travel, Mrs. Stone, who by the way is a great-granddaughter of Robert Owen, wrote under a pseudonym to protect a married daughter then living in Axis territory.

ESCAPE. 1939. B.R.D. 6+, 2- Little. $2.50.   180
The escape was from imprisonment by the Nazis.

"An exciting, fast-moving story that most readers won't believe and won't think any the less of for that."—*New Republic.*

"The thrills of the story are managed with triumphant skill. They provide reading of the kind fairly described as breathless; the latter half of the book is best gulped at a sitting. But Miss Vance offers more than that. The play of character and motive through all the collisions of love and loyalty which she devises is deeply revealing of the emotional tension of life in Nazi Germany."—*Times* (London) *Literary Supplement.*

Van Doren, Carl   1885-

American editor-critic. Brother of Mark Van Doren. Born in Hope, Illinois; educated at the University of Illinois, at Columbia, and by foreign travel with Stuart P. Sherman. He taught English at Columbia from 1911 to 1930. In 1916 he became headmaster of the Brearley School. From 1919 to 1925 he engaged in editorial work for the *Nation* and the *Century Magazine*. The following year he helped to found and became editor-in-chief of the Literary Guild of America, continuing in this position till 1934. He is the author of a dozen books and has edited probably as many more.

BENJAMIN FRANKLIN. 1938. B.R.D. 10+, 3– Viking.
$3.75.   **424**

"A review of Mr. Van Doren's *Benjamin Franklin* can be nothing short of a eulogy. The greatest American has found a biographer worthy of him."—*Nation*.

"The most comprehensive and the most intelligently sympathetic biography of Franklin that we have."—H. S. Commager, in *New York Times*.

"There are many reasons for welcoming Mr. Van Doren's distinguished life of Benjamin Franklin. In style and arrangement it is a biography in the best classic traditions of that art."—Burton J. Hendrick, in *Atlantic*.

MUTINY IN JANUARY; the Story of a Crisis in the Continental Army Now for the First Time Fully Told from Many Hitherto Unknown or Neglected Sources, Both American and British. 1943. B.R.D. 4+, 0– Viking. $3.50.   **100**

Several regiments of the Pennsylvania Line were involved, in the winter of 1780-81.

"Mr. Van Doren has a good story to tell, and he tells it with many new facts and sustained narrative verve."—Allan Nevins, in *Saturday Review of Literature*.

"It is a definite if miniature contribution to our understanding of the perils and difficulties that attended the birth of the republic."—*New Yorker*.

"Historians . . . will gratefully recognize the complete reliability of this dispassionate and well-balanced production by one of America's foremost literary masters."—*American Historical Review.*

SECRET HISTORY OF THE AMERICAN REVOLUTION; an Account of the Conspiracies of Benedict Arnold and Numerous Others, Drawn from the Secret Service Papers of the British Headquarters in North America, Now for the First Time Examined and Made Public. 1941. B.R.D. 11+, 1– Viking. $3.75.
240

973.3
V245

Based chiefly on the Clinton MS. papers in the Clement Library at the University of Michigan.

"No one will attempt to justify Arnold ever again."—*Commonweal.*

"A piece of scholarship, solid and austere."—Albert Guérard, in *Nation.*

"This is first-hand history, not smart popularization."—*New Yorker.*

"A most valuable contribution to the history of the Revolution, and a most interesting narrative, scholarly, thorough, and admirably written."—Allan Nevins, in *Books.*

"Thanks to Van Doren's skillful handling, his history is no less readable, as well as far more satisfying, than the brilliant but mainly undocumented writings of Trevelyan." —B. Knollenberg, in *New Republic.*

THREE WORLDS. 1936. B.R.D. 10+, 3– Harper. $3.
136

818.5
V24

Autobiography of the schoolboy, college professor, critic; in the prewar, postwar and depression periods.

"As a rich cross-section of our literary life, and as a cheerful and revealing record of a strongly affirmative mind, *Three Worlds* should be read by every student of our times."—*Catholic World.*

"It is a pleasure, in these days of autobiographical tear-squeezing, to discover an author who had a grand time as a boy, and plenty to eat, and no Freudian hallucinations, and a father who made a good living and was his own boss."—H. L. Mencken, in *Nation*.

Van Doren, Mark   1894-

Poet and critic. Younger brother of Carl Van Doren. Born at Hope, Illinois, he was educated at the University of Illinois and at Columbia, and served two years in the infantry in World War I. He has taught English at Columbia since 1920, and is the author of about twenty-five books and editor of half as many more. Member, National Institute of Arts and Letters.

COLLECTED POEMS, 1922-38. 1939. B.R.D. 4+, 1– Holt. $3.50.   **161**

In this book, which won the Pulitzer Prize for poetry in 1940, the author has collected all but forty-five of the poems which have appeared in the six volumes of his poetry already published, as well as twenty-one new poems.

"Mr. Van Doren is modest in the best sense—modest in his intelligence. . . . He is an unaffected lover of the countryside. . . . And he has a remarkable command of form in his verse."—W. R. Benét, in *Saturday Review of Literature*.

"The subject matter is almost always the American scene in one way or another—landscape and climate, animals and people, incidents and legends and faiths. . . . As a poet representing his nation and time Mr. Van Doren holds a most considerable position."—*Books*.

LIRERAL EDUCATION. 1943. B.R.D. 7+, 0– Holt. $2.50. **176**

Written at the request of the Association of American Colleges and with the assistance of the Carnegie Corporation.

"His meditations upon liberal education are in effect an interpretation of the theory and practice of teaching as it now goes on at St. John's College. And so suitable is his style to his theme that he has done more than explain what liberal education is. He has also exemplified it."—Alexander Meiklejohn, in *New Republic*.

"If Mark Van Doren's *Liberal Education* is not widely read, that is because Mr. Van Doren's judgment of us is correct—that we have not yet learned what a true liberal education must necessarily be and are too slovenly and lackadaisical to find out."—Clifton Fadiman, in *New Yorker*.

Van Loon, Hendrik Willem   1882-1944

American author. Born in Rotterdam, Holland; came to America in 1903; educated at Cornell, Harvard, Munich; lectured on history and art in many American universities and served as war correspondent in Russia (1906) and (1916-18) in England, France, Italy, Switzerland, Holland, Norway, Sweden and Denmark. He spoke and wrote ten languages. He was a member of the National Institute of Arts and Letters.

THE ARTS. 1937. B.R.D. 8+, 1— Simon. $3.95. **144**

709
V26

Illustrated with two hundred drawings by the author whose subject matter in this book includes all the arts from the cave dweller to the Renaissance.

"It must be a rare reader who does not catch something of the author's enthusiasm for his subject."—*Springfield Republican*.

"Any reader of this book will have absorbed the fundamentals concerning the intention of art throughout the ages, and the place of the artist in human history."—W. R. Benét and others, in *Saturday Review of Literature*.

"Mr. Van Loon has produced a book which stimulates thought, suggests new and striking points of view, and makes one rather proud of being one of our peculiar race of featherless, furless bipeds. . . . The book, one would say, ought to have a wide following. Its attitudes and judgments can certainly be questioned in many places, but they are nowhere arbitrarily expressed."—R. L. Duffus, in *New York Times*.

VAN LOON'S LIVES. 1942. B.R.D. 8+, 2– Simon. $3.95.
105

Witty essays about forty historical personages from Confucius to Jefferson and from Queen Elizabeth to Emily Dickinson, who are entertained in small groups at Saturday night dinner.

Why the title? Well, there's Plutarch for precedent.

"Not so much a book as a biographical-historical-philosophical-literary vaudeville entertainment."—Wilson Follett, in *Atlantic*.

"It is little wonder that this volume leaped overnight into the best seller group. The author's rollicking humor lightens most of the pages he writes, and in this volume his humor is at its best."—*Churchman*.

"The object here is not to be erudite and unbiased, but entertaining and alive—and in being that, to sound the humanist's clarion call again in this present inhuman world. This object, with enormous gusto, *Van Loon's Lives* achieves. It is a considerable achievement. And good fun."—*New York Times*.

Van Paassen, Pierre   1895-

Born in Gorcum, Holland, and educated at Victoria College, Toronto, and L'École des Hautes Études, Paris. He came to Canada in 1911 and served in France with the Canadians in World War I. After the Armistice he became a journalist and eventually a foreign correspondent. He is an ardent Gentile Zionist and anti-Fascist.

DAYS OF OUR YEARS. 1939. B.R.D. 7+, 3– Hillman-Curl. $3.50.
142

An autobiography. Spiritual and intellectual adventures in France, Germany, Morocco, Syria, Palestine, Ethiopia and Spain.

"Ten years ago, or perhaps even five, a writer who suggested that Christianity could again become a militant political force would not have been listened to. The German Führer has revived that hope."—J. B. Phillips, in *Books*.

"He is 'more often led by the heart's inclinations than by cold logic.' But the heart's inclinations have their place in human life, and Mr. Van Paassen has his place as a humanistic observer of an often inhuman world."—R. L. Duffus, in *New York Times*.

"It is the special quality of this book that beneath all its complex unraveling of politics and social forces, . . . one feels what one can only call a spiritual base."—*New Yorker*.

Villard, Oswald Garrison   1872-

Born in Wiesbaden, Germany, and educated at Harvard. He worked on his father's New York *Evening Post*, 1897-1918, and then on the *Nation* till 1935. The grandson of William Lloyd Garrison and son of Henry Villard, he followed always the downright liberal faith of his fathers.

FIGHTING YEARS; MEMOIRS OF A LIBERAL EDITOR.   1939.
B.R.D.   10+, 0-   Harcourt. $3.75.   104

The years covered were the first four decades of the twentieth century.

"A monument of the best in both the American and the German traditions of liberalism."—*Christian Science Monitor*.

"The most exciting chapters by far deal with the war [World War I] and the peace negotiations."—*Boston Transcript*.

"He has no hesitation in saying what he thinks about the great men and events which fill his pages."—Walter Millis, in *Books*.

"A human document through which one may accurately interpret the advanced liberal attitude of the last forty years."—C. G. Bowers, in *New York Times*.

"No one who was in the thick of events during the days of McKinley, the first Roosevelt, Taft, Wilson, Harding, Coolidge and Hoover, has written a braver, finer story about them."—W. A. White, in *New Yorker*.

Wallace, Henry A.   1888-

Born Adair County, Iowa; educated at Iowa State College; associate editor and editor, *Wallace's Farmer*, 1910-29; editor, *Iowa Homestead and Wallace's Farmer* (merged), 1929-33. U.S. Secretary of Agriculture, 1933-40; Vice President, 1941-45; Secretary of Commerce, 1945-46; Presidential candidate of a third party, 1948. His European speeches in 1947 criticising American foreign policy provoked outspoken censure at home. Author of several books in the social science field, and editor of *New Republic*, 1946- .

330.973
W18s

SIXTY MILLION JOBS. 1945. B.R.D. 4+, 1– Simon. $2.   120

Without the artificial stimuli Wallace recommends in this book the United States is already (1947) approaching his goal of *Sixty Million Jobs*.

"A clear, fine book."—Stuart Chase, in *Nation*.

"It contains an immense amount of accurate and highly significant information. . . . To read it is an education in applied economics."—A. H. Hansen, in *New Republic*.

Waller, Willard Walter   1899-

Born at Murphysboro, Illinois, and educated at the University of Illinois, University of Chicago and University of Pennsylvania. Since 1926 he has taught sociology at the Universities of Pennsylvania and Nebraska, the State College of Pennsylvania, at Barnard and Columbia.

355.115
W19v

THE VETERAN COMES BACK. 1944. B.R.D. 6+, 2– Dryden. $2.75.   104

"For the general public, for all who would understand the strange ways war can change men. *Veteran Comes Back* is a 'must'—a plea, a program, a permanent reminder."—*Catholic World*.

Waln, Nora (Mrs. G. E. Osland-Hill)   1895-

American author. Born, Grampian Hills, Pennsylvania; educated at home and at Swarthmore College. A member of the Society of Friends, she was publicity director of the Near East Relief, 1917-19. Many of her Quaker ancestors were in the China trade. This led to her residence and special interest in that country. In 1934 she went to Germany with her husband where he studied music. Four years later they left Germany and returned to their home in Buckinghamshire, England.

REACHING FOR THE STARS. 1939. B.R.D. 5+, 1- Little.   *914.3*
    $3.   114   *W21*

Life in Germany under the Nazis, 1934-38, by an eyewitness who conscientiously attempts tolerance and objectivity. All three copies of this book's manuscript, though mailed from Germany separately, were "lost"; so the book had to be re-written.

"The essence of four years of observation as a resident of Nazi Germany. . . . Portrays the impact of totalitarianism on the German people."—*Saturday Review of Literature.*

"Dear Mrs. Waln, you have seen frightful things, and you are honest enough not to deny it; but often you wipe out the impression you have created by speaking in the next breath of the sunshine or the flowers or the 'transitoriness of human errors.' These errors, these inhuman errors, of the rulers of Germany have not been transitory, and the mildness with which you judge them without ever really condemning them will do little to banish them."— Erika Mann, in *Nation.*

Walsh, Mrs. R. J. *See* **Buck, Pearl S.**

Wecter, Dixon   1906-

Born in Houston, Texas, and educated at Baylor University, Yale, and as a Rhodes Scholar at Oxford. He taught English for many years, beginning in 1930, at the

Universities of Texas, Denver, Colorado and California. A Guggenheim Fellow, 1942-43, he became in 1939 a fellow and associate in residence at the Huntington Library, Pasadena.

WHEN JOHNNY COMES MARCHING HOME. 1944. B.R.D
    7+, 1– Houghton. $3.   **173**

"Study of the return of the American soldiers from three wars; the Revolution, the Civil War and the first World War, with some consideration of the problems of demobilization [after World War II]."—*Book Review Digest.*

"The most interesting pages are the lengthy quotations from Civil War letters and diaries. . . . It devotes far more space to the veterans of the three earlier wars . . . than it does to G. I. Joe."—*New Republic.*

"A distinguished, timely book . . . and, though absorbing reading, it is not in the least frivolous or superficial."— B. DeVoto, in *Weekly Book Review.*

Welles, Sumner   1892-

Born in New York City and educated at Groton and Harvard. American diplomat and State Department official specializing in Central and South American affairs; twice Assistant Secretary of State; Under Secretary of State, 1937-43. Accompanied President Roosevelt at his conference with Churchill at sea in August 1941, when the Atlantic Charter was formulated.

909.82
W44i

(ed) INTELLIGENT AMERICAN'S GUIDE TO THE PEACE. 1945.
    B.R.D. 5+, 2– Dryden. $3.75.   **108**

"A brief picture of every independent nation and of every major dependent people in the world."—Introduction.

"Written in compact, fact-filled, textbook style."—*Annals American Academy.*

"This reviewer marvels at the accuracy, conciseness and balanced statement of facts."—*Survey Graphic.*

"A good and surprisingly honest book for a democracy to be able to produce in the middle of a war. For it is no blueprint of any specifically American plan for peace."—*Weekly Book Review.*

"A reference book . . . to be turned to for an outline account of such countries and peoples as happen to come into the morning's headlines. . . . The notes . . . on 'the stakes in the peace' possessed by each country are . . . an excellent additional feature."—Norman Angell, in *Saturday Review of Literature.*

TIME FOR DECISION. 1944. B.R.D. 13+, 3– Harper. $3.   472

327. 73 W44t

Discussion of recent American foreign policy and the author's plan for the coming peace which involves world organization based on regional systems.

"Written by one of the best informed men of our time on the interrelations of governments."—*New York Times.*

"Unquestionably one of the more important books of the day. . . . Though it cannot be described as indiscreet this book abounds in hitherto unpublished information."—*Foreign Affairs.*

"A book which is not merely a best seller but by far the most important work on American foreign policy in the last twenty-five years, and by far the most far-sighted plan for the post-war world that has emerged from World War II."—*New Statesman.*

Werfel, Franz   1890-1945

Austro-Czech-Jewish poet, novelist, dramatist. Born in Prague. Educated at the University of Prague, he studied also at Leipzig and Hamburg. He was teaching at the University of Leipzig when World War I called him to service on the Russian front, 1915-17. Between the wars he lived in busy retirement in Vienna until he fled from the Nazis to the United States in 1940, visiting Lourdes on the way.

F
W488s

Song of Bernadette; translated by Ludwig Lewisohn.
     1942. B.R.D. 10+, 1– Viking. $3.   242

During the harrassed author's visit to Lourdes, as a
refugee, he vowed reverently to write this novel as his
declaration even in this inhuman era of "the divine mystery
and holiness of man."

"*The Song of Bernadette* is calculated to do an immense
amount of good."—*Catholic World*.

"*The Song of Bernadette* enchants us with the magic
of children's voices, raised in a mediaeval hymn."—*Saturday Review of Literature*.

"Instead of arguing . . . Franz Werfel has reconstructed
the whole scene with such wonderful art that it seems to
me impossible for anybody to read his book without being
completely convinced of the reality of the series of appari-
tions of Our Lady seen by the fourteen-year-old girl in
1858."—Theodore Maynard, in *Commonweal*.

Wescott, Glenway   1901-

American novelist. Born in Kewaskum, Wisconsin, of
old American stock. Studied at the University of Chicago,
where he was president of the Poetry Society but left without taking his degree. He has lived much of his later life
in England, Germany and France. Like Sinclair Lewis
he is far from satisfied with his native Middle West. He
now lives on a farm in New Jersey.

Apartment in Athens. 1945. B.R.D. 11+, 4– Har-
     per. $2.50.   144

The English title of this novel, which deals with the
Nazi occupation of Greece in 1943, is *Household in Athens*.
It has been called the best novel of its year.

"It may be remembered twenty years hence, as the
finest book whose roots were in World War II."—A. C.
Spectorsky, in *Book Week*.

"It holds you spellbound, as you see into the hearts of
the Greeks in their effort to fathom the character of the
German. Their keen analysis of the mentality of the Ger-

mans may well be a message to all freedom-loving peoples."
—*Library Journal.*

"A work of honest, unembarrassed good literature. It is useful in the sense that no good work of art can ever be anything but useful, and timely because it can never come too early or too late."—K. A. Porter, in *Weekly Book Review.*

PILGRIM HAWK. 1940. B.R.D. 6+, 3– Harper. $1.50.
                                                        100

This somewhat enigmatic novelette dealing with love in a Paris suburb in the late twenties has been called "a brilliant *tour de force.*"

"Extremely interesting. A tightly bound little tale that has depths and flights far beyond the surface of the human entanglements it covers."—*Books.*

"In thought, pace and memory his odd little work stays close to the captive pilgrim hawk, which we see here as figure of allegory, catalyst or character in a tale."—*New York Times.*

West, Rebecca (pseudonym of Cecily (Fairfield) Andrews) (Mrs. Henry Maxwell Andrews) 1892-
Born in County Kerry, Eire, and educated at George Watson's Ladies' College, Edinburgh, and at a London dramatic academy, Miss West was for a time on the stage, acting as the heroine of Ibsen's "Rosmersholm," etc. Then came journalism, through which she entered upon her career as literary critic and political writer.

BLACK LAMB AND GREY FALCON; A JOURNEY THROUGH JUGOSLAVIA. 2 vols. 1941. B.R.D. 5+, 3– Viking. $7.50.   **370**
The author devoted five years to the writing of this philosophic travel book which fills twelve hundred pages. It has been hailed as its year's "finest book of non-fiction" and even as "one of the great books of a troubled century."

"That it is Miss West's *magnum opus* goes without saying, but I am almost as sure that, of its sort, it is also one of the great books of our time."—Clifton Fadiman, in *New Yorker*.

"It is not only the magnification and intensification of the travel book form, but, I may say, its apotheosis."—*New York Times*.

"It is an analysis of our culture, the world of ideas and emotions in which we live. It is the story of our present sickness and an examination of the futures our past has stored up for us."—*Books*.

Weston, Christine (Goutière)   1904-

Born in Unao, India, in which country she was educated and married, her father being an officer of the Imperial Indian Police. She came to the United States in 1923, was naturalized in 1928 and now lives in Maine. She was a Guggenheim Fellow in 1940.

INDIGO. 1943. B.R.D. 6+, 2– Scribner. $2.50.   121

This novel chiefly concerns the relations between educated Hindus and Europeans in India.

"It is hard, offhand, to think of any Indian novel, except perhaps *A Passage to India* that has so authentic a feeling for the country. This sense of veracity, added to a sound literary style, ought to have made the book more interesting than it is."—Clifton Fadiman, in *New Yorker*.

"One of the best novels ever written about India and one of the finest novels I have read for years in any language. . . . For me at least every word of it is passionately absorbing. If anyone wants to find out about India, I can recommend *Indigo*."—Louis Bromfield, in *Books*.

White, Elwyn Brooks   1899-

American humorist and poet. Born at Mount Vernon, New York, and educated at Cornell. He served as private in World War I and thereafter became a journalist. For eleven years he wrote most of the "Talk of the Town" copy in the *New Yorker* and married its literary editor, Katharine Sergeant Angell. They are now living in retirement in the country.

ONE MAN'S MEAT. 1942. B.R.D. 7+, 1– Harper. $2.50.   **168**

Forty-five quiet, intelligent, amusing essays written from the country. An enlarged edition with ten new essays was published in 1944.

"Rage in print is one of the finest things a man can write—doesn't Mr. White ever get mad?"—Edward Weeks, in *Atlantic*.

"They are extraordinarily fresh and permanent pieces, and they turn out to be pieces of a whole. . . . They reveal facets of one man's spirit."—Irwin Edman, in *Books*.

"The viewpoint is straight E. B. White throughout—and to the readers of the *New Yorker* and *Harper's Magazine* this recommendation is all the bush needed to set off the volume's heady wine."—*Catholic World*.

White, Elwyn Brooks, and White, Katharine Sergeant Angell, editors

SUB-TREASURY OF AMERICAN HUMOR. 1941. B.R.D. 7+, 1– Coward-McCann. $3.   **160**

Eight hundred and fourteen pages of funny pieces from Benjamin Franklin to F.P.A.

"A sure source of pleasant reading to any one with a little time to spare."—*Catholic World*.

"The best assortment of laughable Americana I have ever seen."—Edward Weeks, in *Atlantic*.

"It does not seem to matter much to what Mr. E. B. White sets his hand. It's bound to be good. And this goes for his delightful anthology. His whole remarkable equipment of common sense and uncommon fancy has gone into the preparation of a charming book."—Leonard Brown, in *Saturday Review of Literature*.

White, M. B. *See* **Caldwell, E. jt. auth.**

White, Newman Ivey   1892-

Born at Statesville, North Carolina, and educated at Trinity College (now Duke University) and Harvard. He has taught English at various schools since 1915; at Duke University since 1919.

821.7
S545W

SHELLEY. 2 vol. 1940. B.R.D. 3+, 0– Knopf. $12.50.
130

After twenty years of study the author has produced this life which has been generally recognized as the definitive one.

"A monumental work which will endure as long as the poet's fame—and that is deathless. It is an achievement for American criticism to acclaim, and American scholarship to be proud of."—Frances Winwar, in *New York Times*.

"There have been a few occasions . . . when I have finished a new book with a strong feeling that what I had read was a genuine contribution to literature, a book I intended to keep and to reread and to introduce to other readers. This is how I feel about Mr. White's *Shelley*."
—Richard Aldington, in *Saturday Review of Literature*.

White, William Allen   1868-1944

American publicist and author. Member, National Institute of Arts and Letters. Born in Emporia, Kansas, where he became the editor of the most famous small-town newspaper in the United States. Educated at the College of Emporia and the University of Kansas. His editorial on the Populists, "What's the Matter with Kansas?" first brought him into national prominence. He was a leader in Theodore Roosevelt's Progressive Party and was much in Europe during and after World War I. Before the United States entered World War II he founded and was the first chairman of the Committee to Defend America by Aiding the Allies. He was never able to take much interest in making money, yet was by no means a poor man when he died.

A PURITAN IN BABYLON; THE STORY OF CALVIN COOLIDGE. 1938. B.R.D. 9+, 0– Macmillan. $3.50.   207

973.915
C77w

"The gist of the story is that Mr. Coolidge was a 'museum piece' who survived into an age with which in the end he was not competent to deal."—*New York Times.*

"The richest and most engrossing story we have had yet of the prosperous, gilded and 'Babylonian' years which made up the decade of the twenties."—M. Josephson, in *New Republic.*

"His skill in putting down one little word after another is approached by few serious writers today. Where others merely see White perceives; where others curl up and get comfortable in their prejudices, White makes an honest effort to keep his balance, and invariably does."—Norman Cousins, in *Current History.*

"This is the first time, as a reviewer, I have had to park my hammer and axe. I can find nothing about the book to knock. ... I like it. ... I'm glad that I read it. I enjoyed it better than any biography that I've read published during the past quarter-century."—J. F. Dineen, in *Saturday Review of Literature.*

White, William Lindsay   1900-

Son of William Allen White. Born at Emporia, Kansas; educated at the University of Kansas and Harvard. After college came journalism, with work on the *Emporia Gazette* and other papers. He was a war correspondent in World War II, 1939-41, and became a roving editor of the *Reader's Digest* in 1942. He is a frequent contributor to leading magazines and the author of six books.

THEY WERE EXPENDABLE. 1942. B.R.D. 7+, 0– Harcourt. $2.   315

The true story of an American squadron of motor boats in the Philippine campaign in World War II. It was told to the author by four of the squadron's young officers. Often spoken of as "the non-fiction book of its year," it was labeled "imperative" by the Council of Books in War-time.

"A short, grim, glorious book."—*New Yorker*.

"A really thrilling story of heroic achievement by Americans in this war."—*New Republic*.

"Mr. White has done a really extraordinary job in writing this book; it will stand up in the ranks of literature for a long time."—*Books*.

"A tale of gallantry, hardship, action, ingenuity. Simply and carefully told, it ranks with the great tales of war. These were the men and this what they did."—S. V. Benét, in *Saturday Review of Literature*.

Wilder, Thornton   1897-

American novelist and playwright. Member, National Institute of Arts and Letters. Born in Madison, Wisconsin, he is the son of an editor, the brother of a poet, the grandson of a Presbyterian minister. His boyhood was spent in China. He studied at Oberlin College, Yale, Princeton and the American Academy at Rome, and taught seven years at Lawrenceville School, and later at the University of Chicago. Served in Coast Artillery in 1918, and in the U. S. Air Corps Intelligence Service, 1942-44.

OUR TOWN; A PLAY. 1938. B.R.D. 4+, 1– Coward-McCann. $2.   117

The Pulitzer Prize play of 1938.

"An exceedingly well-written play. . . . Gives the atmosphere of a small New England town with knowledge and sympathetic fidelity."—*Commonweal*.

"When the reader has finished it . . . he will feel a stirring in his imagination, a stirring like the beating of ethereal wings lifting his spirit to those upper regions where men have fellowship with the Eternal."—Fred Eastman, in *Christian Century*.

Willison, George Findlay   1896-

Born in Denver; educated at the University of Colorado (where he graduated *magna cum laude*), at Oxford as a Rhodes Scholar, and at the University of Paris. After enlisting in a machine-gun corps in World War I he attained a commission before being discharged. His army service was followed by some years of study and travel. He returned to the United States in 1925 and taught at St. John's College, Annapolis, and Hessian Hills School, Croton, New York, 1928-35. He joined the Federal Writers' Project in 1936, where he became editor-in-chief of the American Guide Series.

SAINTS AND STRANGERS. 1945. B.R.D. 12+, 2– Reynal.
    $3.75.   **168**

A history of the Pilgrims, beginning with the youth of William Brewster in Scrooby, Nottinghamshire, England, in the late 1500's, and ending a hundred years later with the absorption of the Plymouth Colony into Massachusetts.

"No one since Bradford has done the job so well."—*New Republic*.

"It was the Victorians who rescued the Pilgrims from obscurity and who named them, and now comes Mr. Willison to rescue them from the Victorians."—Esther Forbes, in *New York Times*.

"A straightforward and readable account of the Pilgrims, thoroughly documented and quoting largely from original sources, it represents the Founding Fathers as the determined, vigorous, human men they must have been."—*U. S. Quarterly Booklist*.

Willkie, Wendell Lewis   1892-1944

Lawyer and statesman. Born in Elwood, Indiana, and educated at Indiana University and Oberlin College. He volunteered for World War I the day war was declared and served as first lieutenant and captain. He was the Republican nominee for President in 1940.

940.5
P92

ONE WORLD. 1943. B.R.D. 11+, 0− Simon. $2. Paper
    edition, $1.   253

Of this book, based on the radio talks which followed
his forty-nine-day world tour in 1942, more than three million copies have been sold.

"Mr. Willkie is a keen observer, and some of his most
casual reflections on men and events betray a remarkable
grasp of the essential realities. . . . His estimates of
both personalities and social forces strike one as true."—
Reinhold Niebuhr, in *Nation*.

"*One World* will be widely read both in this country
and abroad. Its basic emphasis upon the nearness and inter-
dependence of the peoples of all countries, the importance
of strengthening the ties between the United Nations now,
and the need of following through in a definite, continuing
United Nations organization for peace, justice and progress,
is right."—H. E. Stassen, in *New York Times*.

Wilson, Edmund   1895-

Literary and social critic and novelist. Born in Red
Bank, New Jersey; educated at the Hill School, Pottstown,
Pennsylvania, and at Princeton. For eighteen months during World War I he served in France with a hospital unit.
He was a reporter on the New York *Sun*, 1916-17; managing editor, *Vanity Fair*, 1920-21; and associate editor, *New
Republic*, 1926-31. Formerly an avowed Communist, he
rendered a favorable report in 1936 on what he had seen
in Russia. Not long thereafter, however, he became dis-
illusioned with the Soviets. Since 1944 he has been literary
editor of the *New Yorker*.

TO THE FINLAND STATION; STUDY IN THE WRITING AND
    ACTING OF HISTORY. 1940. B.R.D. 6+, 4− Har-
    court. $4.   170

A discussion of radicals and radical thought from the
French Revolution to Bolshevism. Includes excellent character studies, especially of Marx, Engels, Lenin and Trotsky.

"As brilliant and muddled a book as one may meet."—
Lewis Gannett, in *Boston Transcript*.

"The most discerning guide to the faith and vision of
communism that we have."—Louis Hacker, in *Saturday
Review of Literature*.

"There emerges from the story of communism a stern
verdict upon those who, beginning with slogans of liberation, have ended by constructing new instruments of en-
slavement."—*Christian Century*.

WOUND AND THE BOW; SEVEN STUDIES IN LITERATURE.
1941. B.R.D. 9+, 4– Houghton. $3.   **120**

Critical essays and amateur psychiatries of Sophocles,
Dickens, Kipling, Casanova, Wharton, Hemingway and
Joyce.

"Mr. Wilson is about the best literary critic now at work
in our country, and this is one of his most penetrating
books."—*New Yorker*.

"These essays are by far the most interesting criticism
of the year. They combine exact information and scholarship with shrewd and searching penetration into the personal life of the artist."—*New York Times*.

"It is only when Mr. Wilson lapses into the petulant
dogmatism which has lately appeared in his work, where he
becomes merely assertive, as in the Hemingway essay, that
he shocks us into an awareness of his limitations."—Alfred
Kazin, in *Books*.

Wilson, Forrest   1883-1942

Journalist, historian, novelist, playwright, biographer.
Born in Warren, Ohio, he studied at Cambridge University
and served, 1918-20, in Chemical Warfare.

CRUSADER IN CRINOLINE; THE LIFE OF HARRIET BEECHER
STOWE. 1941. B.R.D. 8+, 3– Lippincott. $4.50.
                                              170

This book won the Pulitzer Prize for biography in 1942.
The author died six days after receiving it. He believed

that Mrs. Stowe was, as Lincoln (perhaps) said, "the little woman who made a great war."

"Long, brilliant and well-documented life of Mrs. Stowe."—*Christian Science Monitor*.

"A fascinating book about a unique figure in American history."—*Boston Transcript*.

"Mr. Wilson has at least this in common with his heroine, that he can tell a story."—H. S. Commager, in *Saturday Review of Literature*.

"This reviewer, though not attracted by the subject, found himself compelled to admit that he had discovered the best biography of an American that he had ever read." —*Commonweal*.

Wolfe, Thomas   1900-1938

American novelist. Born, Asheville, North Carolina; educated at the University of North Carolina and Harvard; taught English at New York University, 1924-30; studied in Europe on Guggenheim Fellowship, 1930-31. For years Scribner's editor, Maxwell Perkins, wrestled valiantly with him and his manuscripts. Member, National Institute of Arts and Letters.

THE WEB AND THE ROCK. 1939. B.R.D. 7+, 7– Harper. $3.   123

Wolfe said of this story of a long, tempestuous love affair that it was the most objective novel he had written; yet its critics continued to complain of his lack of objectivity.

"A disappointment. . . . It leaves him still caught in the furious whirl of his own immediate reactions and emotions."—J. D. Adams, in *New York Times*.

"If *The Web and the Rock* had stopped at page 170, it would have been a far finer book."—Clifton Fadiman, in *New Yorker*.

"If *The Web and the Rock* had been published as two volumes it would be possible to say that the first half was

Wolfe's best novel, and the second half his most disappointing. . . . But in spite of everything Wolfe was a genius."
—*Saturday Review of Literature*.

"At once the best and the worst of Wolfe's novels. For some obscure reason he thought he could avoid the charge of excessive autobiography by changing Eugene Gant's name to George Webber. It is the same Gant career, however, and always the same Wolfe."—A. Kazin, in *Books*.

"From this current novel, one can only get the impression of a great oaf stumbling around the earth, trying to kid first himself, then the public that he was on a constant journey of miraculous discovery. . . . Like the curate's egg, however, *parts* of the book are excellent."—*Commonweal*.

You Can't Go Home Again. 1940. B.R.D. 6+, 4–
    Harper. $3   **200**

This last book of Wolfe's, a sequel to *The Web and the Rock*, is a story about the collapse of false values in the late 1920's and the half dozen years which followed.

Wolfe's novels, like *Leaves of Grass*, the Grand Canyon, and *Moby Dick*, are very American. All are impressive, wild and very large. All lack utterly the pleasing, civilized qualities of Greek art—moderation, balance, proportion.

"Had Wolfe lived he would have become the greatest of all American novelists. . . . This is the book of a man who had come to terms with himself, who was on the way to mastery of his art."—J. D. Adams, in *New York Times*.

"Wolfe had wonderful talents but no mastery of either himself or his materials. It would be gracious and pleasant to be able to say that in his last labor he was beginning to achieve this mastery, but it would, I fear, be untrue."—Clifton Fadiman, in *New Yorker*.

Wolfert, Ira   1908-

Journalist and war correspondent in World War II. Born in New York City and educated at the Columbia

School of Journalism, he is a contributor to leading magazines and the author of five books about World War II, one of which won the Pulitzer Prize.

TUCKER' PEOPLE. 1943. B.R.D. 7+, 3– L. B. Fischer. $3. **100**

Realistic first novel about New York's underworld—the Harlem "numbers" racket in the nerve-shattering days of the Great Depression.

"The book is depressing—but it is also convincing."—*Atlantic*.

"The faults, like the virtues of the book, are the result of generosity and eagerness. Like Dreiser, Wolfert can afford to write badly on occasion."—*New Republic*.

Woodward, William E. 1874-

American novelist, biographer, historian and publicist. Born, Ridge Spring, South Carolina; graduate, South Carolina Military Academy. After two years of journalism in Atlanta and New York, he went into the advertising business in New York. He was Vice President of the Industrial Finance Corporation, 1916-20. He turned to the writing of books in 1920. As a former advertising man he regrets that he invented the word *debunk*.

917.3
W91w

THE WAY OUR PEOPLE LIVED; AN INTIMATE AMERICAN HISTORY. 1944. B.R.D. 12+, 7– Dutton. $3.95. **104**

Contains eleven chapters—each a story-essay picturing a time, a place and a group of appropriate Americans—from Boston in 1640, to New York in 1908. There are thirty-two pages of illustrations.

"The basic idea is excellent—a portrait of the average American down the ages."—*Nation*.

"Social history in a form which is painless to the layman and at the same time inoffensive to the historian."—*New England Quarterly*.

"We now know why Grandma was happy, even without so many flavors of ice-cream."—*Book Week*.

Woolf, Virginia (Stephen)   1882-1941

English novelist. Born in London, a daughter of the noted scholar, Sir Leslie Stephen. She is closely related to so many other distinguished English men and women that James Russell Lowell, her father's friend, wrote at her birth,

> "I simply wish the child to be
> A sample of heredity."

She was reared in the academic atmosphere of her own home and attended no other university. Her novels are psychological and intellectual but like no others though she was much influenced by Joyce and Proust and Freud. Her books have little space for action. She is concerned with "reflections in the moving mirror of consciousness." She is "a metaphysical poet who has chosen prose fiction for her medium." Before the manuscript of *Between the Acts* was completely finished she drowned herself because she feared the recurrence of a mental breakdown. Some critics have pronounced her the foremost woman writer of her time.

BETWEEN THE ACTS. 1941. B.R.D. 7+, 2– Harcourt. $2.50.   130

England on a summer day. A county family, their guests and the villagers, who present a pageant.

"This short novel, by no means melancholy but often a humorously lively study of futility, was left by its author without final revision. . . . It has the beauty, the elating beauty, of the assured, matured Virginia Woolf."—*Manchester Guardian*.

"While all her novels are strange, there is no other so strange or so sad as this last puzzling vagary of her temperament that voyaged always alone. . . . Her call is to the heart. Her novels are neither narrative nor pictorial; they are more like cries, broken but never unmelodious."—Clifton Fadiman, in *New Yorker*.

DEATH OF THE MOTH, AND OTHER ESSAYS. 1942. B.R.D.
5+, 0− Harcourt. $3.   116

"The riches of the book are both overwhelming and
companionable."—*Christian Science Monitor*.

"Exquisitely written, if at times too rarified."—*New
Yorker*.

"There is poetry in every line of them, or anyhow in
every other line; and their beautiful quick perceptions are
thrown on objects that every one can recognize."—*Manchester Guardian*.

HAUNTED HOUSE, AND OTHER STORIES. 1944. B.R.D. 9+,
4− Harcourt. $2.   115

Eighteen short stories; five hitherto unpublished.

"The volume . . . holds the essence of her art. As in
her longer works, her writing has the rare quality of a
precious gem, alive with light and deep with shadows."—
Weekly Book Review.

"Trying always to match words to life, Mrs. Woolf
proved through the years that she could do almost anything
with words, and in these brief stories you will find her
skill."—*Saturday Review of Literature*.

"They show her brilliant fantasy, her subtle sense of
humor and, above all, her competent understanding of men
and women."—*New Statesman*.

THE YEARS. 1937. B.R.D. 11+, 2− Harcourt. $2.75.
153

This "novel" is a pattern of a half century of English
upper-middle-class life, 1880-1930.

"The writing throughout has a serene distinction; although there is little deliberate description of persons and
places the whole book seems to breathe the very essence of
English life; and, for any one whose tale in days coincides
with that of the Pargiters, the earlier chapters, more especially, must evoke an almost unbearable nostalgia."—Wilfred Gibson, in *Manchester Guardian*.

"That Mrs. Woolf has discovered no answer to her problem, either in herself or her characters, is not necessarily disconcerting. She does not know the answer to the riddle of the universe, and does not profess to know it. But she is able to clothe the riddle in a rare, poetic loveliness."
—*Springfield Republican.*

Wright, Richard   1908-

Born near Natchez, Mississippi. When he was five his father deserted his mother who was a country schoolteacher. His was an unhappy childhood, doing odd jobs for relatives and in asylums. He learned to read at fifteen and was for a time a post office clerk. He worked on the Federal Writers' Project (W.P.A.) in Chicago and New York, 1935-37. Having become a Communist he wrote for the *Daily Worker* and *New Masses.* He was a Guggenheim Fellow in 1939 and won the Spingarn Medal, 1940, "for achievement in the field of Negro interests."

BLACK BOY; A RECORD OF CHILDHOOD AND YOUTH. 1945.
    B.R.D. 15+, 4— Harper. $2.50.   **278**

This autobiography extends only to the point where the youth "heads north."

"Nowhere except in America could it have been written. Nowhere except in America could such a rebel thrive. But what made him a rebel should be on America's conscience."
—*Boston Globe.*

"Richard Wright, thirty-six, is generally accounted the most gifted living American Negro writer. His new book makes it clearer than ever that he has one of the most notable gifts in U. S. writing, black or white: a narrative style that is simple, direct, almost completely without pretense or decoration, yet never flat."—*Time.*

"If the book is meant to be a creative picture and a warning . . . it misses its possible effectiveness, because it is as a work of art so patently and terribly overdrawn."
W. E. B. DuBois, in *Weekly Book Review.*

NATIVE SON. 1940. B.R.D. 7+, 5– Harper. $2.50. **250**

Story of the violent life and death of a Chicago Negro boy.

"Certainly *Native Son* declares Richard Wright's importance, not merely as the best Negro writer, but as an American author as distinctive as any now writing."—P. M. Jack, in *New York Times*.

"*Native Son* is a shocker. It is brutal, frank, sordid. It is no book for adolescents or for squeamish adults. But this brutality is skillfully subordinated to a wider purpose."—*Commonweal*.

"Some will call it sentimental propaganda, but to me the scope and passionate sincerity of this book give it a grandeur, a moral importance, at least as great as that of *An American Tragedy*."—Rosamond Lehmann, in *Spectator*.

Ybarra, Thomas Russell   1880-

His father was a Venezuelan general, his mother a Bostonian. Born in Boston and educated at the Roxbury and Cambridge Latin Schools and Harvard. He spent his youth and adolescence partly in Caracas and partly in Boston. On leaving college he became a reporter on the *New York Times*. He was a foreign correspondent, 1924-39, and later a news commentator and lecturer.

YOUNG MAN OF CARACAS. 1941. B.R.D. 5+, 0– Washburn. $3.   **100**

"Here is a chapter of autobiography you could place on the same shelf with Clarence Day's *Life with Father*."—Elmer Davis, in the Introduction.

"Thomas Ybarra, in describing his affectionate and tempestuous household, has given us a memoir rich in anecdote and authentic in color—a passkey that will unlock Venezuela for many a Northerner."—Edward Weeks, in *Atlantic*.

"The book should do more to cement the Pan-American front than any congress or conference or any number of good-will ambassadors. Indeed, Mr. Ybarra is a living personification of that front."—*Books.*

Zinsser, Hans   1878-1940

American bacteriologist. Born, New York City; educated at Columbia. Served in New York hospitals, 1903-1910; taught bacteriology at Stanford, Columbia and Harvard after 1910, save for time devoted to medical assignments at home and abroad during World War I and thereafter. Member American Academy of Arts and Sciences.

As I Remember Him. 1940. B.R.D. 13+, 1– Little. $2.75.   **240**

Another of those autobiographies in which the bashful author makes a transparent pretense of writing about some other fellow. (Why do they do it?)

"Its anecdotes are rich with affection and the continual humor of a man who is never done with learning."—Muriel Rukeyser, in *New Republic.*

"There is mountain air in this book. It is months since I have read anything that gave me as much stimulation and delight."—Lewis Gannett, in *Boston Transcript.*

"A biography carried through to the exit curtain must necessarily have some seriousness. But this one does not become solemn at any time. It makes both life and death appear a part of the order of an orderly Nature."—R. L. Duffus, in *New York Times.*

Zweig, Stefan   1881-1942

German author. His works have been translated into several foreign languages. Born in Vienna, of Jewish parents. He studied philosophy at the University, but was largely educated by residence in the European capitals and by his travels in Asia, Africa and America. During World

War I his suppressed pacifism found discreet but effective expression in the drama, *Jeremiah*. He went to England in the early thirties to write *Marie Antoinette*, but stayed on because it was a free country. He made an extended lecture tour through the United States in 1938 and returned to settle here in 1940. The next year, however, he wandered on to Brazil, and in 1942 he perished there with his young wife in a suicide pact.

WORLD OF YESTERDAY; AN AUTOBIOGRAPHY. 1943. B.R.D.
    2+, 0– Viking. $3.   **100**

"The very success with which this book evokes both the beauty of the past and the futility of its passing is what gives it its tragic effectiveness. It is not so much the memory of a life as it is the memento of an age."—Irwin Edman, in *New Republic*.

CLASSIFIED LISTS

Nota Bene: In the headings of the tables which follow, the word *best* means *selected by a consensus of expert opinion as most worthy the attention of modern American readers with at least a high school background.*

THE TWENTY-FIVE BEST AUTHORS OF THE DECADE WITH THE AGGREGATE SCORES OF THEIR BOOKS

		No. of Books	Points
1.	Brooks	4	1711
2.	Steinbeck	4	1068
3.	Mencken	4	947
4.	Marquand	4	919
5.	Van Doren, C.	4	900
6.	Hemingway	2	815
7.	Sandburg	2	660
8.	Roberts, K.	3	633
9.	Santayana	4	624
10.	Gunther	3	604
11.	Koestler	4	585
12.	Freeman	1	583
13.	Huxley	5	583
14.	Welles	2	580
15.	Canby	2	575
16.	Beard	3	572
17.	Wright	2	528

MEMORANDA

Of these twenty-five leading authors only six appeared in the corresponding list for the previous decade: Hemingway, Sandburg, Freeman, Beard, Woolf and Lippmann. None of the twenty-five appeared in the corresponding list for 1901-1925.

Of the twenty-five favorite authors who wrote before 1901, two were women (George Eliot and Charlotte Brontë); of the twenty-five favorite writers, 1901-1925, three were women (Edith Wharton, Willa Cather, May Sinclair); of the twenty-five leaders, 1926-1935, no less than eight were women; of the twenty-five leaders, 1936-1945, only one (Virginia Woolf) was a woman.

Of the twenty-five leading authors before 1901, fourteen were chiefly fictionists; 1901-1925, nineteen were chiefly fictionists; 1926-1935, twelve were chiefly fictionists; 1936-1945, eight were chiefly fictionists.

Of the twenty-five favorite authors who wrote before 1901 only three were American; of the twenty-five favorites who wrote, 1901-1925, thirteen were American; of the twenty-five best authors, 1926-1935, twenty were American; of the twenty-five best writers, 1936-1945, twenty-two were American.

THE FIFTY BEST BOOKS, 1936-1945

				POINTS
1.	Hemingway	*For Whom the Bell Tolls*	1940	680
2.	Steinbeck	*Grapes of Wrath*	1939	589
3.	Freeman	*Lee's Lieutenants*	1942	583
4.	Brooks	*New England: Indian Summer*	1940	560
5.	Brooks	*Flowering of New England*	1936	510
6.	Sandburg	*Abraham Lincoln: the War Years*	1939	484
7.	Hersey	*Bell for Adano*	1944	472
8.	Welles	*Time for Decision*	1944	472
9.	Brooks	*World of Washington Irving*	1944	471
10.	Van Doren, C.	*Benjamin Franklin* ..	1938	424
11.	Schlesinger	*Age of Jackson*	1945	408
12.	Canby	*Thoreau*	1939	390
13.	Bowen, C. D.	*Yankee from Olympus*	1944	380
14.	Shirer	*Berlin Diary*	1941	380
15.	West	*Black Lamb and Grey Falcon*	1941	370
16.	Smith, L.	*Strange Fruit*	1944	368
17.	Leech	*Reveille in Washington*	1941	360
18.	Frost	*Collected Poems*	1939	335
19.	Mauldin	*Up Front*	1945	324
20.	Roberts, K.	*Northwest Passage*	1937	323
21.	White, W. L.	*They Were Expendable*	1942	315
22.	Mitchell	*Gone With the Wind*	1936	312
23.	Rawlings	*The Yearling*	1938	306
24.	Pyle	*Brave Men*	1944	299
25.	Smith, B.	*Tree Grows in Brooklyn* ..	1943	297
26.	Landon	*Anna and the King of Siam*	1944	288
27.	Porter, K. A.	*Leaning Tower*	1944	288
28.	Morison	*Admiral of the Ocean Sea*	1942	284
29.	Wright	*Black Boy*	1945	278
30.	Krutch	*Samuel Johnson*	1944	276
31.	Forbes	*Paul Revere*	1942	273
32.	Marquand	*Late George Apley*	1937	272

FIFTY BEST BOOKS—*Continued*

33. Lippmann   *United States Foreign
         Policy* 1943   264
34. Marquand   *So Little Time* 1943   264
35. Buchan   *Pilgrim's Way* 1940   260
36. Marquand   *H. M. Pulham, Esq.* 1941   260
37. Gunther   *Inside Europe* 1936   256
38. Brown, H. P.   *Walk in the Sun* 1944   253
39. Willkie   *One World* 1943   253
40. Lewis   *Cass Timberlane* 1945   252
41. Llewellyn   *How Green Was My Valley* 1940   250
42. Wright   *Native Son* 1940   250
43. Hitler   *Mein Kampf* 1939   247
44. St. Exupéry   *Wind, Sand and Stars* .. 1939   247
45. Steinbeck   *Of Mice and Men* 1937   246
46. Kazin   *On Native Grounds* 1942   242
47. Werfel   *Song of Bernadette* 1942   242
48. Heiser   *American Doctor's Odyssey* .. 1936   240
49. Van Doren C.   *Secret History of the
         American Revolution* 1941   240
50. Struther   *Mrs. Miniver* 1940   240

NOTE: In the corresponding list for 1901-25 thirty titles
were fiction; in 1926-35, there were twenty-one fiction titles;
in the list above there are eighteen fiction books. This is a
shrinkage of fiction from 60 per cent to 36 per cent. Similarly, there has been a corresponding shrinkage of books of
poetry from 16 per cent to 2 per cent, and of books by
non-Americans from 52 per cent to 12 per cent.

THE TWENTY BEST AMERICAN BOOKS

POINTS

1. Hemingway   *For Whom the Bell Tolls* 1940   680
2. Steinbeck   *Grapes of Wrath* 1939   589
3. Freeman   *Lee's Lieutenants* 1942-44   583
4. Brooks   *New England: Indian Sum-
         mer* 1940   560

5.	Brooks	*Flowering of New England* ..	1936	510
6.	Sandburg	*Abraham Lincoln: the War Years*	1939	484
7.	Hersey	*Bell for Adano*	1944	472
8.	Welles	*Time for Decision*	1944	472
9.	Brooks	*World of Washington Irving*	1944	471
10.	Van Doren, C.	*Benjamin Franklin* ..	1938	424
11.	Schlesinger	*Age of Jackson*	1945	408
12.	Canby	*Thoreau*	1939	390
13.	Bowen, C. D.	*Yankee from Olympus*	1944	380
14.	Shirer	*Berlin Diary*	1941	380
15.	Smith, L.	*Strange Fruit*	1944	368
16.	Leech	*Reveille in Washington*	1941	360
17.	Frost	*Collected Poems*	1939	335
18.	Mauldin	*Up Front*	1945	324
19.	Roberts, K.	*Northwest Passage*	1937	323
20.	White, W. L.	*They Were Expendable*	1942	315

NOTE: Of these titles only five are works of fiction. On the previous decade's corresponding list, eight were fiction; and on the similar list covering 1901-25, fourteen were fiction.

THE TWENTY BEST BRITISH[1] BOOKS

				POINTS
1.	West	*Black Lamb and Grey Falcon*	1941	370
2.	Buchan	*Pilgrim's Way*	1940	260
3.	Llewellyn	*How Green Was My Valley*	1940	250
4.	Struther	*Mrs. Miniver*	1940	240
5.	Hogben	*Mathematics for the Million*	1937	204
6.	Auden	*Collected Works*	1945	199
7.	Maugham	*Razor's Edge*	1944	173
8.	Pearson	*G. B. S.*	1942	168
9.	Marshall	*World, the Flesh and Father Smith*	1945	156

[1] *British* includes English, Irish, Welsh and Scottish.

TWENTY BEST BRITISH BOOKS—*Continued*

10.	Maugham	*Summing Up*	1938	153
11.	Woolf	*The Years*	1937	153
12.	Chesterton	*Autobiography*	1936	152
13.	Housman	*Collected Poems*	1940	150
14.	Churchill	*Blood, Sweat and Tears* ..	1941	150
15.	Brogan	*American Character*	1944	150
16.	Huxley, A.	*Ends and Means*	1937	144
17.	Hogben	*Science for the Citizen*	1938	135
18.	Joyce	*Finnegan's Wake*	1939	133
19.	Cecil	*Young Melbourne*	1939	133
20.	Bowen, E.	*Death of the Heart*	1939	133

THE TEN BEST FOREIGN BOOKS

POINTS

1.	Hitler	*Mein Kampf*	1939	247
2.	St. Exupéry	*Wind, Sand and Stars* ..	1939	247
3.	Werfel	*Song of Bernadette*	1942	242
4.	Curie	*Madame Curie*	1937	212
5.	Koestler	*Darkness at Noon*	1941	200
6.	Asch	*The Apostle*	1943	198
7.	Rauschning	*Revolution of Nihilism* ..	1939	190
8.	Simonov	*Days and Nights*	1945	190
9.	Romains	*Men of Good Will*	1933-45	190
10.	Curie	*Journey Among Warriors*	1943	187

THE TEN BEST NOVELS

POINTS

1.	Hemingway	*For Whom the Bell Tolls*	1940	680
2.	Steinbeck	*Grapes of Wrath*	1939	589
3.	Hersey	*Bell for Adano*	1944	472
4.	Smith, L.	*Strange Fruit*	1944	368
5.	Roberts, K.	*Northwest Passage*	1937	323

6.	Mitchell	*Gone With the Wind*	1936	312
7.	Rawlings	*The Yearling*	1938	306
8.	Smith, B.	*Tree Grows in Brooklyn* ..	1943	297
9.	Porter	*Leaning Tower*	1944	288
10.	Marquand	*Late George Apley*	1937	272

NOTE: All ten are by Americans; six were American in 1926-35; six were American also in 1901-25; none of the ten best novels before 1900 were by Americans.

THE BEST AMERICAN FICTION: FORTY TITLES

				POINTS
1.	Hemingway	*For Whom the Bell Tolls*	1940	680
2.	Steinbeck	*Grapes of Wrath*	1939	589
3.	Hersey	*Bell for Adano*	1944	472
4.	Smith, L.	*Strange Fruit*	1944	368
5.	Roberts, K.	*Northwest Passage*	1937	323
6.	Mitchell	*Gone With the Wind*	1936	312
7.	Rawlings	*The Yearling*	1938	306
8.	Smith, B.	*Tree Grows in Brooklyn* ..	1943	297
9.	Porter	*Leaning Tower*	1944	288
10.	Marquand	*Late George Apley*	1937	272
11.	Marquand	*So Little Time*	1943	264
12.	Marquand	*H. M. Pulham, Esq.*	1941	260
13.	Brown, H. P.	*Walk in the Sun*	1944	253
14.	Lewis	*Cass Timberlane*	1945	252
15.	Wright	*Native Son*	1940	250
16.	Steinbeck	*Of Mice and Men*	1937	246
17.	Glasgow	*In This Our Life*	1941	220
18.	Cather	*Sapphira and the Slave Girl* ..	1940	210
19.	Roberts, K.	*Oliver Wiswell*	1940	210
20.	Santayana	*Last Puritan*	1936	200
21.	Wolfe	*You Can't Go Home Again* ..	1940	200

THE BEST BRITISH FICTION

THE BEST FOREIGN FICTION

			POINTS
1. Werfel	*Song of Bernadette (German)*	1942	242
2. Koestler	*Darkness at Noon (German)*	1941	200
3. Asch	*Apostle (Yiddish)*	1943	198
4. Simonov	*Days and Nights (Russian)*	1945	190
5. Romains	*Men of Good Will (French)*		
	....	1933-45	190
6. Seghers	*Seventh Cross (German)* ..	1942	179
7. Koestler	*Arrival and Departure (German)*	1943	165
8. Asch	*The Nazarene (Yiddish)*	1939	152
9. Mann	*Joseph in Egypt (German)* ...	1938	144
10. Martin du Gard	*The Thibaults (French)*	1939	142

THE BEST BOOKS ON PHILOSOPHY, PSYCHOLOGY, ETHICS AND RELIGION

			POINTS
1. St. Exupéry	*Wind, Sand and Stars* ..	1939	247
2. Werfel	*Song of Bernadette (novel)*	1942	242
3. Asch	*The Apostle (novel)*	1943	198
4. Mumford	*Culture of Cities*	1938	180
5. Wilson, E.	*To the Finland Station* ..	1940	170
6. Koestler	*Arrival and Departure (novel)*	1943	165
7. Shepard	*Pedlar's Progress*	1937	153
8. Asch	*The Nazarene (novel)*	1939	152
9. Huxley	*Ends and Means*	1937	144
10. St. Exupéry	*Flight to Arras*	1942	137
11. Byrd	*Alone*	1938	135
12. Adler	*How to Read a Book*	1940	130

BEST BOOKS ON PHILOSOPHY, ETC.—*Continued*

13.	Lin Yu-tang *Importance of Living* ..	1937	119
14.	Chase, S. *Tyranny of Words*	1938	117
15.	Santayana *Realm of Truth*	1938	108
16.	Dewey *Freedom and Culture*	1939	100
17.	Fosdick *On Being a Real Person* ...	1943	100
18.	Huxley *After Many a Summer Dies the Swan (novel)*	1939	100

THE BEST SOCIAL SCIENCE BOOKS
(Political Science, Economics, Sociology, Education)

			POINTS
1.	Wright *Black Boy (autobiography)*	1945	278
2.	Lynd & Lynd *Middletown in Transition*	1937	238
3.	Holt *George Washington Carver* ...	1943	231
4.	Beard *The Republic*	1943	209
5.	Barzun *Teacher in America*	1945	204
6.	Mumford *Culture of Cities*	1938	180
7.	Van Doren, M. *Liberal Education* ..	1943	176
8.	Wecter *When Johnny Comes Marching Home*	1944	173
9.	Wilson, E. *To the Finland Station* ..	1940	170
10.	Childs *Sweden: the Middle Way* ...	1936	154
11.	Ottley *New World A-Coming*	1943	143
12.	Roosevelt *Public Papers and Addresses. 5 vols.*	1938	142
13.	Dos Passos *State of the Nation*	1944	138
14.	Agar *Time for Greatness*	1942	137
15.	Burnham *Managerial Revolution* ...	1941	130
16.	Chase, S. *Rich Land, Poor Land*	1936	128
17.	Harvard University *General Education in a Free Society*	1945	120
18.	McWilliams *Prejudice: Japanese-Americans*	1944	115

19. McWilliams   *Brothers Under the Skin*   1943   110
20. Myrdal   *American Dilemma: the Negro Problem* 1944   110
21. Russell   *Power: a New Social Analysis*   1938   108
22. Laski   *American Presidency* 1940   100

NOTE: All but the last three are by American authors.

THE BEST BOOKS ON SCIENCE

			POINTS
1.	Heiser *American Doctor's Odyssey* ..	1936	240
2.	Audubon *Audubon's America*	1940	240
3.	Zinsser *As I Remember Him*	1940	240
4.	Curie *Madame Curie*	1937	212
5.	Hogben *Mathematics for the Million*	1937	204
6.	Hogben *Science for the Citizen*	1938	135
7.	Smyth *Atomic Energy*	1945	132
8.	Peattie *Green Laurels*	1936	121
9.	Audubon *Birds of America*	1937	119
10.	Parran *Shadow on the Land: Syphilis*	1937	119
11.	Flexner *William Henry Welch*	1941	110
12.	Einstein *Evolution of Physics*	1938	108
13.	Jaffe *Men of Science in America* ...	1944	104

THE BEST ART BOOKS

			POINTS
1.	Leonardo da Vinci *Notebooks*	1938	162
2.	Cheney *World History of Art*	1937	161
3.	Craven *Treasury of Art Masterpieces*	1939	161
4.	Van Loon *The Arts*	1937	144
5.	Covarrubias *Island of Bali*	**1937**	**127**
6.	Audubon *Birds of America*	1937	119
7.	Delacroix *Journals*	1937	119

THE BEST BOOKS ON LITERATURE AND LANGUAGE

			Points
1.	Brooks	*New England: Indian Summer*	1940	560
2.	Brooks	*Flowering of New England*	1936	510
3.	Brooks	*World of Washington Irving*	1944	471
4.	Kazin	*On Native Grounds*	1942	242
5.	Mencken	*American Language: First Supplement*	1945	216
6.	Canby	*Walt Whitman in America*	1943	176
7.	White, E. B.	*One Man's Meat*	1942	168
8.	Matthiesen	*American Renaissance*	1941	150
9.	Adams, H.	*Letters*	1938	144
10.	Emerson	*Letters*	1939	142
11.	Adler	*How to Read a Book*	1940	130
12.	Schuster, ed.	*Treasury of the World's Great Letters*	1940	130
13.	Glasgow	*Certain Measure*	1943	121
14.	Chase, S.	*Tyranny of Words*	1938	117

NOTE: All of these are by American authors.

THE BEST BOOKS OF POETRY

			Points
1.	Frost	*Collected Poems*	1939	327
2.	Auden	*Collected Works*	1945	199
3.	Sandburg	*The People, Yes*	1936	176
4.	Jeffers	*Selected Poems*	1938	171
5.	Miller, A. D.	*White Cliffs*	1941	170
6.	Benét, S. V.	*Western Star*	1943	165
7.	Van Doren, M.	*Collected Poems*	1939	161
8.	Benét, W. R.	*Dust Which Is God*	1941	160
9.	Millay	*Conversation at Midnight*	1937	153
10.	Housman	*Collected Poems*	1940	150

11. Frost   *Witness Tree* 1942   137
12. Davenport, R.   *My Country* 1944   127
13. Millay   *Collected Sonnets* 1941   120
14. Eliot   *Collected Poems* 1936   120
15. Cummings   *Collected Poems* 1938   117
16. Shapiro   *Essay on Rime* 1945   108

THE BEST PLAYS

		POINTS

1. Millay   *Conversation at Midnight* ... 1937   153
2. Sherwood   *Abe Lincoln in Illinois* ... 1937   123
3. Wilder   *Our Town* 1938   117
4. Sherwood   *There Shall Be No Night* 1940   110
5. MacLeish   *Fall of the City* 1937   102

THE BEST ESSAYS

		POINTS

1. Mencken   *Happy Days* 1940   190
2. White, E. B.   *One Man's Meat* 1942   168
3. Lin Yu-tang   *Between Tears and Laughter* 1943   143
4. Koestler   *Yogi and the Commissar* .. 1945   120
5. Wilson, E.   *Wound and the Bow* ... 1941   120
6. Woolf   *Death of the Moth* 1942   116
7. Peattie   *Road of a Naturalist* 1941   110
8. Adams, J. D.   *Shape of Books to Come* 1944   103

THE BEST BOOKS OF HUMOR

		POINTS

1. Mauldin   *Up Front* 1945   324
2. Hargrove   *See Here, Private Hargrove* 1942   189
3. Ross   *Education of Hyman Kaplan* .. 1937   170

Best Books of Humor—*Continued*

4. White, E. B. & White, K. S. A.   *Sub-*
   treasury of American Humor   1941   160
5. Skinner & Kimbrough   *Our Hearts*
   Were Young and Gay   1942   143
6. Day   *Life with Mother*   1937   119
7. Halsey   *With Malice Toward Some* ..   1938   117
8. Nash   *I'm a Stranger Here Myself* ..   1938   108

Note: All by American authors.

THE BEST BOOKS OF TRAVEL AND DESCRIPTION

			Points
1. West	*Black Lamb and Grey Falcon*	1941	370
2. Paul	*Life and Death of a Spanish Town*	1937	238
3. Lindbergh	*Listen! the Wind*	1938	234
4. Daniels	*Southerner Discovers the South*	1938	207
5. Rawlings	*Cross Creek*	1942	189
6. Cross	*Connecticut Yankee*	1943	187
7. Carmer	*The Hudson*	1939	171
8. Paul	*Last Time I Saw Paris*	1942	168
9. Dos Passos	*State of the Nation*	1944	138
10. Byrd	*Alone*	1938	135

Note: All by American authors.

THE BEST BIOGRAPHIES

			Points
1. Freeman	*Lee's Lieutenants*	1942	583
2. Sandburg	*Abraham Lincoln: the War Years 4 vols.*	1939	484
3. Van Doren, C.	*Benjamin Franklin* ..	1938	424
4. Canby	*Thoreau*	1939	390

5.	Bowen, C. D. *Yankee from Olympus* [Justice Holmes]	1939	390
6.	Landon *Anna and the King of Siam*	1944	288
7.	Morison *Admiral of the Ocean Sea* [Columbus]	1942	284
8.	Wright *Black Boy* [Autobiography]	1945	278
9.	Krutch *Samuel Johnson*	1944	276
10.	Forbes *Paul Revere*	1942	273
11.	Buchan *Pilgrim's Way* [Autobiography]	1940	260
12.	Heiser *American Doctor's Odyssey* [Autobiography]	1936	240
13.	Nevins *John D. Rockefeller*	1940	240
14.	Mencken *Newspaper Days* [Autobiography]	1941	240
15.	Zinsser *As I Remember Him* [Autobiography]	1940	240
16.	Holt *George Washington Carver* ...	1943	231
17.	James *Andrew Jackson*	1937	221
18.	Pringle *Life and Times of William H. Taft*	1939	218
19.	Curie *Madame Curie*	1937	212
20.	Mencken *Happy Days* [Autobiography]	1940	190
21.	Santayana *Persons and Places* [Autobiography]	1944	184
22.	Seagrave *Burma Surgeon* [Autobiography]	1943	175
23.	Chase, M. E. *Goodly Fellowship* [Autobiography]	1939	173
24.	Fowler *Good Night, Sweet Prince* [John Barrymore]	1944	173
25.	Armstrong *Trelawney*	1940	170
26.	Wilson, F. *Crusader in Crinoline* [Harriet Beecher Stowe]	1942	168
27.	Pearson *G. B. S.* [Shaw]	1942	168

NOTE: All but three are by Americans.

THE BEST HISTORIES

			Points
1.	Schlesinger *Age of Jackson*	1945	408
2.	Leech *Reveille in Washington*	1941	360
3.	Gunther *Inside Europe*	1936	256
4.	Van Doren, C. *Secret History of the American Revolution*	1941	240
5.	Beard & Beard *America in Midpassage*	1939	237
6.	Gunther *Inside Asia*	1939	228
7.	Stewart *Names on the Land*	1945	192
8.	Rauschning *Revolution of Nihilism*	1939	190
9.	DeVoto *Year of Decision*	1942	175
10.	Carmer *The Hudson*	1939	171
11.	Willison *Saints and Strangers*	1945	168

Note: All but one are by Americans.

THE BEST WAR BOOKS

			Points
1.	Shirer *Berlin Diary*	1941	380
2.	Mauldin *Up Front*	1945	324
3.	White, W. L. *They Were Expendable*	1942	315
4.	Pyle *Brave Men*	1944	299
5.	Brown, H. *Walk in the Sun*	1944	253
6.	Hitler *Mein Kampf*	1939	247
7.	Paul *Life and Death of a Spanish Town*	1937	238
8.	Stowe *They Shall Not Sleep*	1944	219
9.	Snow *People on Our Side*	1944	196
10.	Rauschning *Revolution of Nihilism*	1939	190
11.	Hargrove *See Here, Private Hargrove*	1942	189
12.	Curie *Journey Among Warriors*	1943	189
13.	Carlson *Under Cover*	1943	187
14.	Seagrave *Burma Surgeon*	1943	175

15.	Pyle	*Here Is Your War*	1943	165
16.	Ingersoll	*Battle Is the Pay-off*	1943	154
17.	Lawson	*Thirty Seconds over Tokyo*	1943	143
18.	Smith, H. K.	*Last Train from Berlin*	1942	137
19.	Brown, C.	*Suez to Singapore*	1942	126
20.	Brown, J. M.	*Many a Watchful Night*	1944	126

THE BEST BOOKS ON WORLD AFFAIRS

POINTS

1.	Welles	*Time for Decision*	1944	472
2.	Lippmann	*U.S. Foreign Policy*	1943	264
3.	Willkie	*One World*	1943	253
4.	Gunther	*Inside Asia*	1939	228
5.	Snow	*People on Our Side*	1944	196
6.	Lippmann	*United States War Aims*	1944	173
7.	Streit	*Union Now*	1939	161
8.	Lattimore	*Solution in Asia*	1945	156
9.	Huxley	*Ends and Means*	1937	144
10.	Lin Yu-tang	*Between Tears and Laughter*	1943	143
11.	Nehru	*Toward Freedom*	1941	140
12.	Welles, ed.	*Intelligent American's Guide to the Peace*	1945	108

THE BEST BOOKS ON RUSSIA AND THE RUSSIANS

POINTS

1.	Koestler	*Darkness at Noon (Fiction)*	1941	200
2.	Snow	*People on Our Side*	1944	196
3.	Simonov	*Days and Nights (Fiction)*	1945	190
4.	Lyons	*Assignment in Utopia*	1937	170
5.	Snow	*Red Star Over China*	1938	135
6.	Snow	*Pattern of Soviet Power*	1945	120
7.	Lauterbach	*These Are the Russians*	1945	108
8.	Valtin	*Out of the Night*	1941	100

THE PUBLISHERS OF THE BEST BOOKS OF THE DECADE

As in the previous decade, some fourteen publishers issued about three quarters of our four hundred best books. The remaining one hundred titles were divided among thirty-two other publishers.

1936-45		1926-35	
No. of Books		No. of Books	
1. Harper	41	Macmillan	42
2. Harcourt	40	Harcourt	40
3. Little	37	Doubleday	36
4. Viking	27	Scribner	26
5. Knopf	24	Houghton	26
6. Macmillan	22	Knopf	26
7. Simon	21	Harper	24
8. Random	20	Little	22
9. Scribner	19	Viking	18
10. Houghton	17	Simon	14
11. Doubleday	16	Putnam	8
12. Holt	11	Liveright	8
13. Farrar	9	Bobbs	8
14. Day	8	Boni	8

There are four new-comers among this decade's fourteen leaders: Random House (in eighth place), and Holt, Farrar and Day (twelfth, thirteenth and fourteenth places). The non-appearance of Putnam, Liveright, Bobbs and Boni has made room for them. And there have been some noteworthy gains: Harper has risen from seventh to first place; Little from eighth to third; Viking from ninth to fourth. It would be unkind to call attention to changes of the other sort.

The poor showing made by the university presses is surprising. Together they have published only ten of our four hundred best books, and only seven of these presses are represented at all: three by two books each, the other four by one apiece.

SOME OF THE IMPECCABLES

The *Book Review Digest* indicates by plus and minus signs the tenor of most of its quoted reviews. The list below includes only such books as (1) can boast a record in the *Book Review Digest* which is unsullied by a single minus sign, and (2) have also accumulated an unusually high score in points.

			B.R.D.	Points
Barzun	*Teacher in America*	1945	11+	204
Brooks	*World of Washington Irving*	1944	9+	471
Buchan	*Pilgrim's Way*	1940	12+	260
Churchill	*Blood, Sweat and Tears*	1941	13+	150
Curie	*Madame Curie*	1937	6+	212
Daniels	*Southerner Discovers the South*	1938	9+	207
Ferber	*Peculiar Treasure*	1939	8+	161
Grew	*Ten Years in Japan*	1944	12+	161
Heiser	*American Doctor's Odyssey*	1936	11+	240
Holmes	*Holmes-Pollock Letters*	1941	9+	140
Lawson	*Thirty Seconds Over Tokyo*	1943	8+	143
Marquand	*Late George Apley* ..	1937	13+	272
Mencken	*Happy Days*	1940	11+	190
Mumford	*Culture of Cities*	1938	9+	180
Paul	*Life and Death of a Spanish Town*	1937	8+	238
Phelps	*Autobiography*	1939	8+	152
Porter	*Leaning Tower*	1944	10+	288
Pyle	*Brave Men*	1944	11+	299
Rawlings	*Cross Creek*	1942	10+	189
Ross	*Education of Hyman Kaplan*	1937	5+	170
St. Exupéry	*Wind, Sand and Stars*	1939	8+	247

APPENDIX

"THE RUNNERS-UP"

Six hundred books of the decade (1936-1945) which were praised by many critics, though none of their scores (53 to 99) were large enough to win them places among the four hundred best.

			POINTS
Adamic, L.	*My America*	1938	54
Adamic, L.	*Nation of Nations*	1945	72
Adamic, L.	*Two-way Passage*	1941	60
Adams, J. T.	*Album of American History*	1944	69
Adams, J. T.	*Emperor of the Seven Seas*	1940	70
Adams, J. T.	*The Living Jefferson*	1936	56
Adams, J. T., ed.	*Dictionary of American History* 6v.	1940	80
Adams, S. H.	*Incredible Era*	1939	66
Adler, M.	*How to Think about Peace and War*	1944	58
Agar, H.	*Pursuit of Happiness*	1938	54
Alcott, B.	*Journals*	1938	90
Aldanov, M.	*Fifth Seal*	1943	55
Aldington, R.	*The Duke*	1943	88
Aldridge, J.	*Signed with Their Honour*	1942	74
Alegria, C.	*Broad and Alien Is the World*	1941	60
Algren, N.	*Never Come Morning*	1942	63
Allen, H.	*Action at Aquila*	1938	72
Allen, H.	*Forest and the Fort*	1943	77
Almedingen, E. M. von	*Frossia*	1943	55
Anderson, M.	*Eleven Verse Plays*	1940	70
Anderson, M.	*Eve of St. Mark*	1942	55
Anderson, M.	*High Tor*	1937	68
Armstrong, L. V.	*We Too Are the People*	1938	72

POINTS

Arnold, T. W.	*Bottlenecks of Business* ...	1940	60
Arnold, T. W.	*Folklore of Capitalism*	1937	85
Auden, W. H.	*On This Island*	1937	68
Auden, W. H., ed.	*Oxford Book of Light Verse*	1938	54
Auden, W. H. and Isherwood, C.	*Journey to a War*	1939	66
Auden, W. H. and MacNeice, L.	*Letters from Iceland*	1937	68
Bailey, T. A.	*Woodrow Wilson and the Lost Peace*	1944	69
Bakeless, J. E.	*Christopher Marlowe*	1937	68
Bakeless, J. E.	*Master of the Wilderness* ..	1939	95
Baker, R. S.	*American Chronicle*	1945	84
Baldwin, H. W.	*What You Should Know about the Navy*	1943	55
Barbour, T.	*Naturalist at Large*	1943	66
Baring, M.	*Have You Anything to Declare?*	1936	60
Barry, P.	*War in Heaven*	1938	54
Barzun, J.	*Of Human Freedom*	1939	85
Barzun, J.	*Romanticism and the Modern Ego*	1943	66
Basso, H.	*Mainstream*	1943	66
Bates, E. S.	*American Faith*	1940	80
Bates, E. S., ed.	*Bible Designed to be Read as Living Literature*	1936	56
Bates, H. E.	*Fair Stood the Wind for France*	1944	58
Bates, R.	*Olive Field*	1936	78
Beals, C.	*America South*	1937	60
Beals, C.	*Coming Struggle for Latin America*	1938	90
Beard, C. A. and Beard, M. R.	*American Spirit*	1942	74
Becker, C. L.	*How New Will the Better World Be?*	1944	84

POINTS

Beebe, C. W., ed.	*Book of Naturalists*	1945	84
Belden, J. R.	*Still Time to Die*	1944	81
Belden, J. R.	*Retreat with Stilwell*	1943	55
Bell, E. T.	*Men of Mathematics*	1937	85
Bemelmans, L.	*The Donkey Inside*	1941	80
Bemis, S. F.	*Diplomatic History of the U. S.*	1936	72
Benchley, R.	*Benchley Beside Himself* ...	1943	77
Benét, S. V.	*America*	1944	92
Benét, S. V.	*Selected Works*	1942	84
Benét, S. V.	*Tales Before Midnight*	1939	95
Bennett, J.	*Virginia Woolf*	1945	96
Benson, S.	*Junior Miss*	1941	60
Bentley, E. R.	*Century of Hero-Worship*	1944	81
Benton, T. A.	*Artist in America*	1937	59
Best, H.	*Young 'un*	1944	81
Beston, H., ed.	*American Memory*	1937	68
Beveridge, Sir W. H.	*Full Employment in a Free Society*	1945	84
Biddle, G.	*American Artist's Story*	1939	57
Binkley, W. E.	*American Political Parties*	1943	66
Binns, A.	*Land Is Bright*	1939	57
Bishop, J. P.	*Selected Poems*	1941	60
Boardman, P.	*Patrick Geddes*	1944	69
Bodley, R. V. C.	*Wind in the Sahara*	1944	58
Bodmer, F.	*Loom of Language*	1944	69
Bogan, L.	*Poems and New Poems*	1941	80
Bogan, L.	*Sleeping Fury*	1937	68
Bolte, C. G.	*New Veteran*	1945	72
Borgese, G. A.	*Common Cause*	1943	55
Boswell, P.	*Modern American Painting* ..	1939	66
Bottome, P.	*Mortal Storm*	1938	63
Bowen, E.	*Bowen's Court*	1942	63
Bowen, E.	*Look at All Those Roses*	1941	70
Boyle, K.	*Crazy Hunter*	1940	90

POINTS

POINTS

Davis, F. and Lindley, E. K. *How War Came*	1942	55
DeKruif, P. *Fight for Life*	1938	54
De la Mare, W. *Collected Poems*	1941	70
De la Roche, M. *Building of Jalna*	1944	69
De La Roche, M. *Wakefield's Course*	1941	60
De Voto, B. *Mark Twain in Eruption*	1940	90
Dewey, J. *Logic: the Theory of Inquiry* ..	1938	81
Diament, G. *Days of Ofelia*	1942	74
Dick, E. *Sod-House Frontier*	1937	68
Dickinson, E. *Bolts of Melody*	1945	96
Di Donato, P. *Christ in Concrete*	1939	76
Dinesen, I. *Out of Africa*	1938	63
Dinesen, I. *Winter's Tales*	1943	88
Dobie, J. F. *Texan in England*	1945	96
Dodd, W. E. *Old South*	1937	76
Dos Passos, J. *Adventures of a Young Man*	1939	76
Dos Passos, J. *Ground We Stand On*	1941	60
Dos Passos, J. *Journeys Between Wars* ...	1938	63
Dos Passos, J. *Number One*	1943	77
Douglas, L. C. *The Robe*	1942	84
Drake, St. C. and Clayton, H. R. *Black Metropolis*	1945	72
Drucker, P. *End of Economic Man*	1939	57
Du Bois, W. E. B. *Dusk of Dawn*	1940	70
Duckett, E. S. *Gateway to the Middle Ages*	1938	63
Duffus, R. L. *Lillian Wald*	1938	54
Duffus, R. L. and Krutch, C. *Valley and Its People*	1944	81
Dunsany, Lord *Guerilla*	1944	58
Earle, E. M. *Makers of Modern Strategy*	1943	66
Eastman, M. *Enjoyment of Laughter*	1936	54
Edman, I. *Philosopher's Holiday*	1938	81
Edmonds, W. D. *Chad Hanna*	1940	80
Eliot, T. S. *Family Reunion*	1939	57
Embree, E. R. *Indians of the Americas* ...	1939	66

POINTS

POINTS

Stegner, W. and Editors of *Look* *One Nation*	1945	96
Steinbeck, J. *Bombs Away*	1942	53
Steinbeck, J. *Cannery Row*	1945	96
Steinbeck, J. *In Dubious Battle*	1936	80
Stephenson, N. and Dunn, W. *George Washington 2v.*	1940	60
Stern, G. B. *Trumpet Voluntary*	1944	92
Stern, G. B. *Young Matriarch*	1942	53
Stettinius, E. R. *Lend-Lease*	1944	69
Stevens, W. *Man with the Blue Guitar*	1937	85
Stevens, W. *Parts of a World*	1942	63
Stone, I. *Immortal Wife*	1944	92
Stone, I. *They Also Ran*	1943	55
Stowe, L. *No Other Road to Freedom*	1941	60
Strunsky, S. *Living Tradition*	1939	85
Strunsky, S. *No Mean City*	1944	58
Stuart, J. *Taps for Private Tussie*	1943	88
Sues, I. R. *Shark's Fins and Millet*	1944	72
Sullivan, M. *Education of an American*	1938	63
Taggard, G. *Collected Poems*	1938	88
Tansill, C. C. *America Goes to War*	1938	54
Tarbell, I. M. *All in the Day's Work*	1939	85
Tate, A. *Selected Poems*	1937	68
Taylor, D. *Treasury of Gilbert and Sullivan*	1941	70
Taylor, D. *Well-Tempered Listener*	1940	80
Taylor, E. *Strategy of Terror*	1940	90
Teasdale, S. *Collected Poems*	1937	68
Thompson, J. M. *French Revolution*	1945	77
Thompson, S. *Gulls Fly Inland*	1941	60
Thomson, V. *State of Music*	1940	70
Thurber, J. *Let Your Mind Alone*	1937	85
Thurber, J. *My World—and Welcome to It*	1942	84
Thurber, J. *Thurber Carnival*	1945	96
Todd, H. *Man Named Grant*	1940	90
Tolischus, O. D. *They Wanted War*	1940	70

INDEX TO TITLES

of the

FOUR HUNDRED BEST BOOKS